# SUSSEX REVISITED

## PHOTOGRAPHIC MEMORIES

**RONALD KERRIDGE**, born in 1938 and a life-long Sussex resident, is married with a daughter, son and three grandchildren. He is a keen local historian with four previous publications to his credit and in 1989 was awarded his masters degree in regional history. As a retired local government officer he now spends his spare time lecturing in local history and following his other interests in archaeology and geology

**MICHAEL STANDING** was born in 1946 and lived in Worthing until recent years when he moved to a village near Chichester. He is married and has two sons, a daughter and three much loved grandchildren. In 1989 he was awarded a masters degree with distinction in regional history and with his co-author, Ronald Kerridge, has written *Georgian and Victorian Broadwater, Ferring Past* and *Worthing - from Saxon Settlement to Seaside Town*.

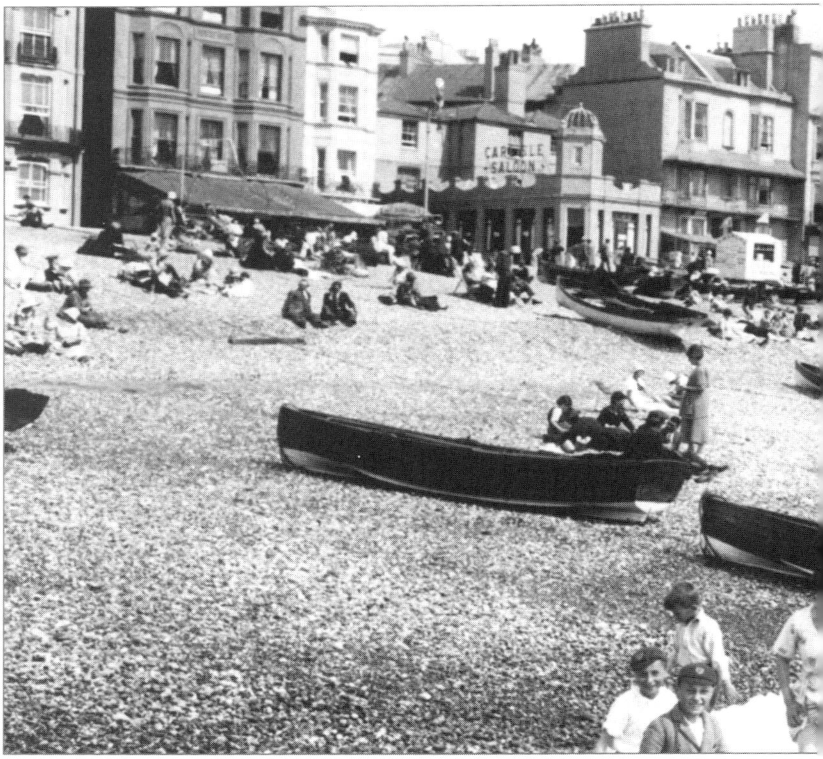

FRANCIS FRITH'S
PHOTOGRAPHIC MEMORIES

# SUSSEX REVISITED

## PHOTOGRAPHIC MEMORIES

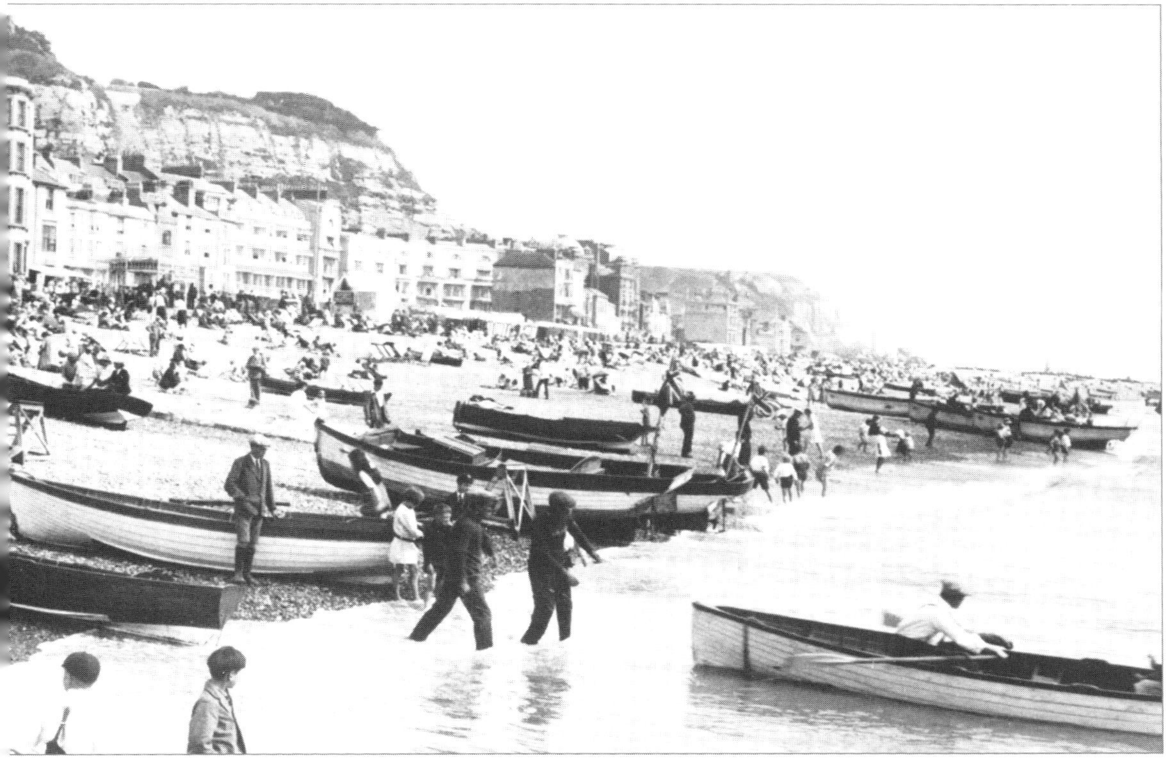

RONALD KERRIDGE
AND MICHAEL STANDING

First published in the United Kingdom in 2004 by
Frith Book Company Ltd

Hardback Edition 2004
ISBN 1-85937-449-2



British Library Cataloguing in Publication Data

Francis Frith's Sussex Revisited - Photographic Memories
Ronald Kerridge and Michael Standing

Frith Book Company Ltd
Frith's Barn, Teffont,
Salisbury, Wiltshire SP3 5QP
Tel: +44 (0) 1722 716 376
Email: info@francisfrith.co.uk
www.francisfrith.co.uk

Printed and bound in Great Britain

Front Cover: **EASTBOURNE,** *The Pier 1910* 62958
Frontispiece: **HASTINGS,** *View from the Pier 1925* 77975

*The colour-tinting is for illustrative purposes only, and is not intended to be historically accurate*

AS WITH ANY HISTORICAL DATABASE THE FRITH ARCHIVE IS CONSTANTLY BEING CORRECTED AND IMPROVED AND THE PUBLISHERS WOULD WELCOME INFORMATION ON OMISSIONS OR INACCURACIES

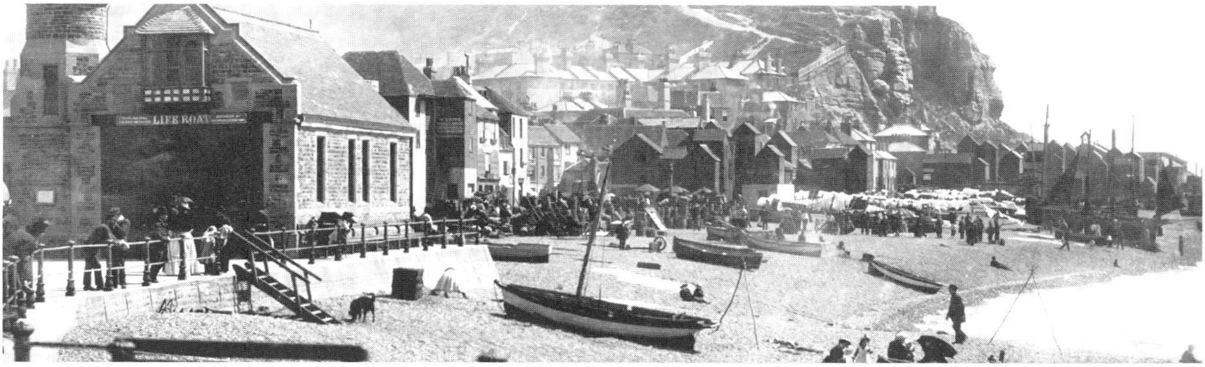


# CONTENTS

# FRANCIS FRITH
## VICTORIAN PIONEER

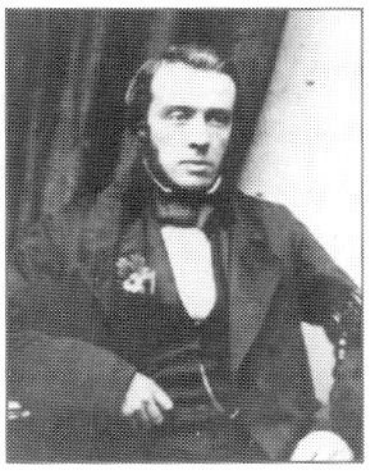

FRANCIS FRITH, founder of the world-famous photographic archive, was a complex and multi-talented man. A devout Quaker and a highly successful Victorian businessman, he was philosophic by nature and pioneering in outlook.

By 1855 he had already established a wholesale grocery business in Liverpool, and sold it for the astonishing sum of £200,000, which is the equivalent today of over £15,000,000. Now a very rich man, he was able to indulge his passion for travel. As a child he had pored over travel books written by early explorers, and his fancy and imagination had been stirred by family holidays to the sublime mountain regions of Wales and Scotland. 'What lands of spirit-stirring and enriching scenes and places!' he had written. He was to return to these scenes of grandeur in later years to 'recapture the thousands of vivid and tender memories', but with a different purpose. Now in his thirties, and captivated by the new science of photography, Frith set out on a series of pioneering journeys up the Nile and to the Near East that occupied him from 1856 until 1860.

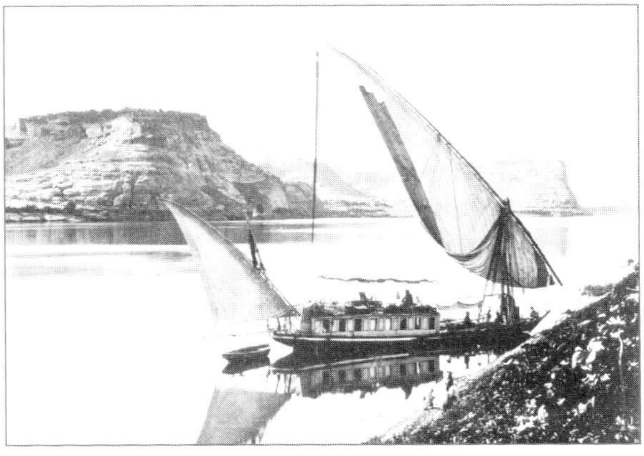

### INTRIGUE AND EXPLORATION

These far-flung journeys were packed with intrigue and adventure. In his life story, written when he was sixty-three, Frith tells of being held captive by bandits, and of fighting 'an awful midnight battle to the very point of surrender with a deadly pack of hungry, wild dogs'. Wearing flowing Arab costume, Frith arrived at Akaba by camel seventy years before Lawrence of Arabia, where he encountered 'desert princes and rival sheikhs, blazing with jewel-hilted swords'.

He was the first photographer to venture beyond the sixth cataract of the Nile. Africa was still the mysterious 'Dark Continent', and Stanley and Livingstone's historic meeting was a decade into the future. The conditions for picture taking confound belief. He laboured for hours in his wicker dark-room in the sweltering heat of the desert, while the volatile chemicals fizzed dangerously in their trays. Back in London he exhibited his photographs and was 'rapturously cheered' by members of the Royal Society. His reputation as a photographer was made overnight.

### VENTURE OF A LIFE-TIME

Characteristically, Frith quickly spotted the opportunity to create a new business as a specialist publisher of photographs. He lived in an era of immense and sometimes violent change.

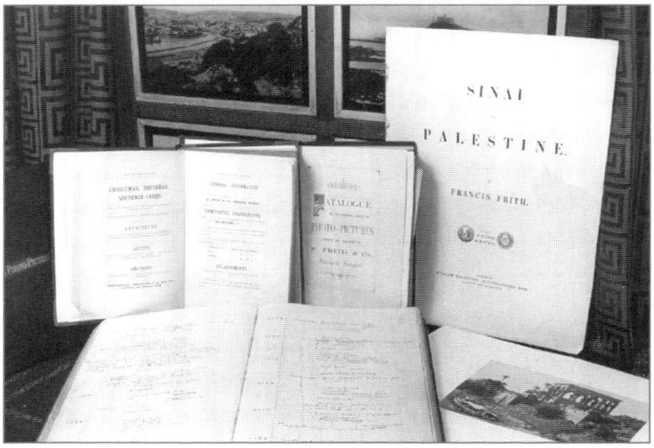


For the poor in the early part of Victoria's reign work was exhausting and the hours long, and people had precious little free time to enjoy themselves. Most had no transport other than a cart or gig at their disposal, and rarely travelled far beyond the boundaries of their own town or village. However, by the 1870s the railways had threaded their way across the country, and Bank Holidays and half-day Saturdays had been made obligatory by Act of Parliament. All of a sudden the working man and his family were able to enjoy days out and see a little more of the world.

With typical business acumen, Francis Frith foresaw that these new tourists would enjoy having souvenirs to commemorate their days out. In 1860 he married Mary Ann Rosling and set out on a new career: his aim was to photograph every city, town and village in Britain. For the next thirty years he travelled the country by train and by pony and trap, producing fine photographs of seaside resorts and beauty spots that were keenly bought by millions of Victorians. These prints were painstakingly pasted into family albums and pored over during the dark nights of winter, rekindling precious memories of summer excursions.

## THE RISE OF FRITH & CO

Frith's studio was soon supplying retail shops all over the country. To meet the demand he gathered about him a small team of photographers, and published the work of independent artist-photographers of the calibre of Roger Fenton and Francis Bedford. In order to gain some understanding of the scale of Frith's business one only has to look at the catalogue issued by Frith & Co in 1886: it runs to some 670 pages, listing not only many thousands of views of the British Isles but also many photographs of most European countries, and China, Japan, the USA and Canada - note the sample page shown here from the hand-written Frith & Co ledgers recording the pictures. By 1890 Frith had created the greatest specialist photographic publishing company in the world, with over 2,000 sales outlets - more than the combined number that Boots and WH Smith have today! The picture on the next page shows the Frith & Co display board at Ingleton in the Yorkshire Dales (left of window). Beautifully constructed with a mahogany frame and gilt inserts, it could display up to a dozen local scenes.

## POSTCARD BONANZA

The ever-popular holiday postcard we know today took many years to develop. In 1870 the Post Office issued the first plain cards, with a pre-printed stamp on one face. In 1894 they allowed other publishers' cards to be sent through the mail with an attached adhesive halfpenny stamp. Demand grew rapidly, and in 1895 a new size of postcard was permitted called the court card, but there was little room for illustration. In 1899, a year after Frith's death, a new card measuring 5.5 x 3.5 inches became the standard format, but it was not until 1902 that the divided back came into being, so that the address and message could be on one face and a full-size illustration on the other. Frith & Co were in the vanguard of postcard development: Frith's sons Eustace and Cyril continued their father's monumental task, expanding the number of views offered to the public and recording more and more places in

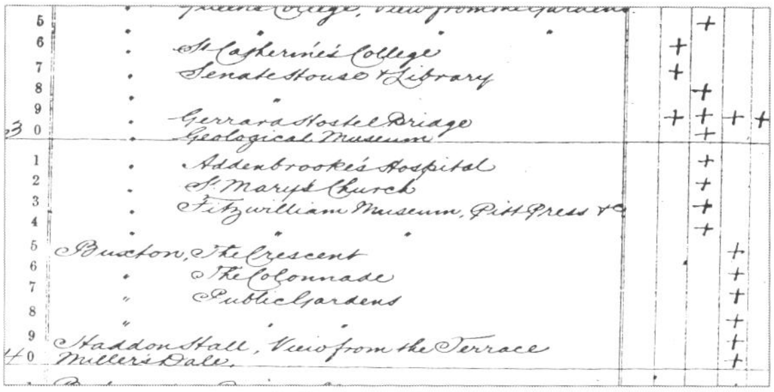

5 Queens College, View from the Gardens
6 St Catherine's College
7 Senate House & Library
8
9 Gerrard Hostel Bridge
30 Geological Museum
1 Addenbrooke's Hospital
2 St Mary's Church
3 Fitzwilliam Museum, Pitt Press &c
4
5 Buxton, The Crescent
6 The Colonnade
7 Public Gardens
8
9 Haddon Hall, View from the Terrace
40 Millers Dale

Britain, as the coasts and countryside were opened up to mass travel.

Francis Frith had died in 1898 at his villa in Cannes, his great project still growing. The archive he created continued in business for another seventy years. By 1970 it contained over a third of a million pictures showing 7,000 British towns and villages.

### FRANCIS FRITH'S LEGACY

Frith's legacy to us today is of immense significance and value, for the magnificent archive of evocative photographs he created provides a unique record of change in the cities, towns and villages throughout Britain over a century and more. Frith and his fellow studio photographers revisited locations many times down the years to update their views, compiling for us an enthralling and colourful pageant of British life and character.

We are fortunate that Frith was dedicated to recording the minutiae of everyday life. For it is this sheer wealth of visual data, the painstaking chronicle of changes in dress, transport, street layouts, buildings, housing, engineering and landscape that captivates us so much today. His remarkable images offer us a powerful link with the past and with the lives of our ancestors.

### THE VALUE OF THE ARCHIVE TODAY

Computers have now made it possible for Frith's many thousands of images to be accessed almost instantly. Frith's images are increasingly used as visual resources, by social historians, by researchers into genealogy and ancestry, by architects and town planners, and by teachers involved in local history projects.

In addition, the archive offers every one of us an opportunity to examine the places where we and our families have lived and worked down the years. Highly successful in Frith's own era, the archive is now, a century and more on, entering a new phase of popularity. Historians consider the Francis Frith Collection to be of prime national importance. It is the only archive of its kind remaining in private ownership. Francis Frith's archive is now housed in an historic timber barn in the beautiful village of Teffont in Wiltshire. Its founder would not recognize the archive office as it is today. In place of the many thousands of dusty boxes containing glass plate negatives and an all-pervading odour of photographic chemicals, there are now ranks of computer screens. He would be amazed to watch his images travelling round the world at unimaginable speeds through internet lines.

The archive's future is both bright and exciting. Francis Frith, with his unshakeable belief in making photographs available to the greatest number of people, would undoubtedly approve of what is being done today with his lifetime's work. His photographs depicting our shared past are now bringing pleasure and enlightenment to millions around the world a century and more after his death.

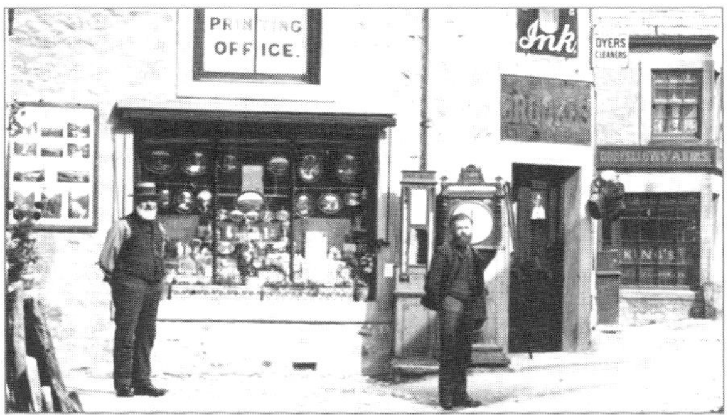

# SUSSEX
## REVISITED
## AN INTRODUCTION

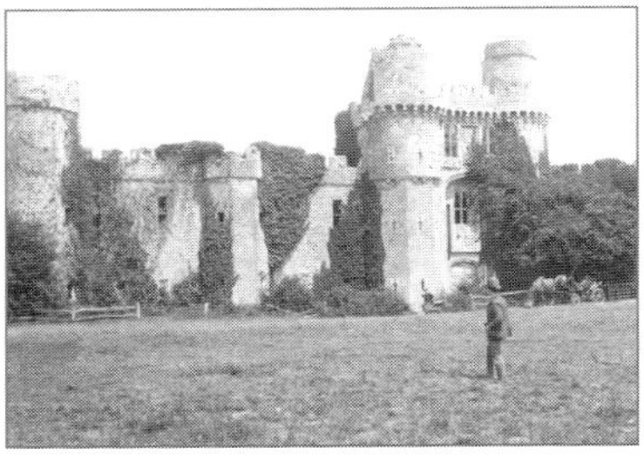

**W G HOSKINS** suggests that 'every few square miles of England has its own marked character.' Sussex is no exception, for there are some quite startling contrasts in the county. Overlying its varying sedimentary rocks are five very distinct natural regions: the history of the county is encapsulated in the regional diversity of the changes and sequence of human settlement which occurred in each of them over the centuries.

The relatively flat, tapering coastal plain, over 64km long, extends from Brighton in East Sussex to the Hampshire border, gradually widening to its maximum width of 16km in the Chichester/Selsey area. For over 2,000 years its easily worked, stoneless, fertile brickearth has supported the wealthiest and most populous communities in the south-east of England.

During the period of Roman occupation, the coastal plain was part of a 'grain factory', which produced corn for export to other parts of the

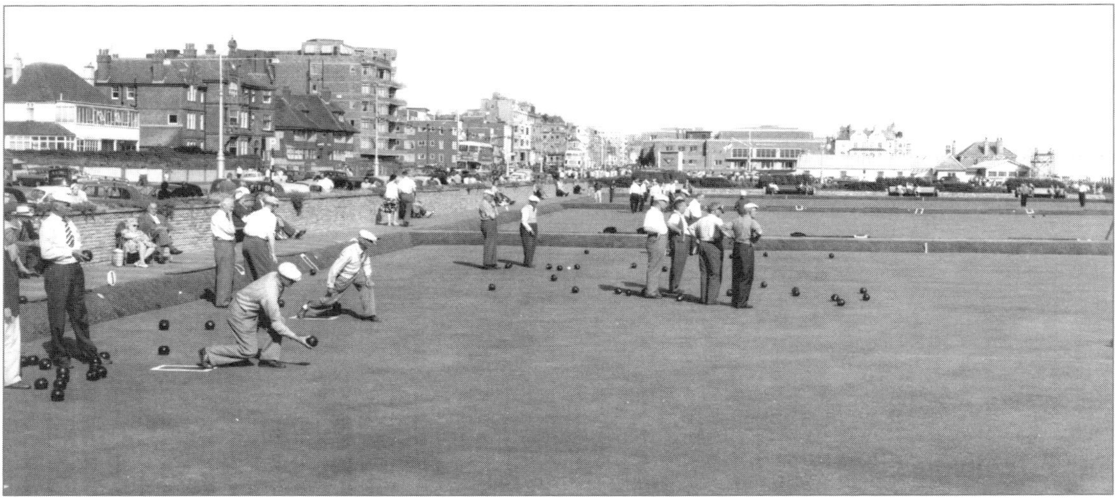

**HOVE,** *The Bowling Green c1960* H128011

Roman Empire. The Roman palace at Fishbourne was an important administrative supply base for the early phases of the Roman conquest, and by the 2nd century AD Chichester (Noviomagus) had developed as a centre of Roman culture and authority.

In the 5th century, Saxon migrants began to settle alongside the wide river estuaries and numerous tidal creeks that were very similar to those of their flooded homelands on the north German and Frisian coast. Sussex derives its name from these migrants: they were quite distinct from those who settled the kingdoms of Kent and Wessex, and are described in the Anglo-Saxon Chronicles as Suose(a)xe. Initially the name only applied to the people, but over the course of time it came to be used as the name of their territory.

Over the centuries the family communities of initial settlement evolved into today's coastal plain hamlets, villages and towns. Continuous improvement of the soil by the introduction of legumes into crop rotations virtually eliminated the need for fallow fields by the 13th century, and ensured arable productivity unrivalled in southern England. Large tenanted holdings sold their surplus barley and wheat, and with the capital raised were able to purchase wagons, ploughs and other husbandry implements.

During the late 18th century, the small towns, agricultural villages and hamlets adjoining the coast began to develop into fashionable Georgian watering places as the fashion for holidays beside the sea gained popularity. Initially, because of the limited number of visitors, only a few places could benefit from the emergence of seaside tourism. Brighton was the first Sussex resort town to develop, but the fashion for sea bathing soon spread to affect adjacent areas of the Sussex coastline. While development at Hastings was slow, and the spectacular investment at Bognor by the entrepreneur Henry Hotham was a financial disaster, Worthing and Eastbourne developed into fashionable Georgian towns.

By the beginning of the Victorian period, resort development was becoming a significant element in the overall economy of Sussex. The opening of the London to Brighton Railway in 1841 rapidly changed Brighton from a fashionable watering place into a centre of mass entertainment. As an antidote to Brighton's lively entertainment, the more select watering place became a particular phenomenon of the Sussex coastline. Both Worthing and Eastbourne continued to actively encourage middle-class Victorian visitors. Today, the urban conurbation that stretches along the Sussex coastline is one of the most developed areas in Britain.

Dividing the coastal plain from the Weald, and covering nearly one third of Sussex, the undulating hills of the South Downs form the most distinctive of the county's natural regions. For thousands of years the physical and chemical nature of the downland chalk - its lack of water and alkaline soil - influenced the environment of those who lived and toiled in this natural region.

Although the hills of Salisbury Plain were the centre of Neolithic civilization, these cattle-raising, food-producing farmers slowly migrated eastwards, and by 4,000 BC communities of Neolithic or New Stone Age man began to settle on the South Downs. Fundamental to their way of life was a good supply of flint axes, essential for forest clearance, agricultural purposes and building shelter. These settlers soon discovered that the flint obtained from within the chalk was far superior to that lying on the surface; by 3,700 BC flint mines had been established at Cissbury (to the north of Worthing), one of the largest flint mining areas in the country, Church Hill (Findon), Blackpatch, and Harrow Hill.

During the Bronze Age, large areas of the Sussex downland were managed as organised farmsteads. These farmers grew crops on sloping hillside terraces, kept animals, and practised a variety of crafts. Alongside the ancient South Downs Way, which runs the entire length of the South Downs from Buriton near Petersfield in the west to Eastbourne, there are more than four hundred tumuli, the round barrows in which these Bronze Age people buried their dead.

Traces of Iron Age cultivation in the form of lynchets (raised field boundaries) can still be seen today on the slopes of the South Downs. This period was far more turbulent, and 19 hill forts, many of them no more than stockaded farms, dominated the downland landscape during this period. The largest of these was at Cissbury Ring, where the oval-shaped fortress covered nearly 60 acres.

The downland was still cultivated during the Roman and Saxon periods. However, as ploughing techniques improved, the difficult chalk soils that yielded indifferent crops were abandoned, and more and more of the heavy remunerative soils of the Weald were cleared of their forest cover to become arable fields. For the next six centuries the South Downs became a vast open sheep pasture. Large flocks of Dorset or Hampshire sheep grazed the more wooded western downland, while to the east there were large flocks of the more hardy Southdown breed. Few village settlements evolved on the southern slopes of the Downs. Most lie along the slightly raised sandstone ridge below the steep northern escarpment, where sheep rearing was integrated with the cultivation of wheat and barley on the deeper soils of the northern dip slope. A large proportion of the older buildings in these small downland hamlets and villages are constructed of flint or the whitish-grey stone called malm, which lies just below the chalk, and many of the smaller settlements still retain the unique quality they possessed over a century ago.

The Weald, which rises some 150 metres above sea level, derives its ancient name from the Germanic word meaning woodland. It was originally part of the great Andredswald, an impenetrable primeval forest that covered the Wealden plateau of Kent, Surrey and Sussex and overflowed west into Hampshire. Unlike the coastal plain, where there was continuity of settlement from at least the Roman era, if not earlier, the Weald was an area of ill-defined pioneering colonization, and was the largest post-Domesday expanse of wild country to be cleared and settled in England.

Although traversed by the Romans in search of iron ore, and used by the Saxons as woodland commons, or 'outliers', for pannage and summer pasture, the Sussex Weald was not perceived as an area to be farmed until the end of the 12th century. Two centuries later, areas within the dense woodland had been cleared by land-hungry pioneering backwoodsmen, and the temporary huts and shelters associated with seasonal woodland commons and summer pasture had evolved into today's isolated farms, hamlets and villages. Foul winter weather made the notorious Wealden roads between the emerging settlements impassable, and placed severe limitations on the agricultural productivity of these hard-won intractable clay fields. Both the Low and High Weald were wood pasture regions, and farming on these depleted Wealden soils involved hard work, worry and the constant investment of capital.

Large areas of the Weald remained heavily wooded, and non-agricultural employment was therefore very important to this region's economy. The vast resource of timber provided employment for wood craftsmen, and was used in shipbuilding and the construction of timber-framed buildings, many of which still survive today. These extensive areas of woodland also provided the fuel for the production of glass and iron smelting. Although a relatively small industry, iron smelting was carried out in various parts of the Weald before the 15th century. The distribution of the ironworks was determined by the quality and availability of the clay-ironstone nodules found in layers at the base of the Wadhurst clay. The introduction of water-powered bloomery forges in the 15th century revolutionized the iron industry in Sussex, and new furnaces and forges were sited on the swift Wealden streams that powered the new bellows or forge hammers. The water was diverted and contained by dams, which created long narrow hammer ponds, and although many are now dry, those that remain form some of the most beautiful man-made features of the Wealden landscape in Sussex. During the 15th century, nobles, gentry and wealthy merchants started to acquire rural retreats amidst the woodland, fields and pastures of the Weald. By the beginning of the Victorian era, London stockbrokers and wealthy migrants from the coast had acquired middle-class villas in new urban settlements such as Haywards Heath, which were beginning to develop alongside the London to Brighton railway and its numerous branch lines. Landscape artists, architects and writers also sought weekend and summer cottages from which to promote a romanticised rural idyll in their paintings, sketches and photographs. They portrayed 'a rediscovered Eden'. In reality, it was already beginning to become threatened by their very presence.

Modern development has, however, been largely contained within the framework of the fields and woodland copses shaped by the pioneering backwoodsmen nearly 800 years ago. In the High Weald there are still steep unspoilt wooded valleys, and isolated farmhouses surrounded by small fields of rich pasture and ploughland. The fields in the Low Weald are often separated or edged by dense oak or hazel coppices, remnants of the former primeval forest.

The numerous springs and streams in the Weald provide the headwater for the six major rivers in Sussex. Four of these have slowly cut through the South Downs, and the most westerly, the Arun, with its fine abandoned river cliffs at Amberley, has possibly the most impressive scenery. The Adur, Arun and Ouse have broad open valleys filled with rich alluvium deposits. For centuries these valleys have been used for grazing cattle and as sheep ranges and raised corn fields by the settlers along their banks. The most easterly is the Cuckmere that slowly meanders its way to the sea.

At the eastern extremity of the county, the Downs eventually give way to the Pevensey and Rye marshes. These, along with the lower valleys of the rivers Brede and Eastern Rother and

Romney Marsh, form a significant area of marshland. During the medieval period these were tidal bays with mudflats and salt marsh and were only used for fishing and fowling, but by 1750 they had become important grazing areas. The owners of this extensive area of marshland were farmers and graziers from elsewhere in Sussex and Kent. 'Lookers' tended large flocks of Kent sheep on Romney Marsh, while the Pevensey marshes were used for the fattening of cattle. This marshland area, however, remained poorly drained and was not, therefore, favoured for settlement.

While the western end of the county has over the centuries been slowly eroded by the sea, at the eastern end the process has been reversed. South-westerly storms and the longshore drift have blocked the harbours and accelerated the silting up of the river valleys. The ancient Cinque Ports, Pevensey, Winchelsea and Rye, now lie stranded miles from the present shoreline.

The pictures that follow of the market towns, ancient ports, villages, isolated hamlets and the coastal resorts of Sussex provide further insight into the evolution of its varied and contrasting natural regions.

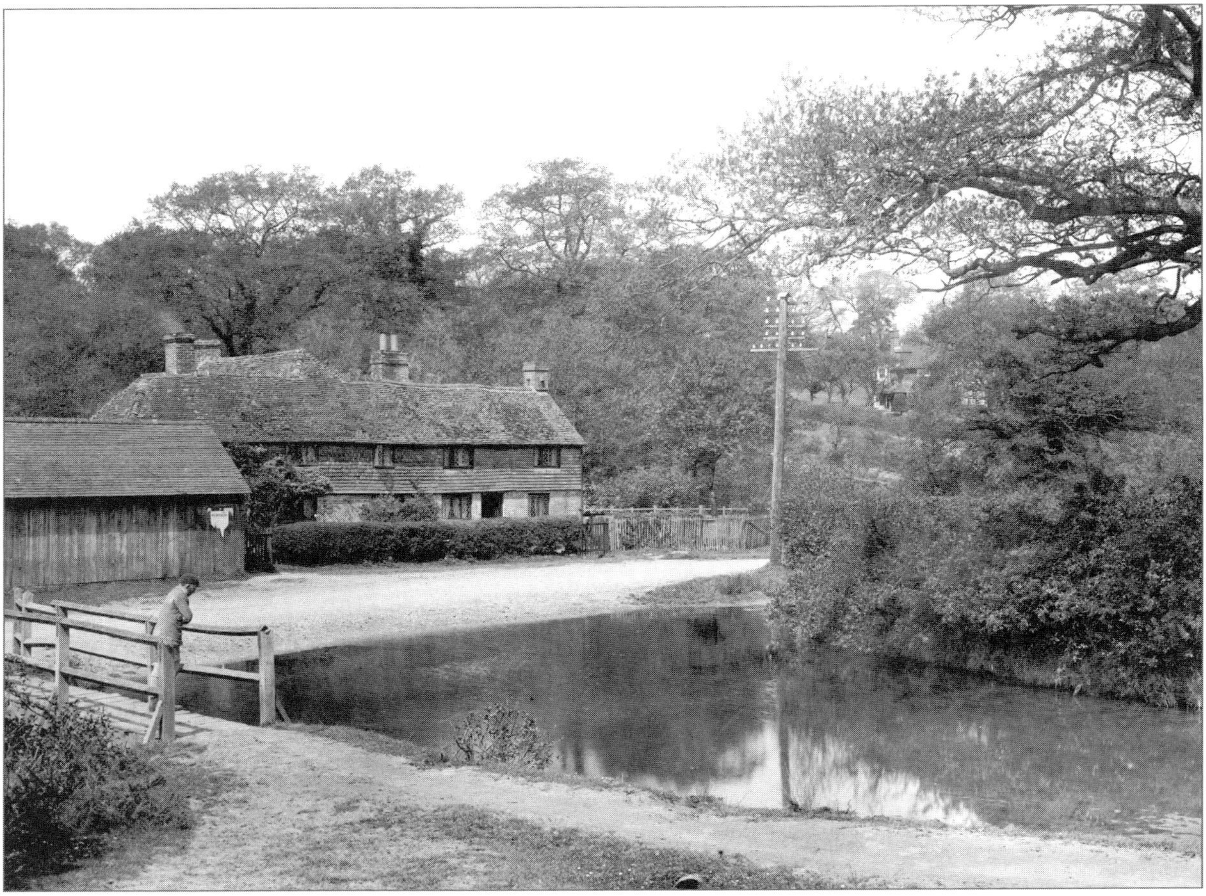

**COLEMANS HATCH,** *The River 1928* 80771

# THE COASTAL RESORTS

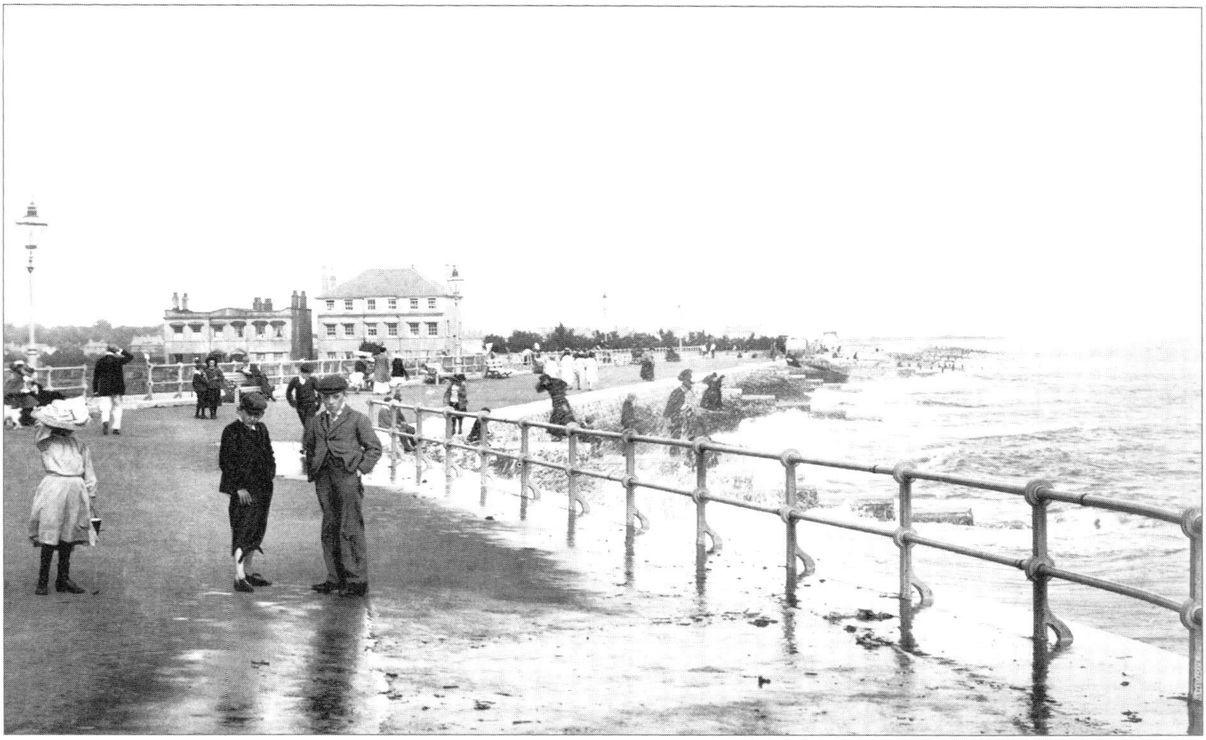

**BOGNOR REGIS,** *East Parade 1903* 50189

In 1791 Bognor was re-named Hothamton after Sir Richard Hotham, whose intention was to change the village into 'a desirable sea-bathing resort' for those of the nobility and gentry wishing to avoid the larger and noisier resorts. To protect the resort against the sea, a concrete wall and promenade had been built by 1870. This offered enjoyment to those of all ages willing to brave the elements.

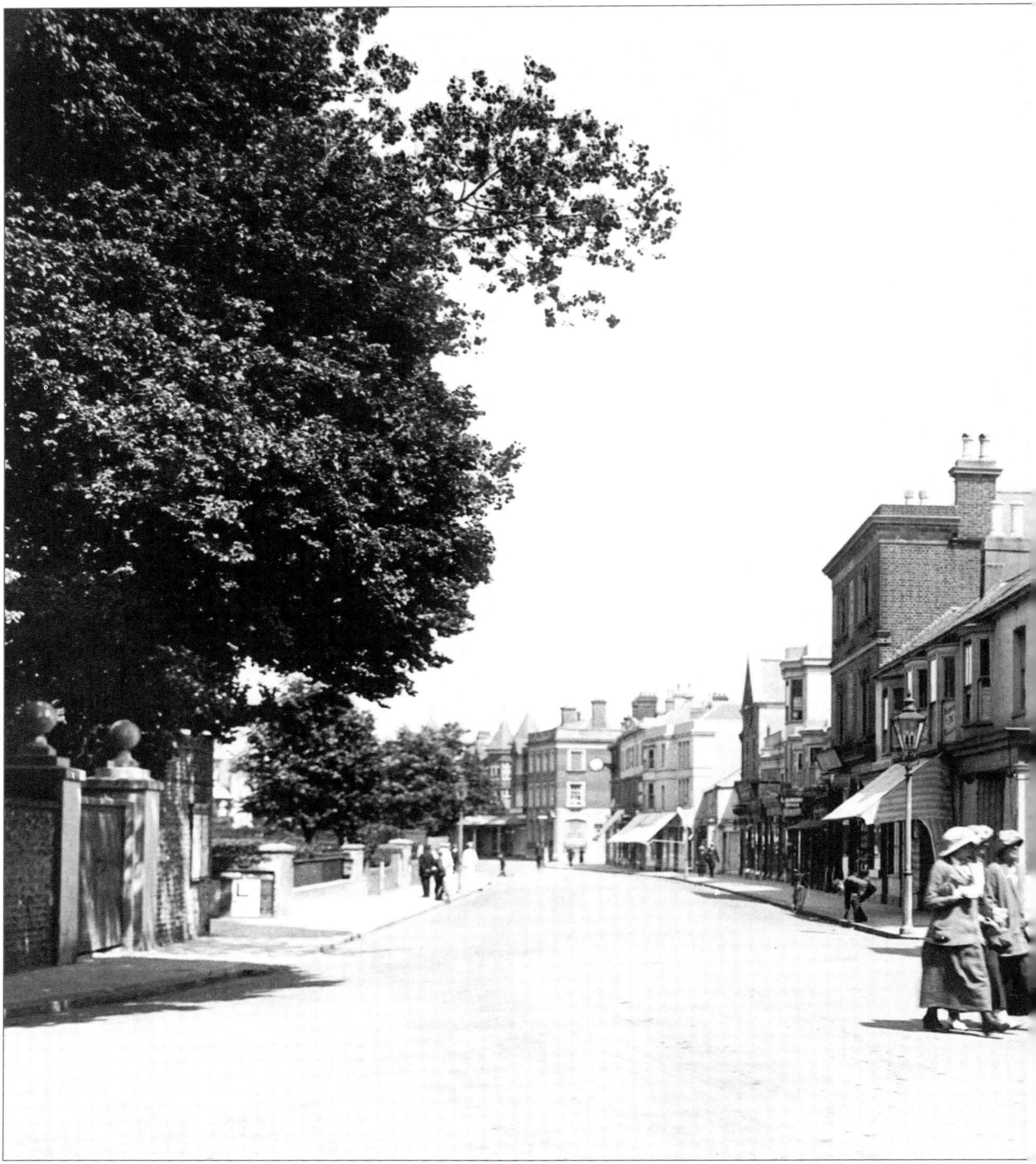

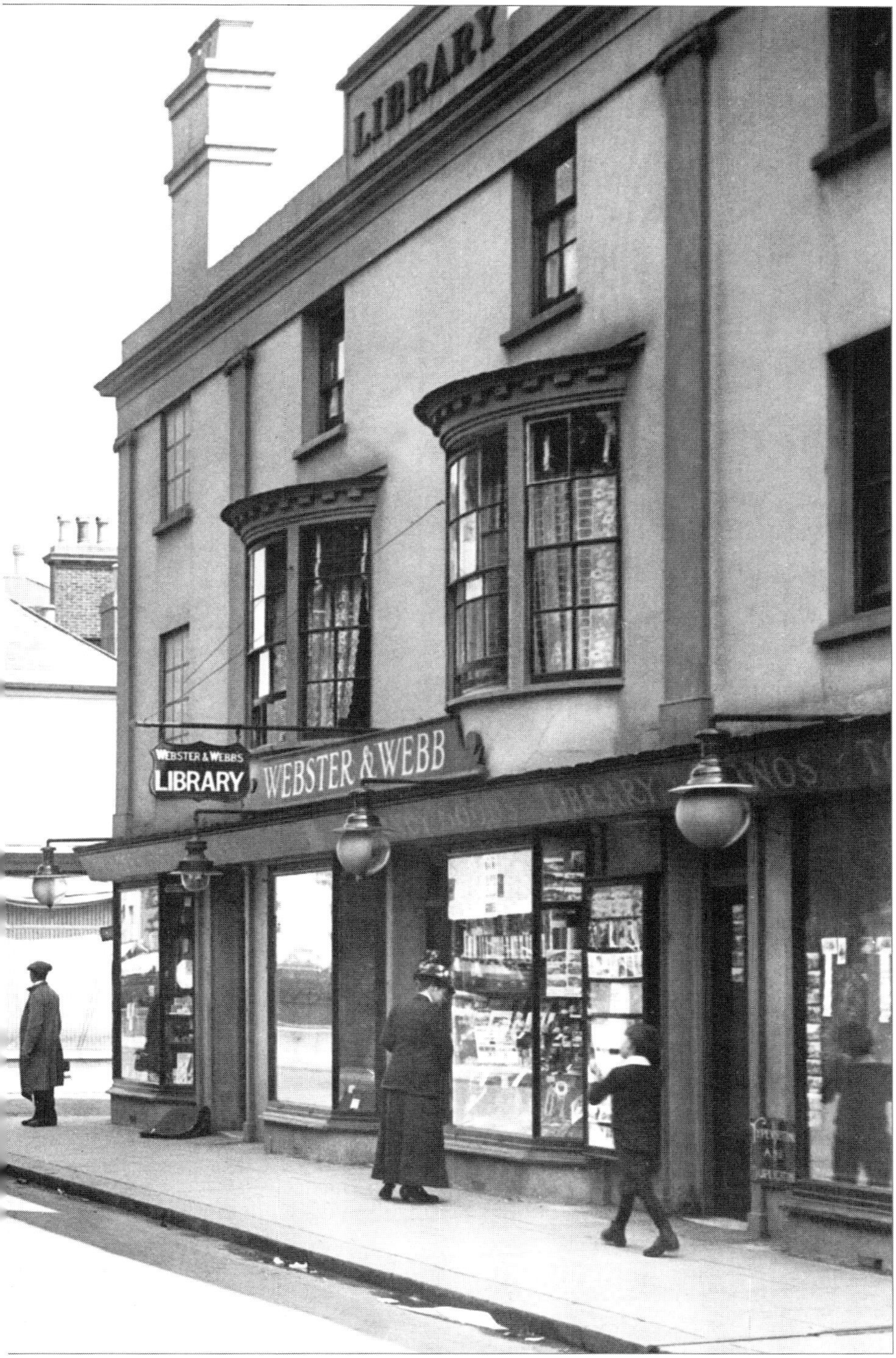


**BOGNOR REGIS**
*High Street 1914* 66934

By 1830 the name Hothamton had been dropped in favour of Bognor. The High Street was part of the original lane which ran through the old village to the sea. The old library on the right (later named Webster and Webb) was built in the 1820s by Robert Knapton; it was visited by Princess Augusta Sophia, daughter of King George III. It was known as The Coffee House in 1983.

**BOGNOR REGIS**
*The Beach 1890*
22627

From the beginning of the 19th century most resorts had bathing machines in which bathers could change while being dragged into the sea, initially by horses and later by winches. Bathing machines were still very popular at Bognor in 1890 - it was not until the Edwardian era that people changed and swam from the beach.

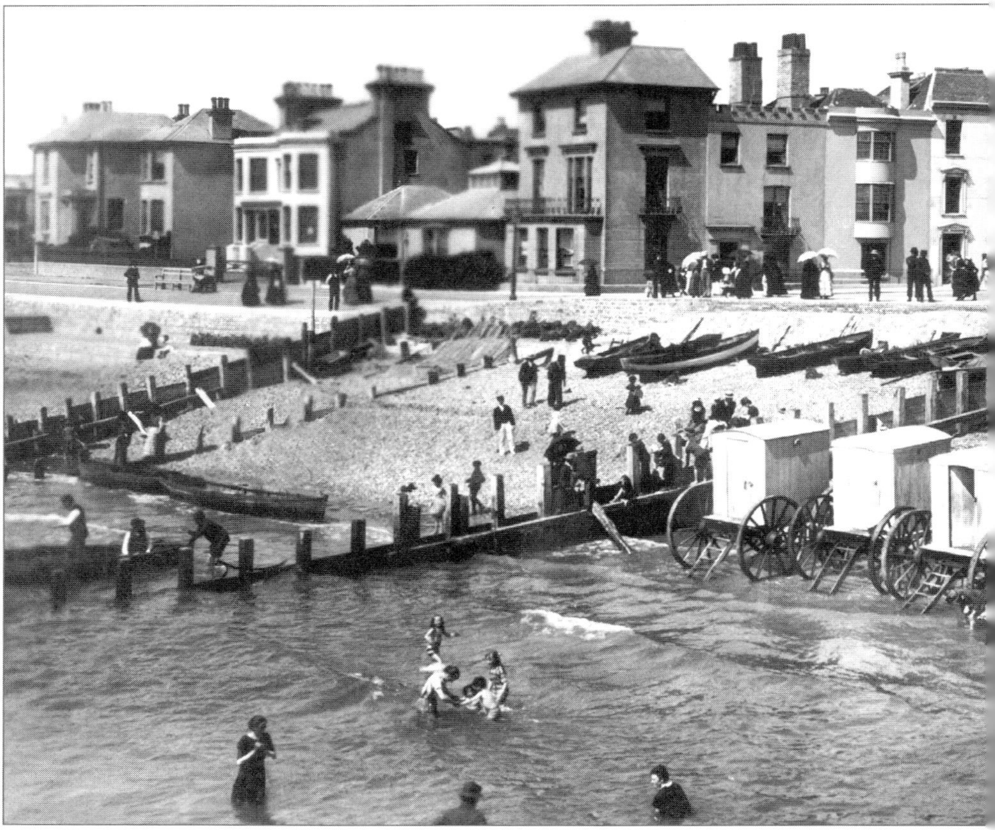

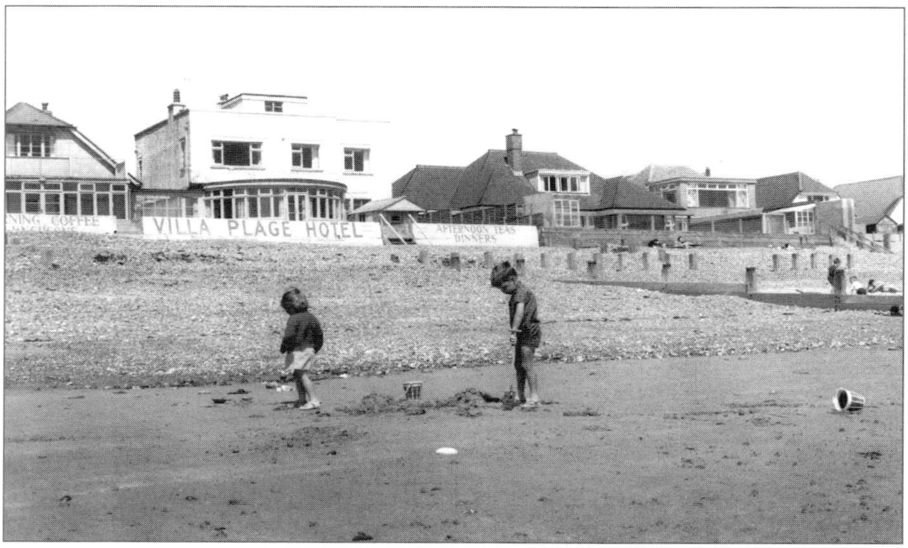


**ELMER**
*The Beach c1960*
E133054

The lack of people on this quiet beach at Elmer, near Bognor Regis, does not appear to distract from the enjoyment of these two young children. At low tide all that matters is the irresistible combination of a bucket and spade for digging holes and making sand castles.

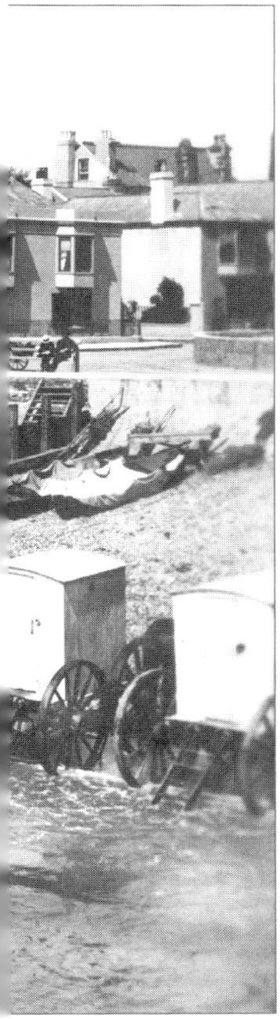

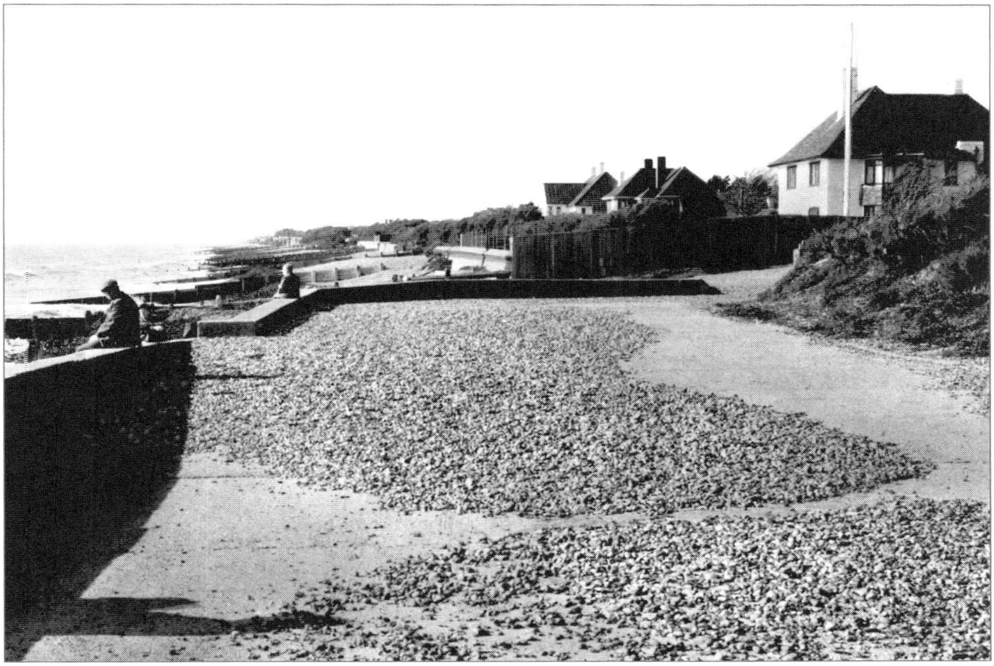

▲ **ANGMERING-ON-SEA,** *The Beach c1955* A327054

This almost deserted beach at the village of Angmering-on-Sea dramatically contrasts with the crowds at the larger and more popular resorts. Nevertheless, a few people appear to be enjoying the sunshine in the peaceful tranquillity, devoid of any deckchairs or boat trips.

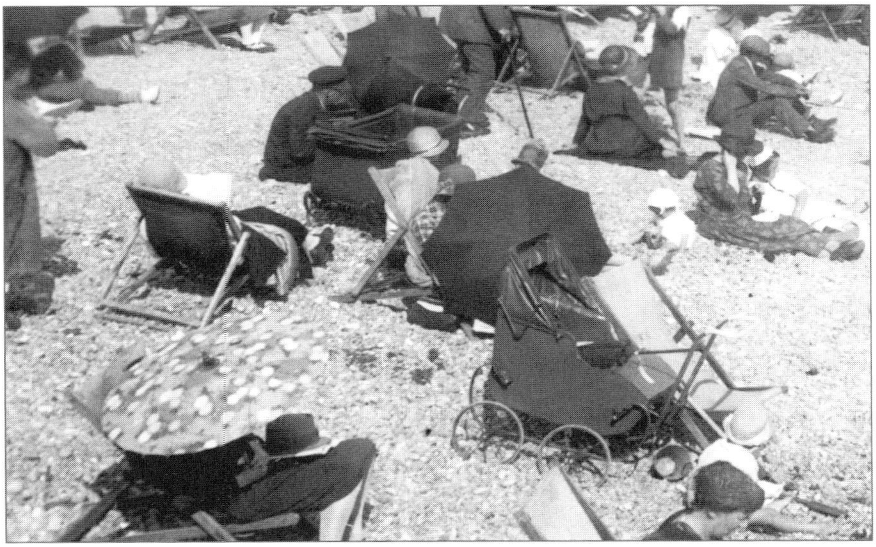

◄ **WORTHING**
*Perambulators on the Beach 1925* 78826X

During the first quarter of the 20th century Worthing's beach was very popular with visitors and inhabitants alike. Here we see it packed with families relaxing in the sunshine, many of them in hired deckchairs. Even the very young, conveyed to the beach in their perambulators, were encouraged to enjoy the sun and sea air.

**WORTHING,** *The Pier 1899* 43953A

Seaside piers were unique to Britain. They initially consisted of a jetty leading to a landing stage for boats, but they soon became fashionable promenades extending over the sea. By the 1860s, their popularity, combined with technical innovation derived from the railways, led to the construction of purpose-built pleasure piers. Worthing Pier, opened in 1862, was the first of these new-style piers in Sussex.

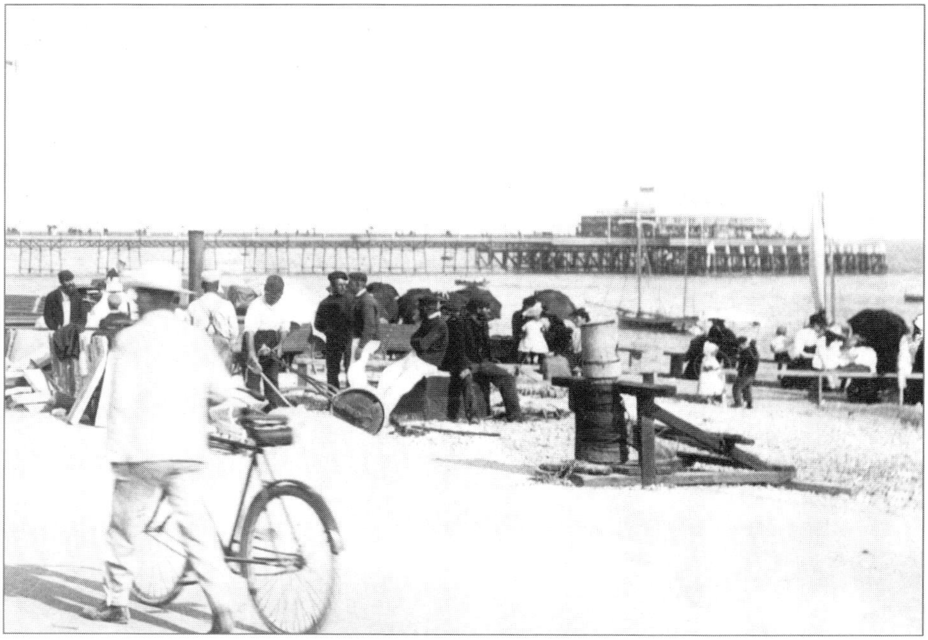

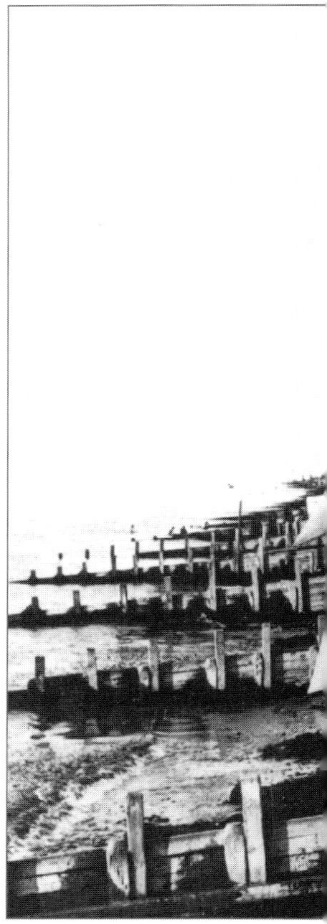

**WORTHING**
*The Bandstand and the Pier 1919* 68985

By the end of the Victorian period, band concerts were a popular form of entertainment at most resorts. This resulted in the erection of a wide variety of ornate iron bandstands, many of which were selected from illustrations in pattern books issued by the various ironworks. W Macfarlane of Glasgow erected the iron 'birdcage' bandstand on the Esplanade at Worthing in 1897.

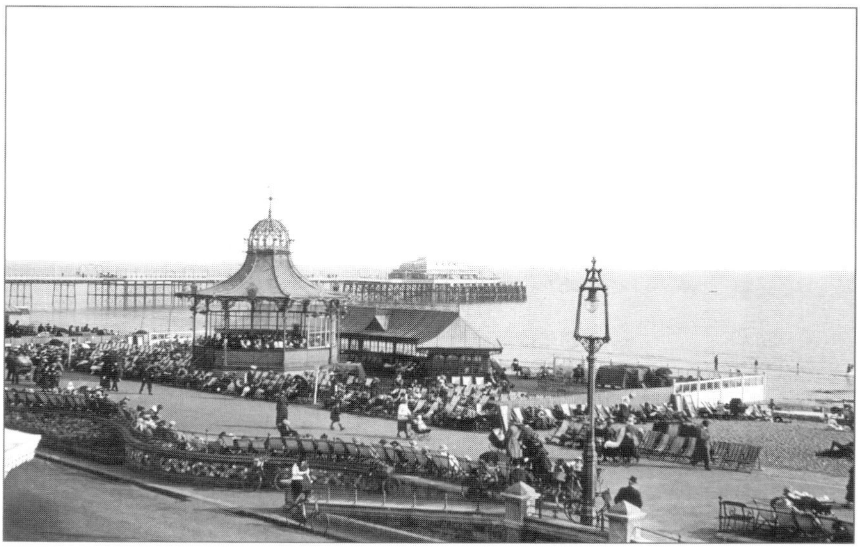

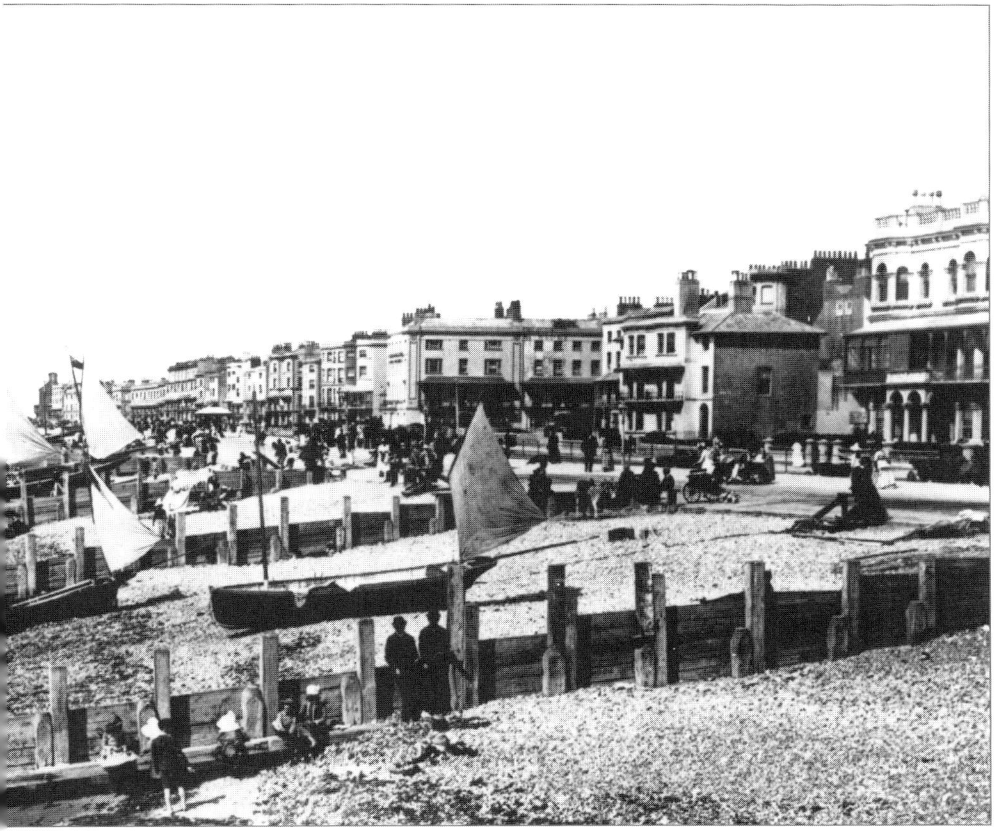

◄ **WORTHING**
*Marine Parade*
*1890* 22677

The architecture captured in late Victorian and early Edwardian photographs often provides an indication of the resort's origins. In 1890, visitors looking westwards from Worthing's pier would have seen terraces of Georgian lodging houses interspersed with a few newly erected Victorian buildings, such as the Clear View Hotel shown on the right.

► **HOVE**
*The Promenade*
*1921* 71500

Although Brighton and Hove have now been amalgamated into a city, in the past Hove was a much quieter and more conservative town than its neighbour. It deliberately provided fewer mass entertainment facilities than Brighton, which presumably accounts for the nearly deserted promenade and beach we see in this picture.

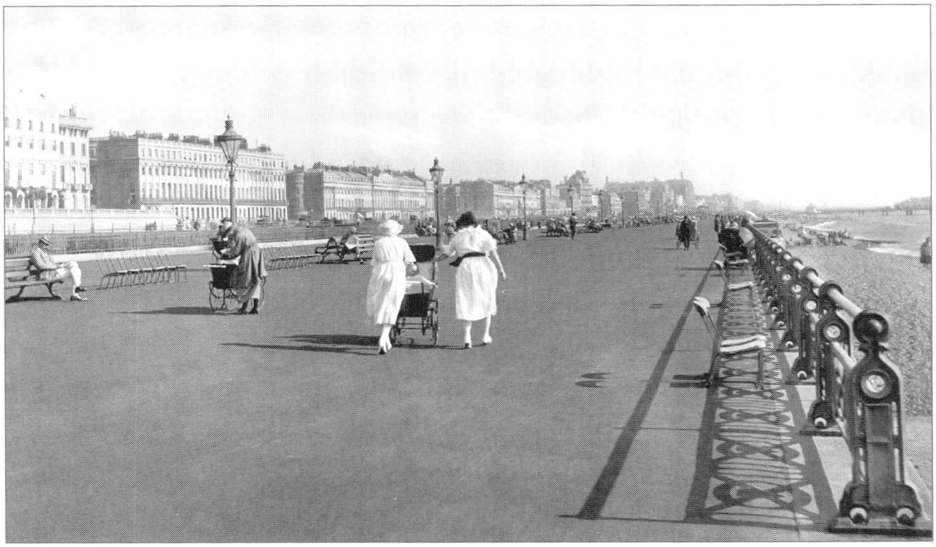

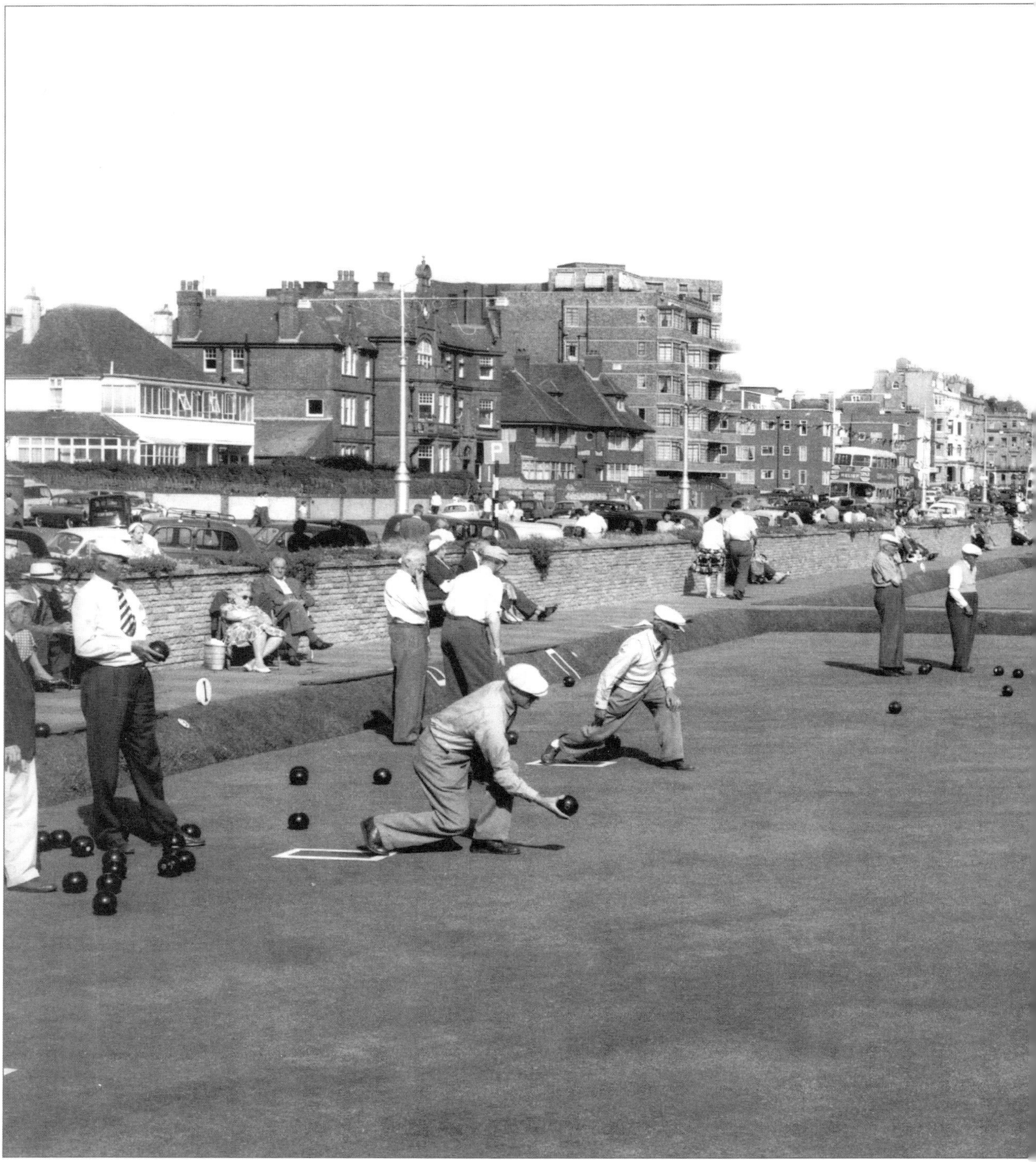

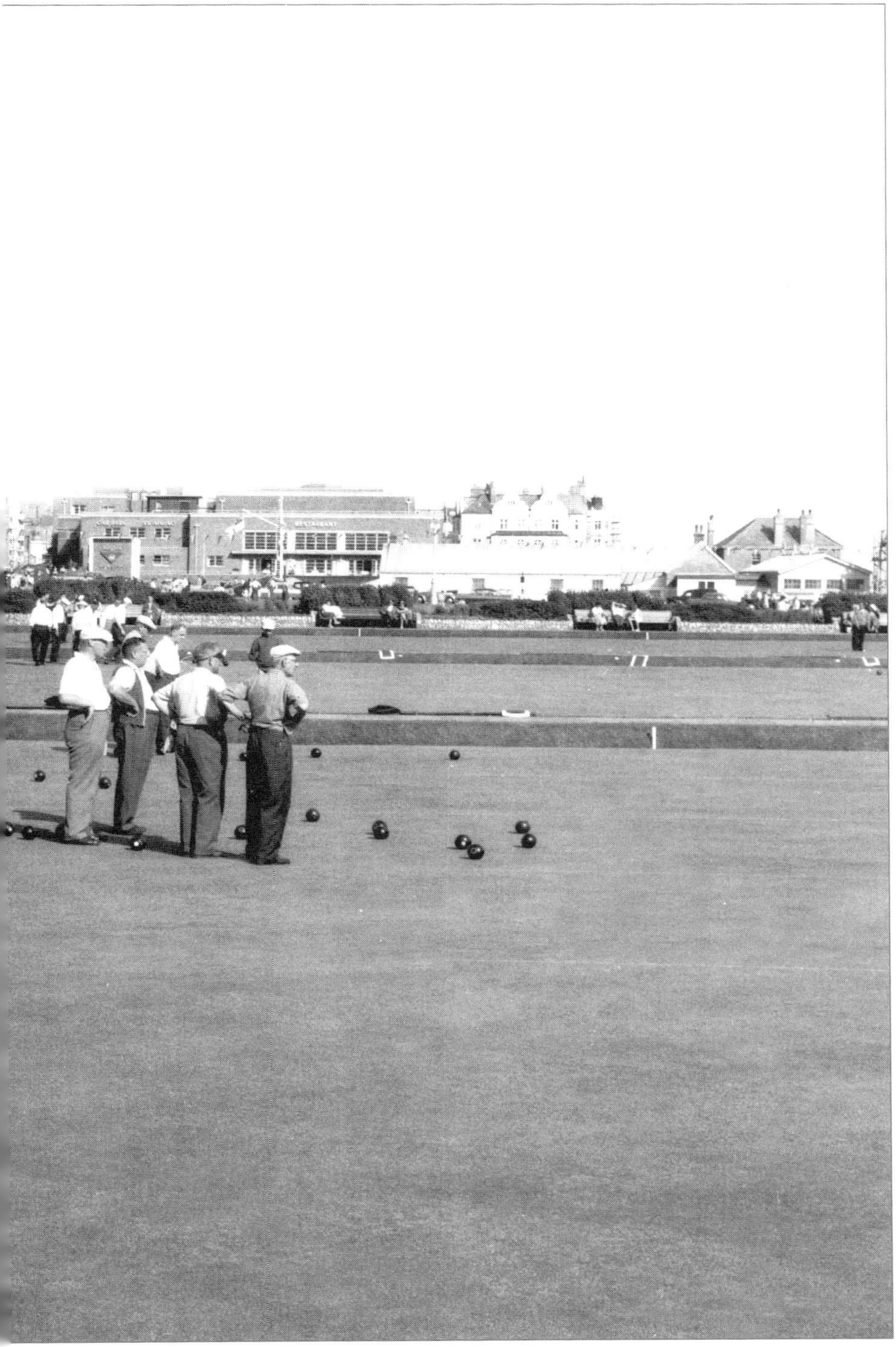

**HOVE**
*The Bowling Green c1960* H128011

The Sussex coast normally has high levels of sunshine combined with a mild and equable climate. These conditions are not only attractive to visitors, but also to those who have chosen to live in the coastal towns of Sussex following their retirement, some of whom can be seen enjoying a competitive game of bowls in this picture.

**BRIGHTON**
*The Pavilion 1889*
22245

Brighton Pavilion is a fitting reminder of this town's emergence as a seaside resort. When Dr Richard Russell moved to Brighthelmstone in 1754 to supervise his sea-water cures, he publicised the resort, and the patronage of the Prince Regent glamorised it. The nucleus of the Pavilion was built in 1787 as a simple Georgian villa, but it was transformed by Nash into the extravaganza (now a tourist attraction) we see today by 1821.

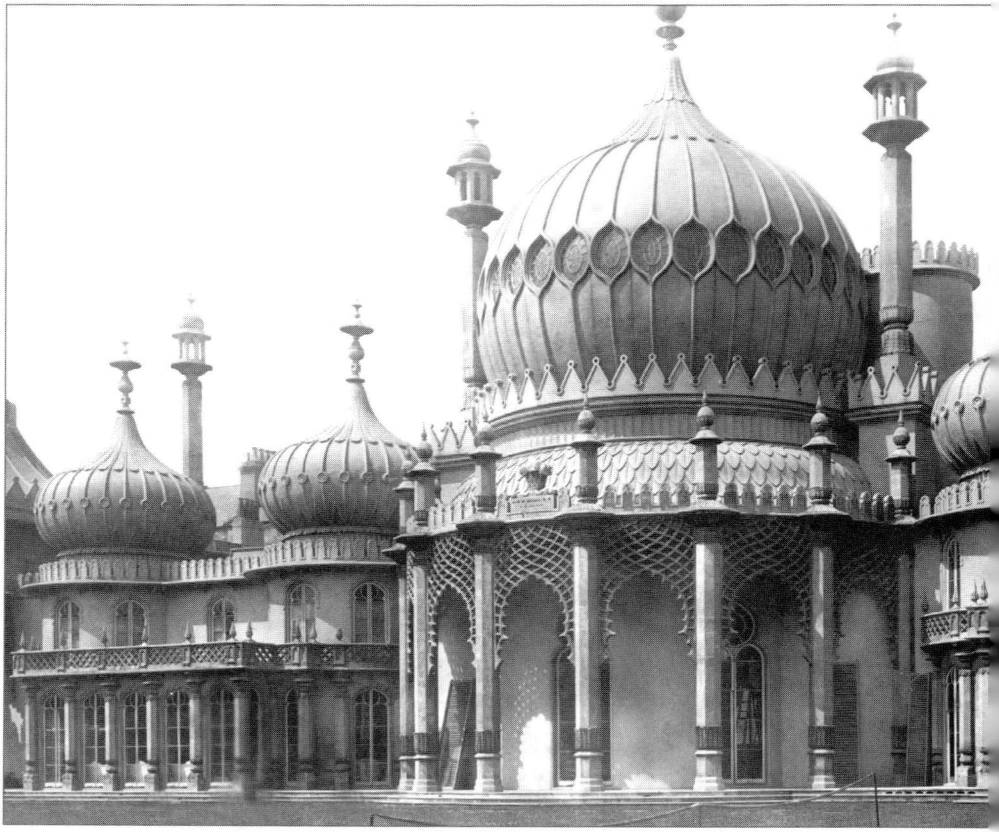

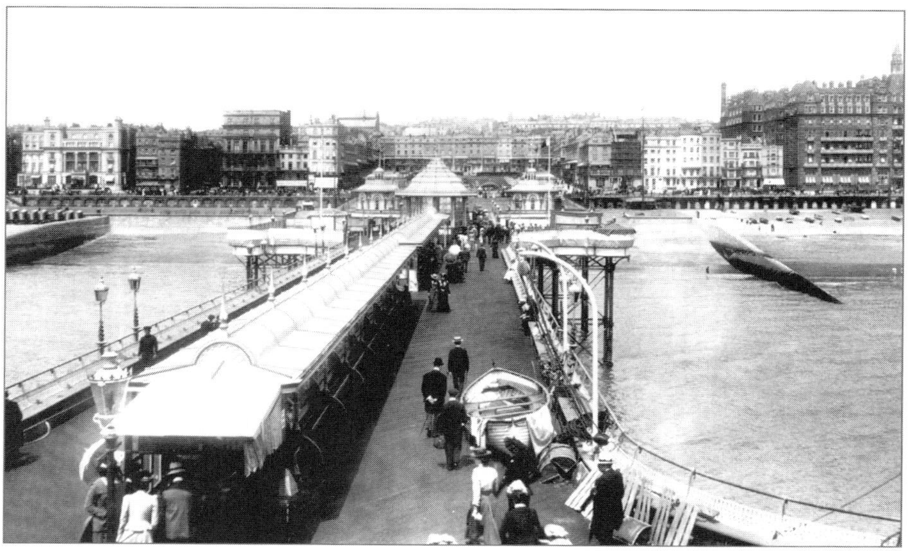

**BRIGHTON**
*West Pier 1902* 48497

Piers allowed the visitor to travel easily over the sea and obtain views of the resort which otherwise would be only possible from a boat, but without any of the attendant discomfort! This is clearly demonstrated in this fine panoramic view of Brighton from the West Pier, which was designed by Eugenius Birch and opened in 1866.

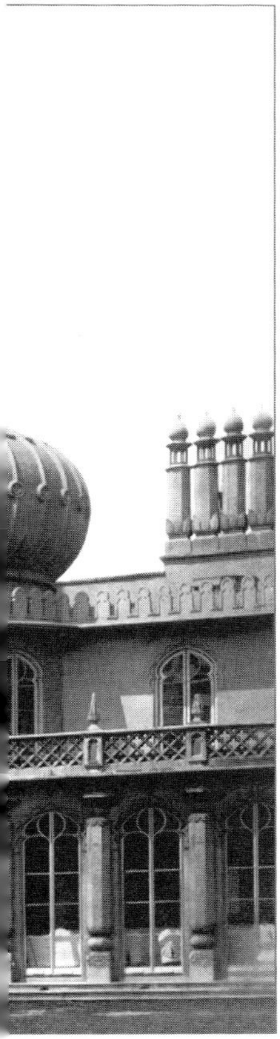

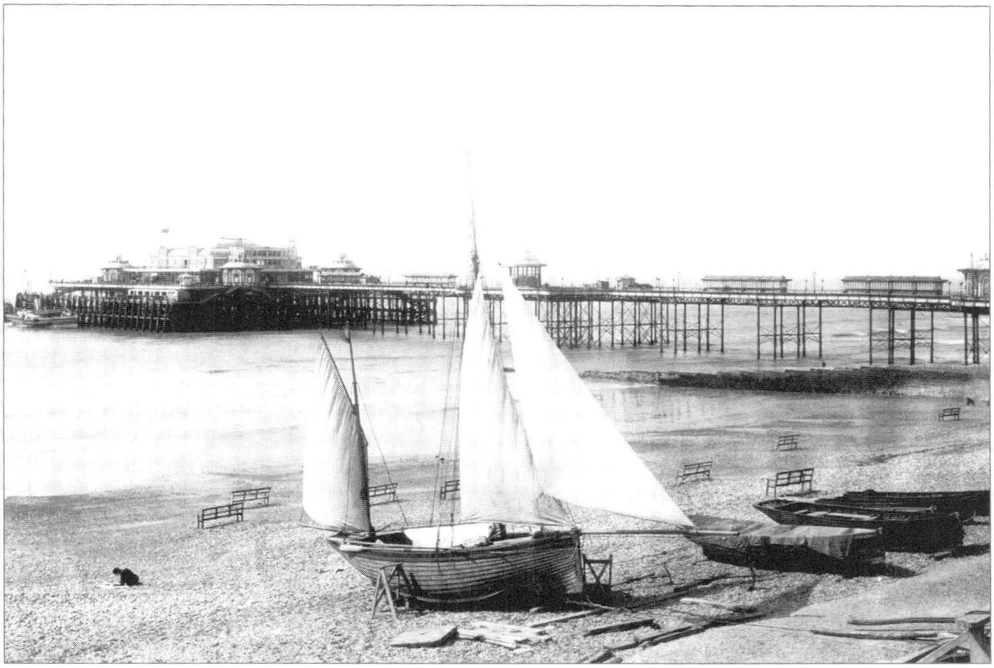

▲ **BRIGHTON,** *West Pier Pavilion from Kings Road 1894* 33763

By 1894 Brighton's West Pier had been extensively rebuilt, and a landing stage had been added together with a new pavilion. Pleasure boats were still available from the beach; these competed for trade with the paddle steamers that had been introduced in the 1880s, after their initial function had been superseded by the railways.

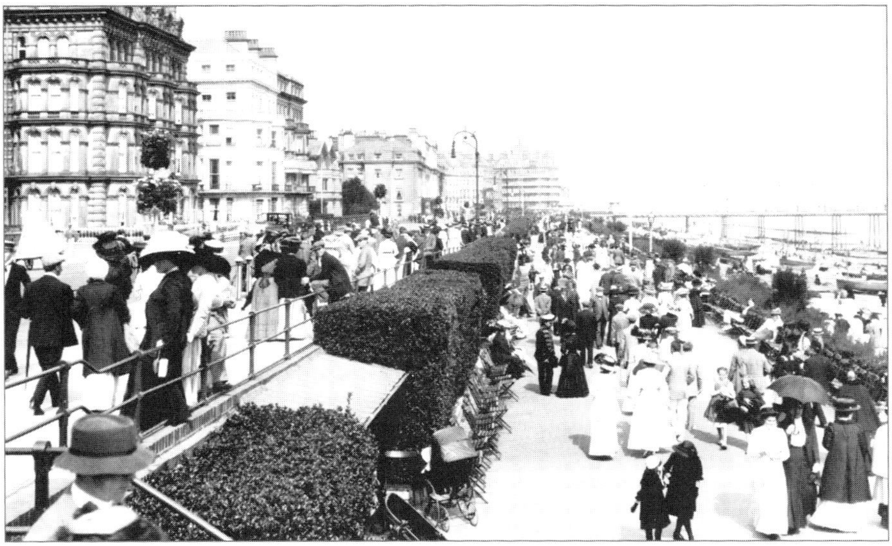

◄ **EASTBOURNE**
*Grand Parade 1910*
62948

The Georgian practice of the leisured classes of promenading along the water's edge for therapeutic reasons continued to be popular during the Victorian and Edwardian eras, and imposing parades were constructed at the larger resorts. Eastbourne's Grand Parade consisted of three terraces stretching from the Wish Tower to the Pier; it has been described as 'one of the finest of its kind in England.'

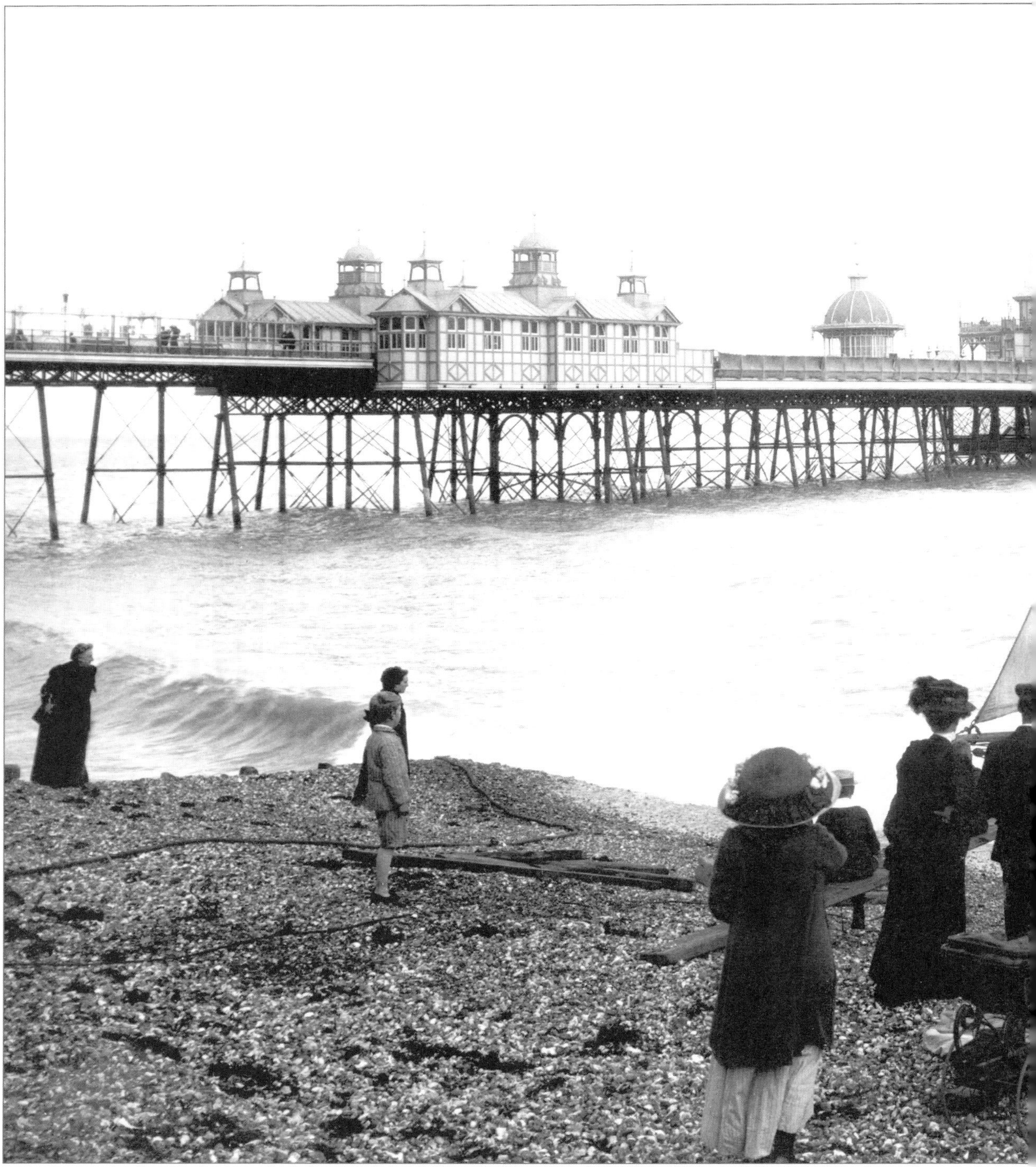

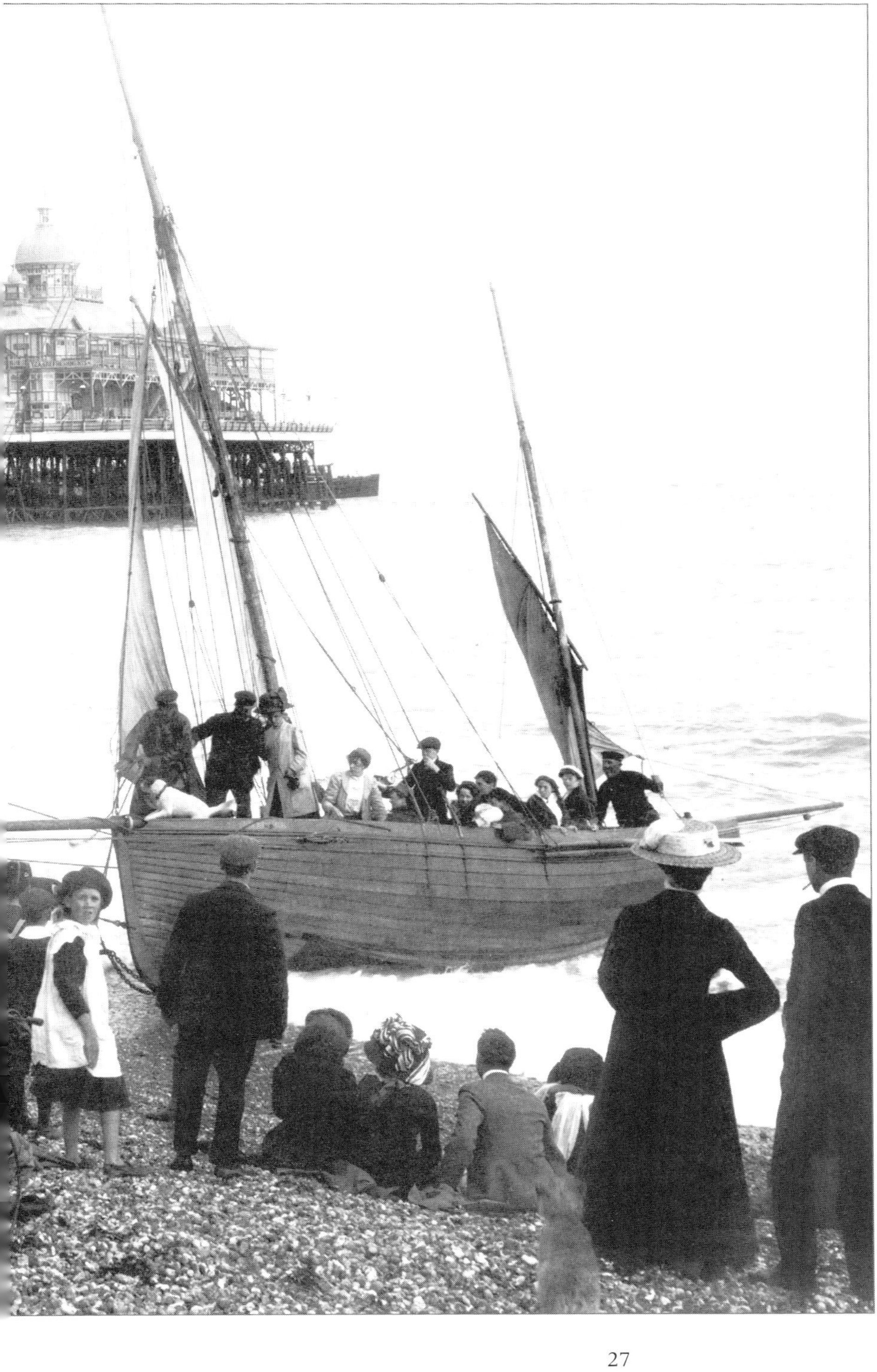

**EASTBOURNE**
*The Pier 1910* 62958

A southern pavilion was added to the seaward end of Eastbourne's pier in 1888 - late Victorian visitors expected piers to be more than just a promenade or an occasional venue for entertainment. Fishermen also benefited from this extra demand for entertainment, as they were still able to supplement their income by offering pleasure boat trips from the beach.

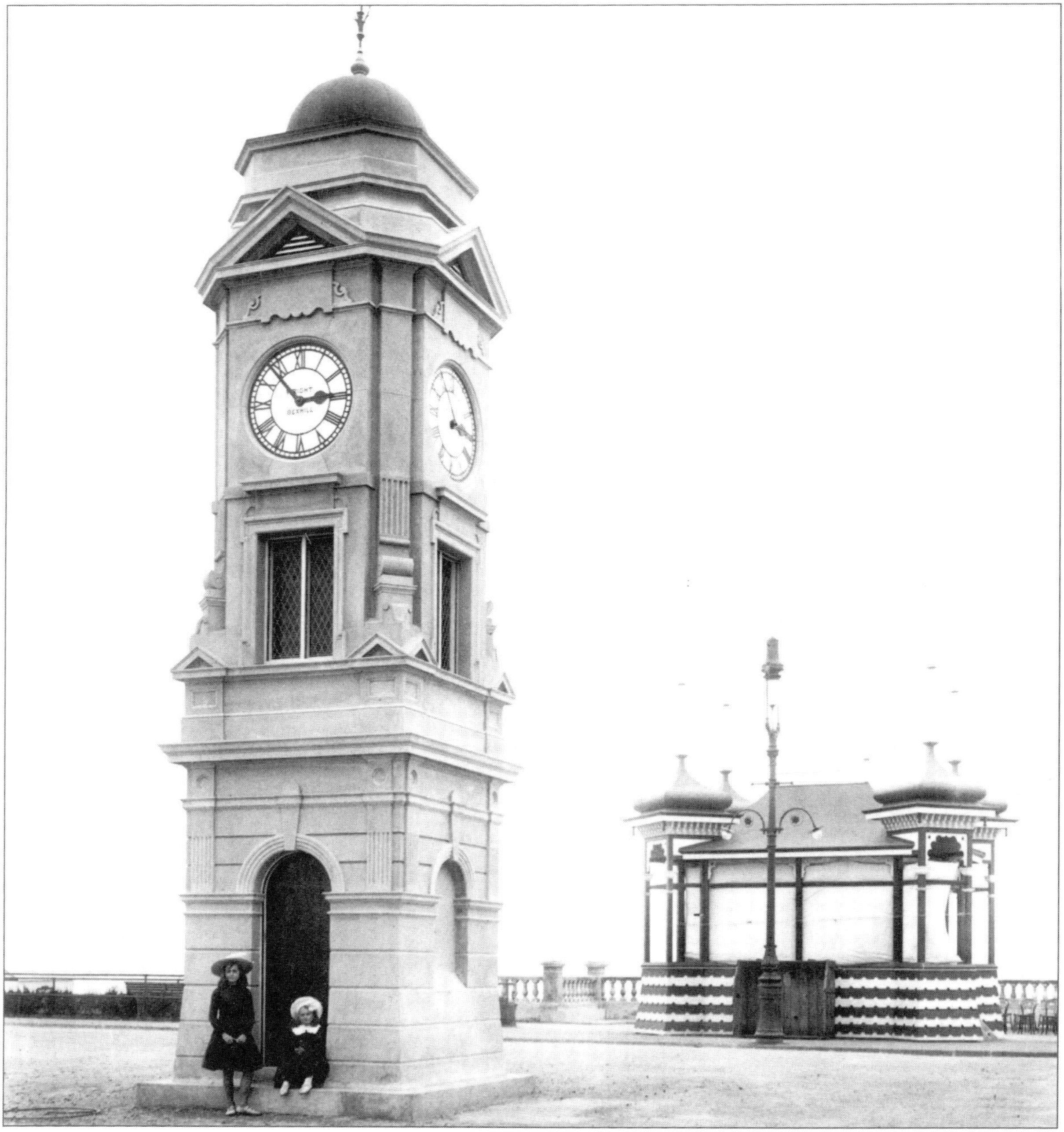

**BEXHILL,** *The Clock Tower and the Bandstand 1904* 52895

The children are standing in front of Bexhill's clock tower, which was erected on the Parade in 1902 to commemorate the Coronation of King Edward VII. Nearby was the town's ornate bandstand, which was very different in style to the ones erected at the other Sussex seaside resorts.

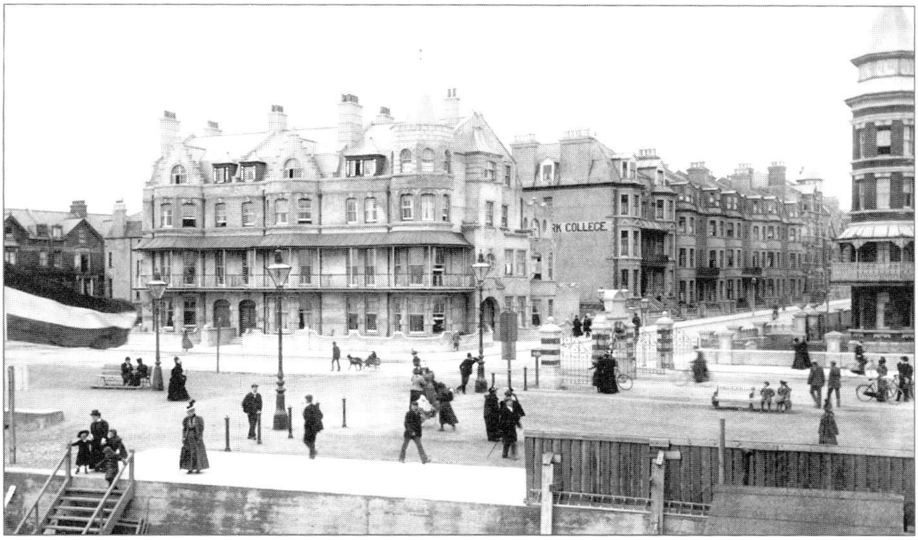

**BEXHILL**
*The Parade 1897*
38989

Bexhill had been a fishing village before 1884, when the words 'on-Sea' were added to its name. Thereafter the resort expanded on to the low-lying ground between the old hillside village and the sea. Bexhill's Parade was constructed on top of the sea wall that had been built in the 1880s as a coastal defence.

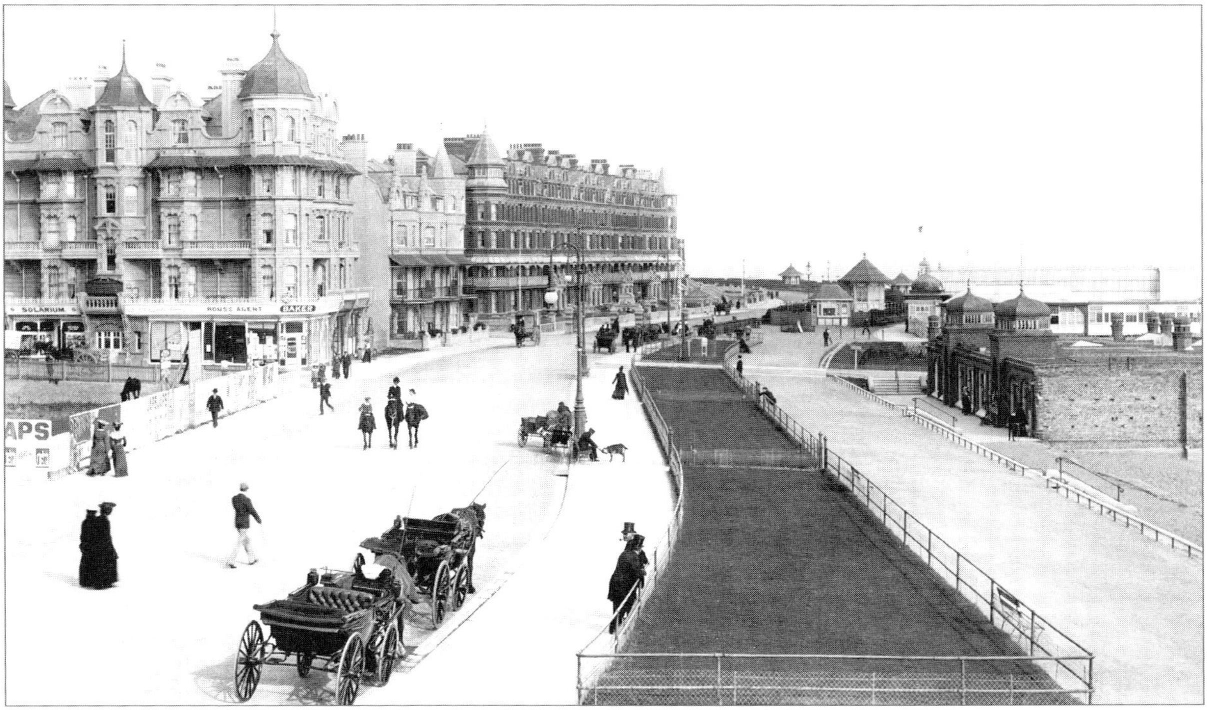


**BEXHILL,** *The Parade 1903* 50305

In direct contrast to other Sussex resorts, the 8th Earl De La Warr did not develop Bexhill as a high-class seaside resort until the late Victorian and Edwardian period. The majority of the buildings fronting the De La Warr Parade were erected between 1891 and 1901, and reflect the late Victorian style of seaside architecture.

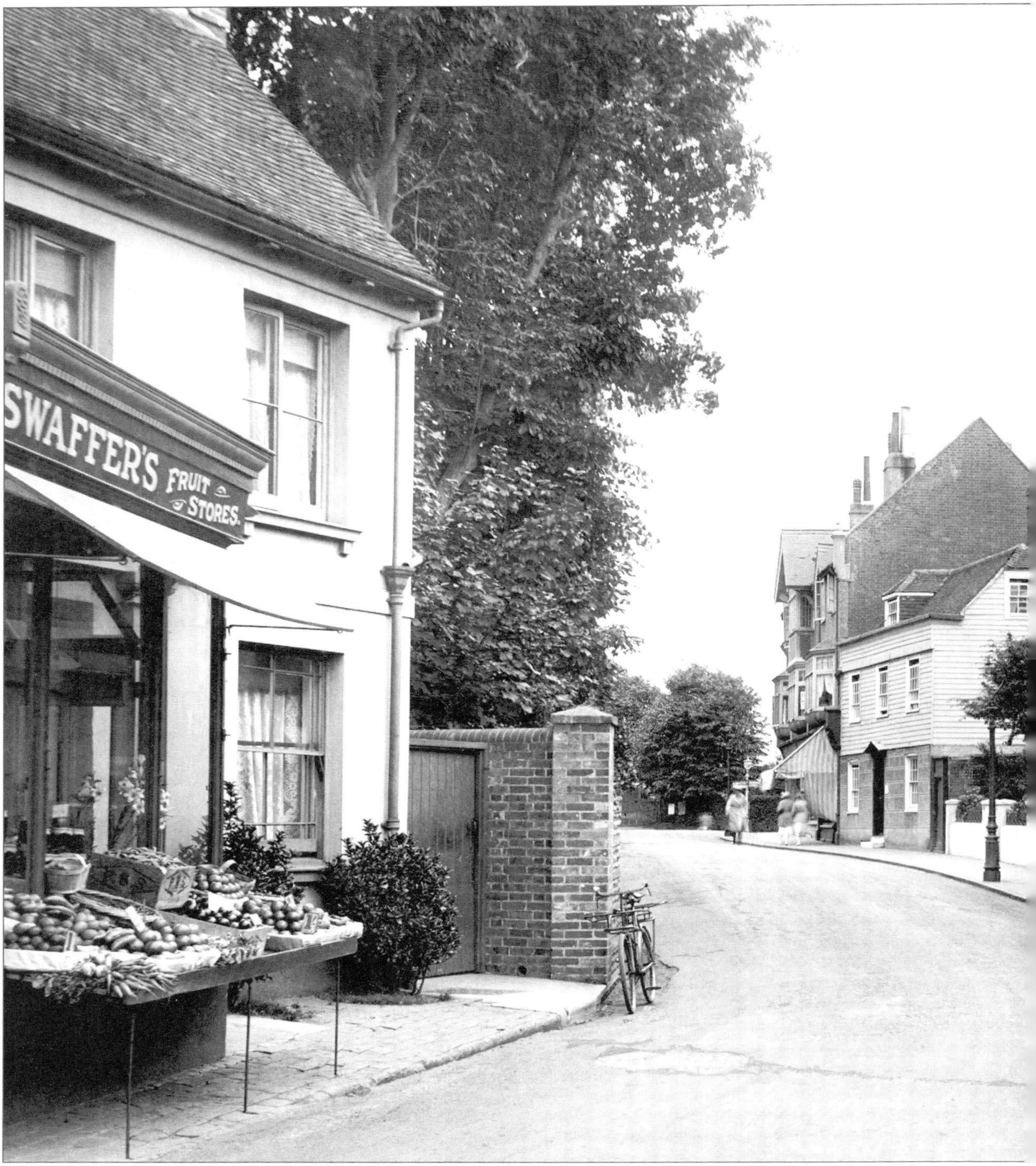
SWAFFER'S FRUIT STORES.

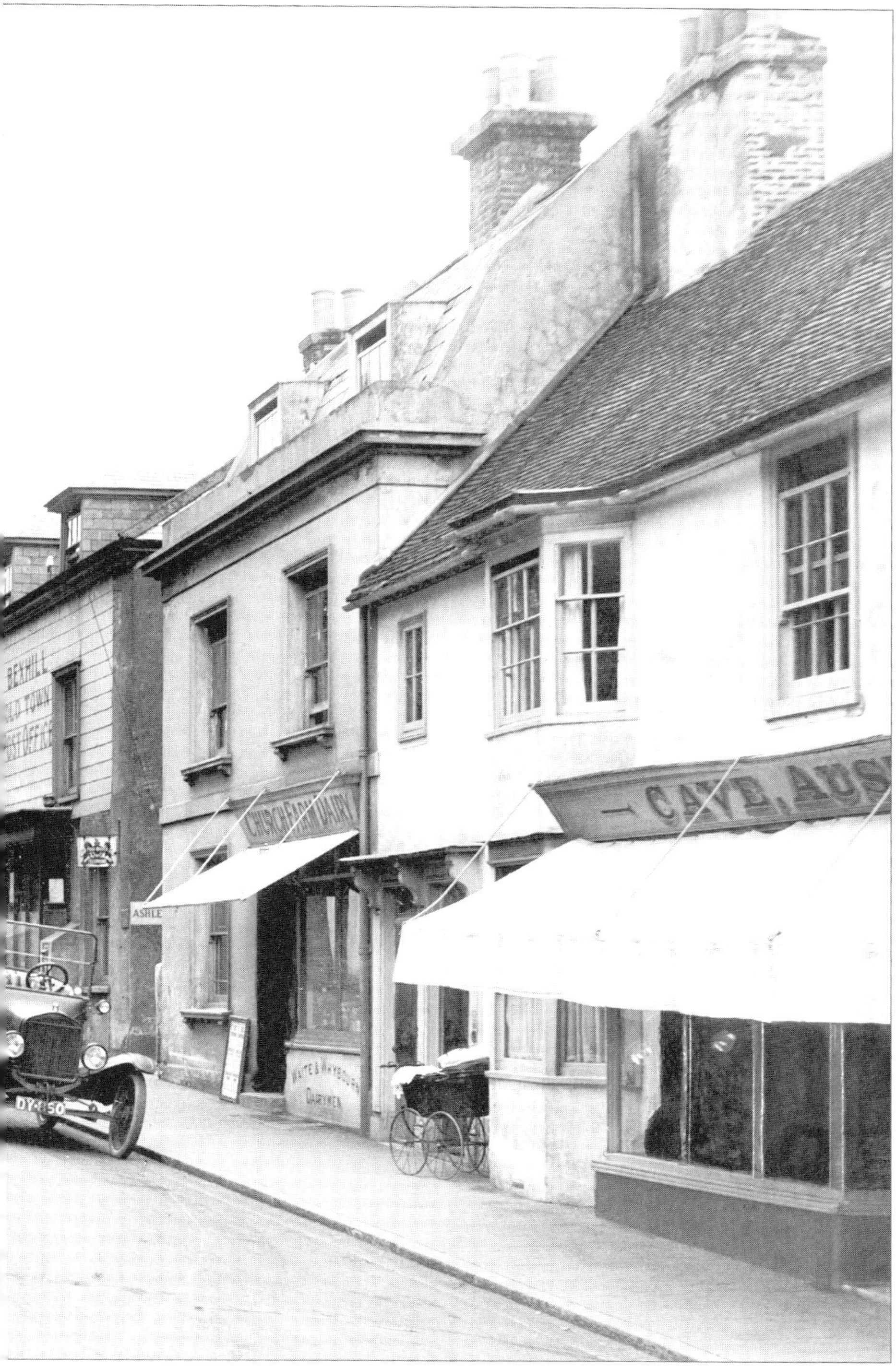


**BEXHILL**
*The Old Town 1921*
70524

By 1921, the now well-established resort of Bexhill-on-Sea had expanded southwards from the ancient fishing village known as the Old Town. The motor car is a fitting reminder that in 1902 Bexhill held the first motor racing trials in England, on a course leading from Galley Hill to the De La Warr Parade.

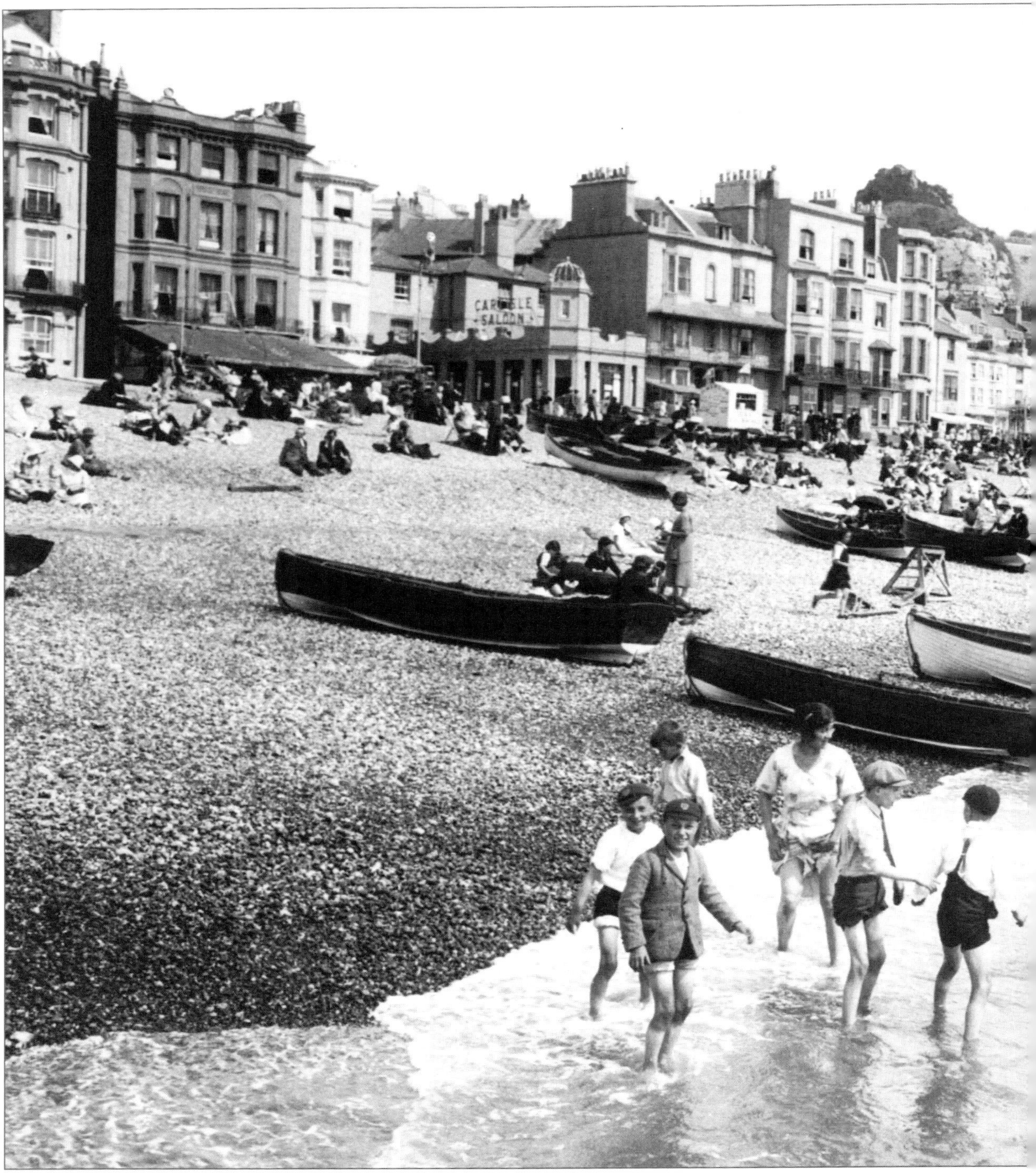

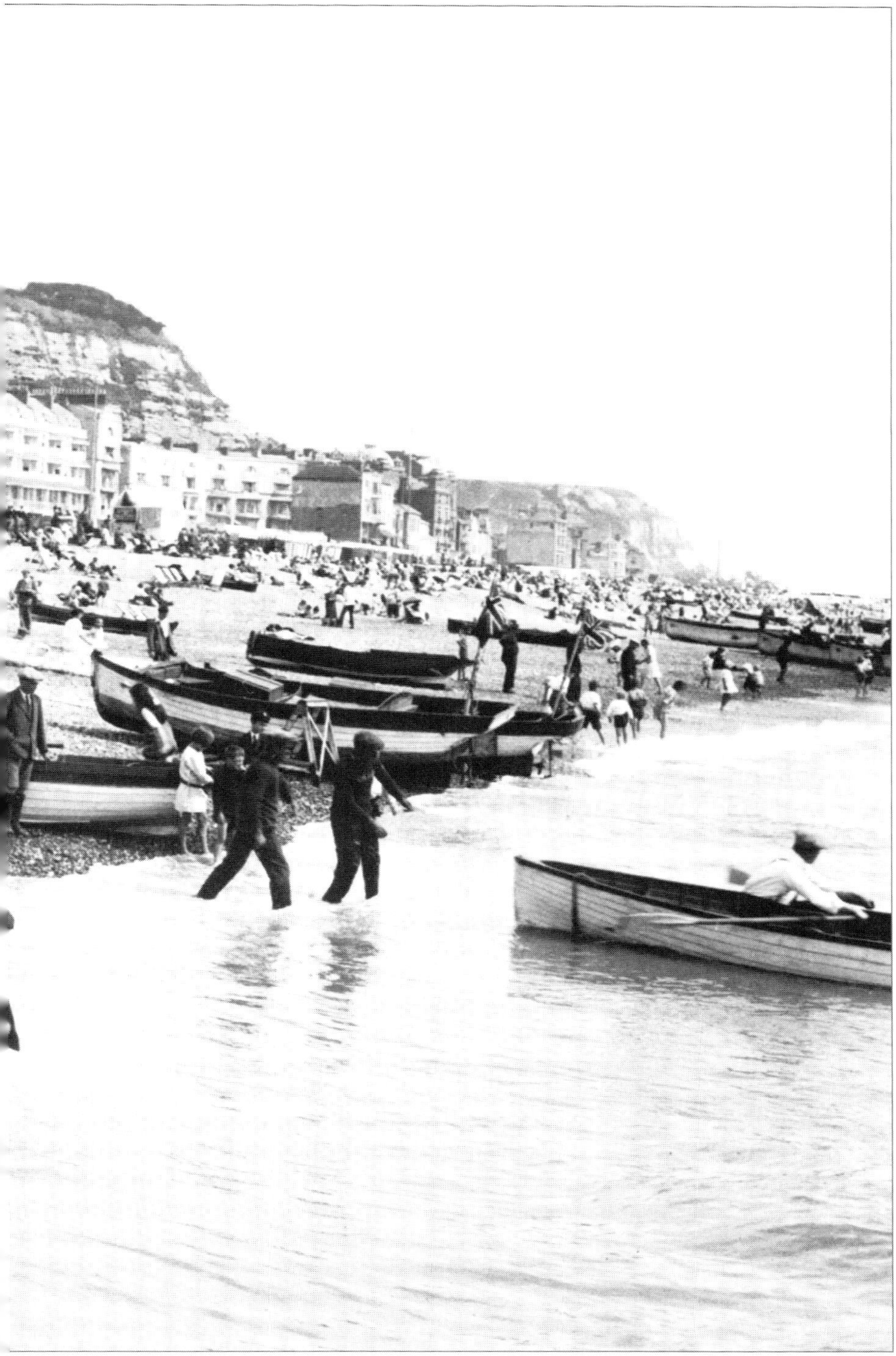

**HASTINGS**
*The View from the Pier 1925* 77975

Children are not generally difficult to please, and at the seaside they create their own entertainment. Paddling in the sea is as popular today as it was at Hastings in 1925. The two men behind them, who appear to be paddling while fully clothed, are actually going to assist a family returning from a rowing boat trip

# THE COASTAL PLAIN

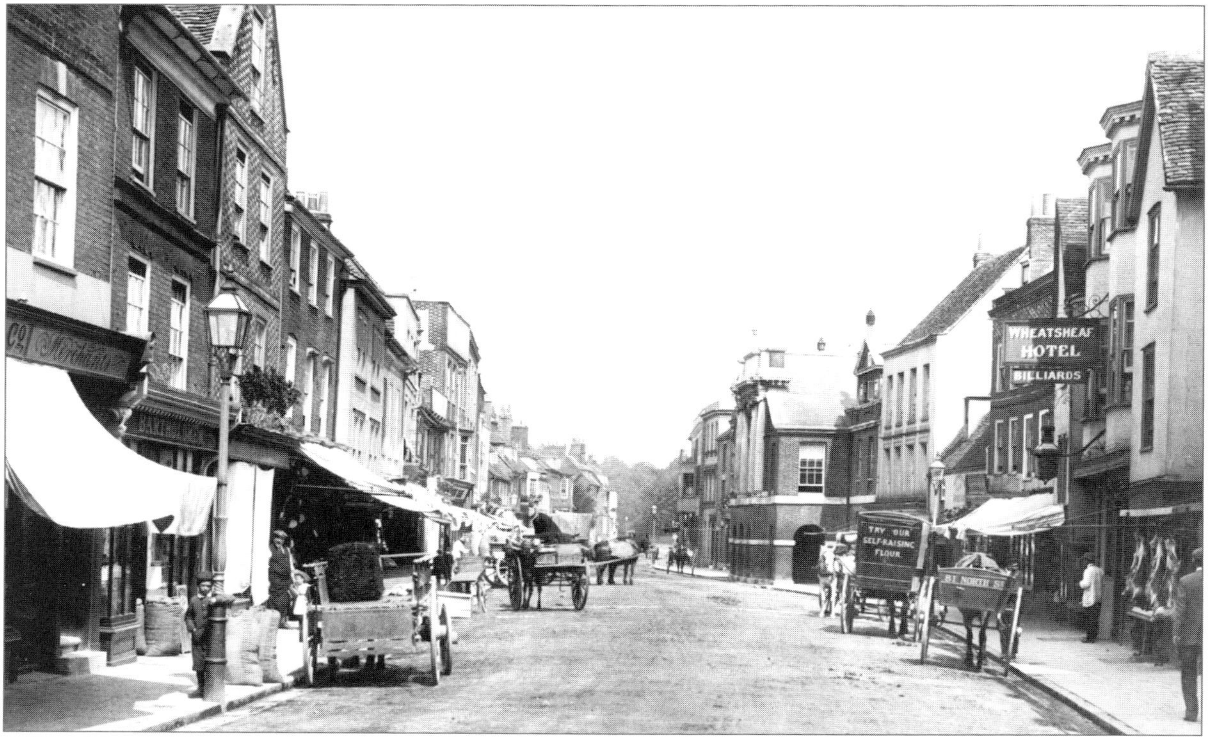


**CHICHESTER,** *North Street 1898* 42677

Little of the Roman town or medieval city remains, as Chichester was almost entirely rebuilt by the end of the 18th century. The Wheatsheaf Hotel (right) displaced an earlier 17th-century victuallers, and the 19th-century properties on the right replaced the early 16th-century shops that had slowly encroached onto the city's medieval market site.

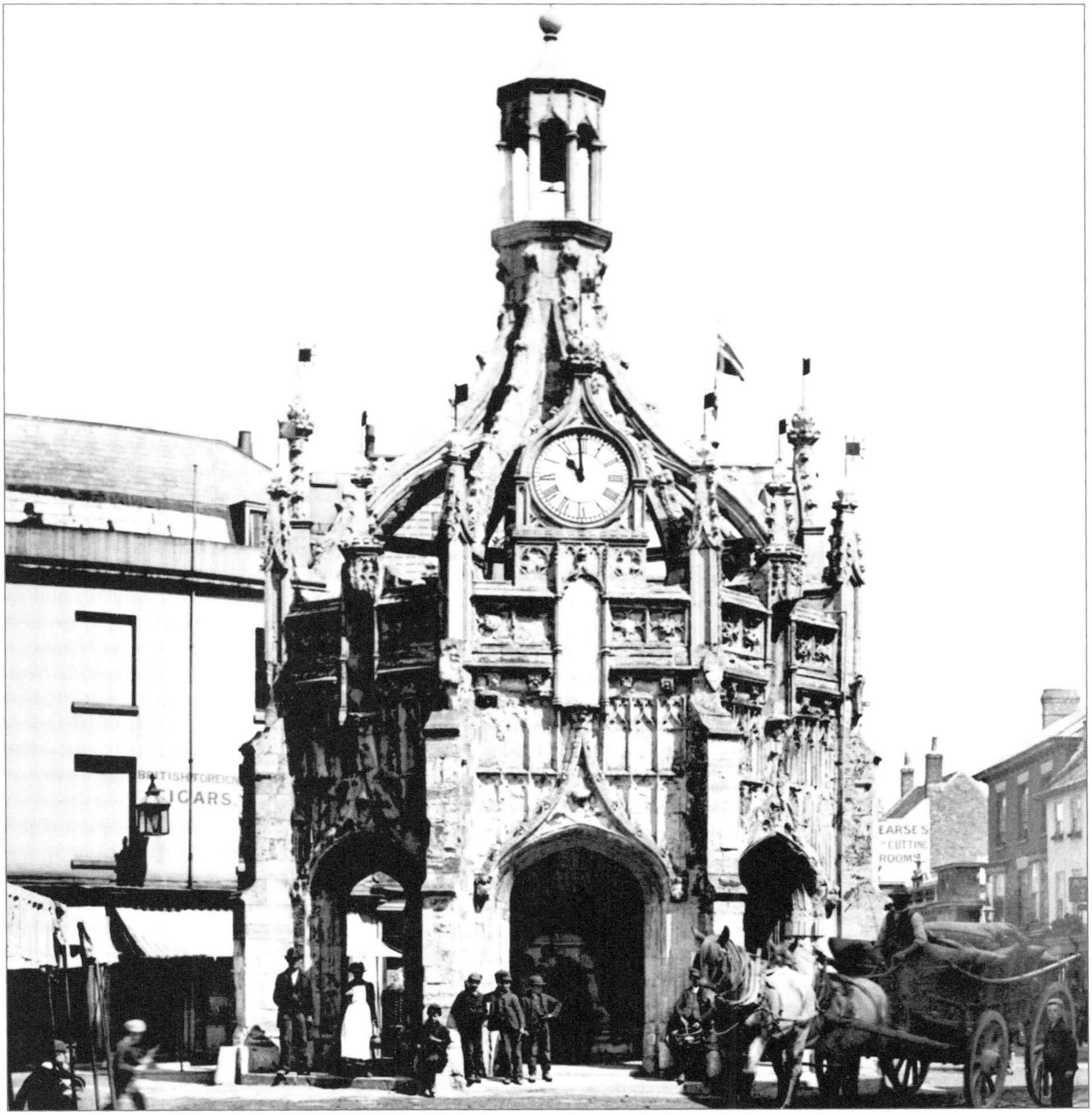


**CHICHESTER,** *The Market Cross 1890* 22615

Chichester's Market Cross is sited at the intersection of its four main roads that date from the Roman period. The eight-sided Caen stone building was built in 1501 by Bishop Storey, so that the poor displaced from the market area by merchants' shops had somewhere to sell their wares. The clock, the ball and the iron weather vane were all added in 1746.

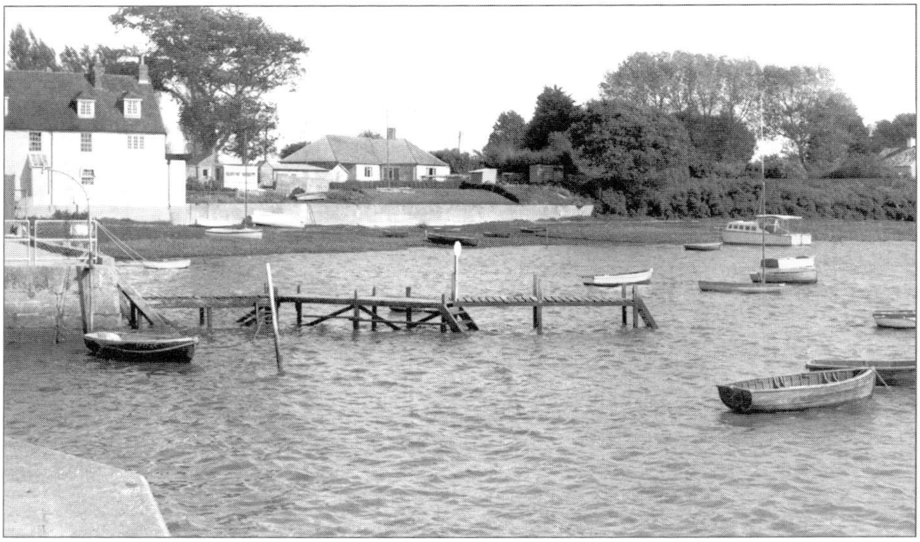

**DELL QUAY**
*c1960* D244040

Dell Quay, at the northern end of Chichester Harbour, was the landing place for cargo ships delivering goods to the market at Chichester. While sitting in the garden of the very popular Rose and Crown public house, visitors can still enjoy this view of the ancient estuary today.

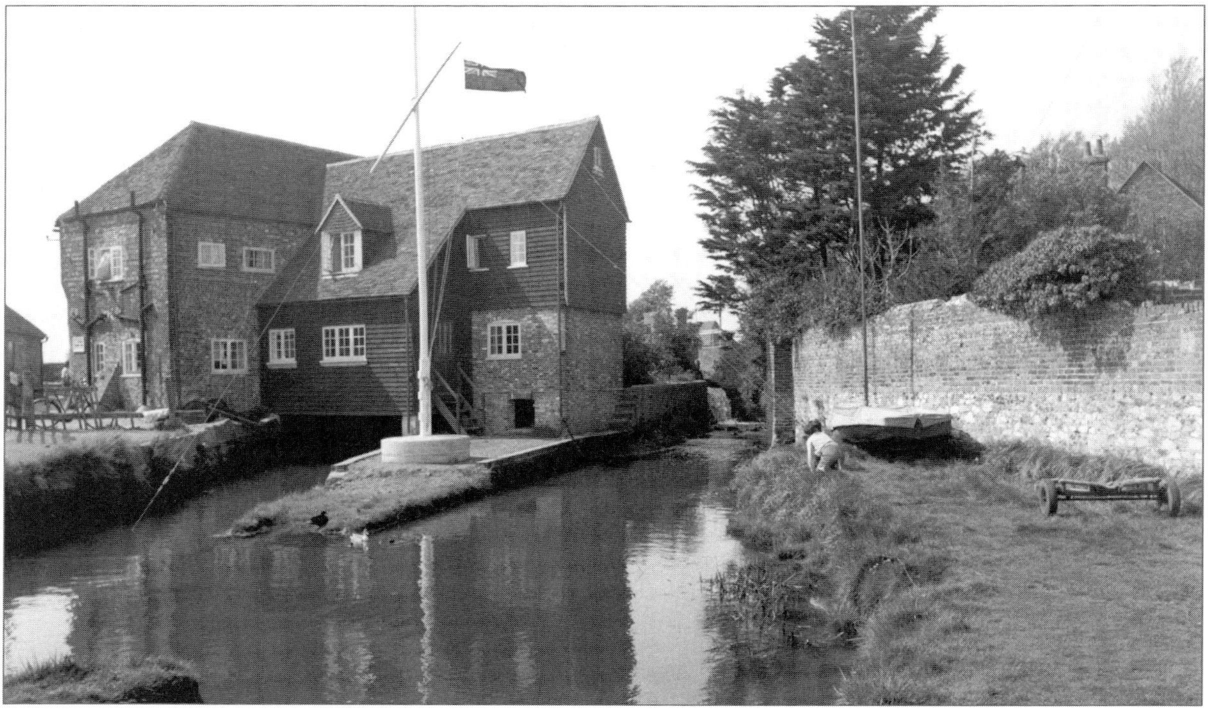

**BOSHAM,** *The Old Mill c1965* B152028

This former ancient tide mill, sited to the south of Dell Quay and at the head of the Bosham Channel, today stands alongside the Bosham Yacht Club quay, and is the haunt of many yachtsmen who enjoy the charm and tranquillity of Chichester Harbour.

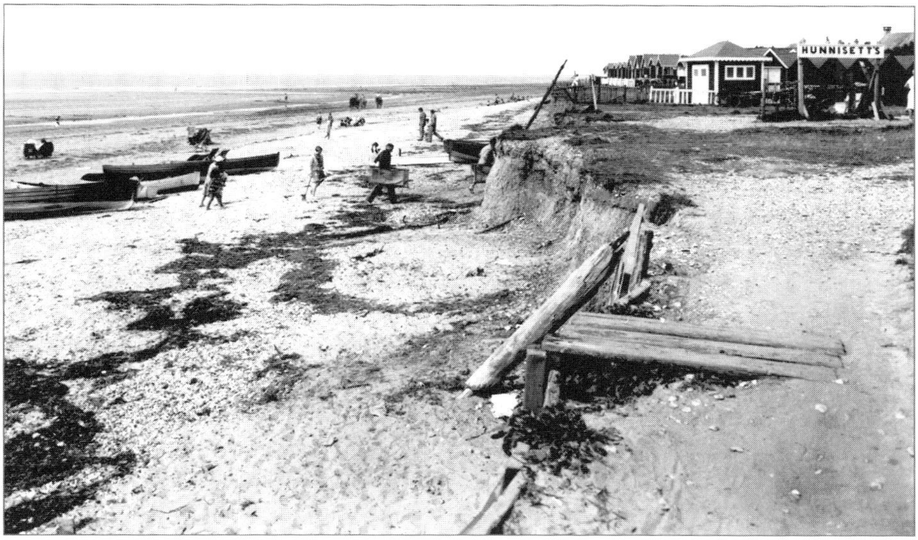


**SELSEY**
*The Beach 1930*
83450

In the 7th century, Selsey was the cultural centre of Sussex. Today the remains of Bishop Wilfrid's Saxon cathedral and the Bishop of Chichester's deer park lie submerged a few hundred yards offshore. The coastline is still being eroded, and as each winter storm breaches the vulnerable unprotected beach, the sea threatens to make Selsey an island again.

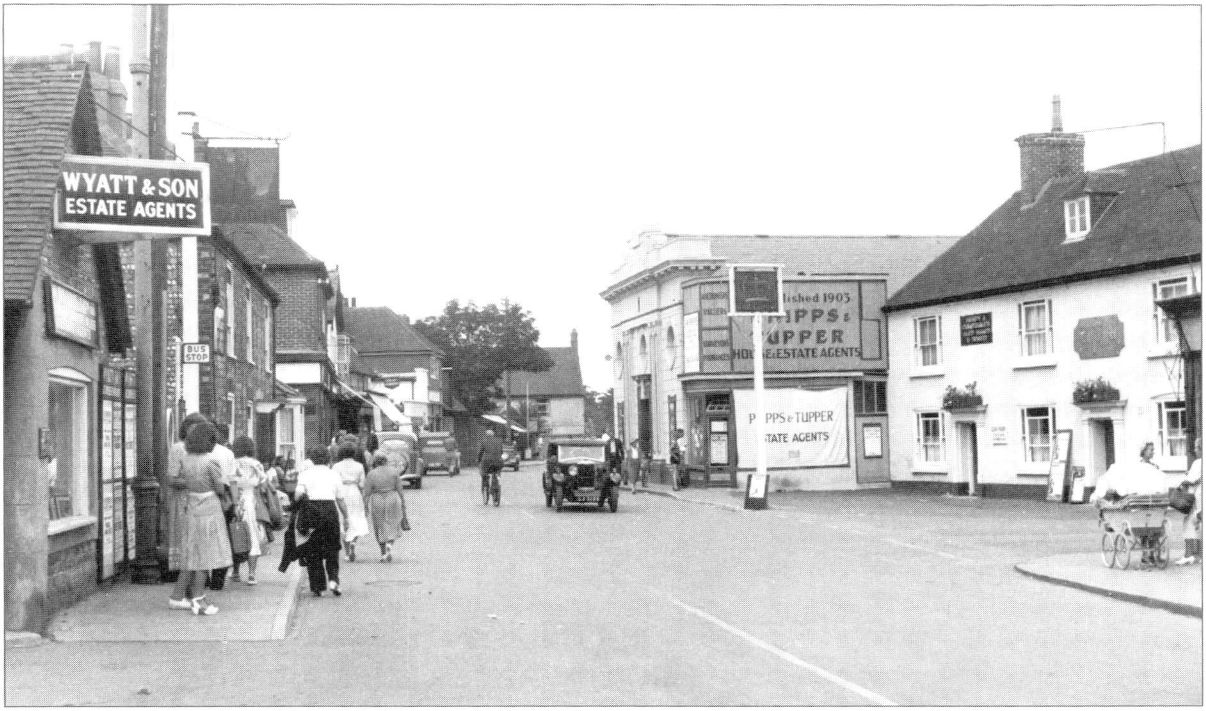


**SELSEY,** *High Street c1955* S91020

On either side of the High Street, some of the former well-stocked shops have become estate agents, marketing the many bungalows and houses that were built for families who came year after year to enjoy the sea air, the fine sands and the seclusion. At least the Crown Inn (right) survives for the visitors' enjoyment!

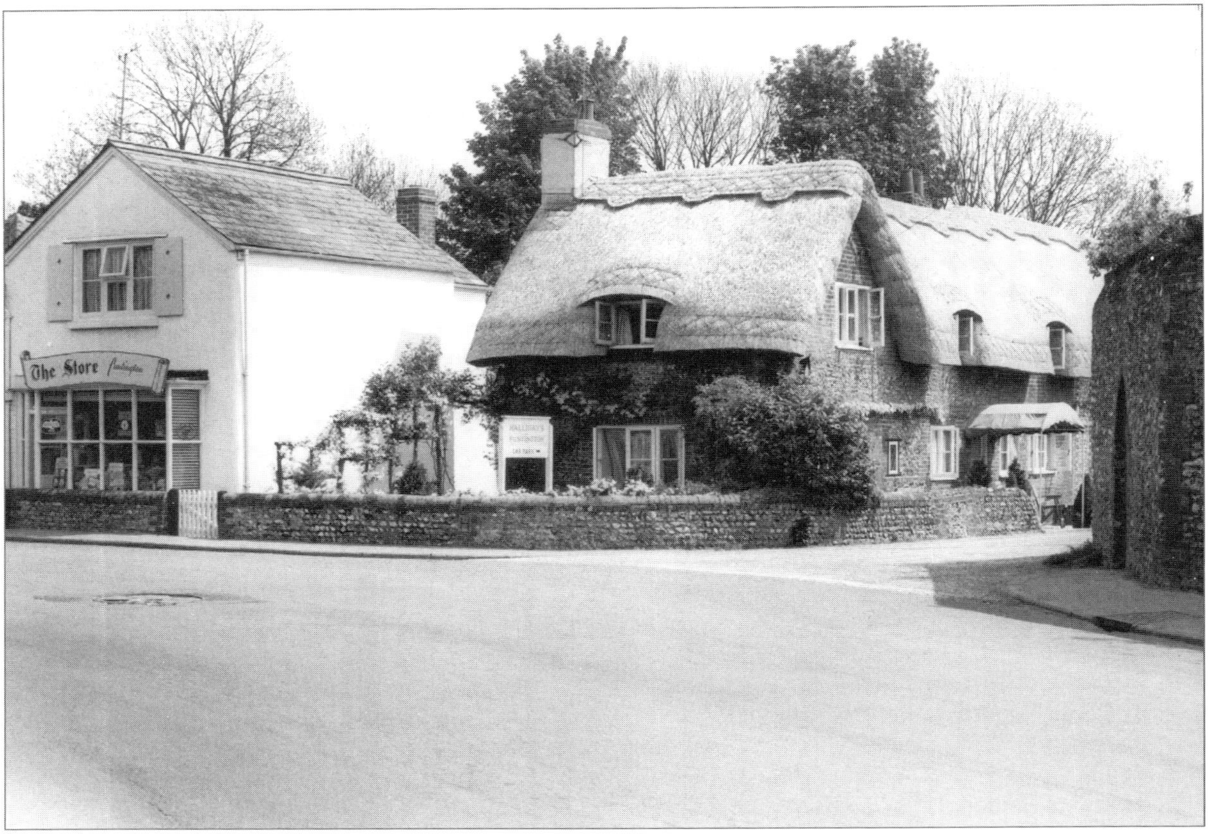


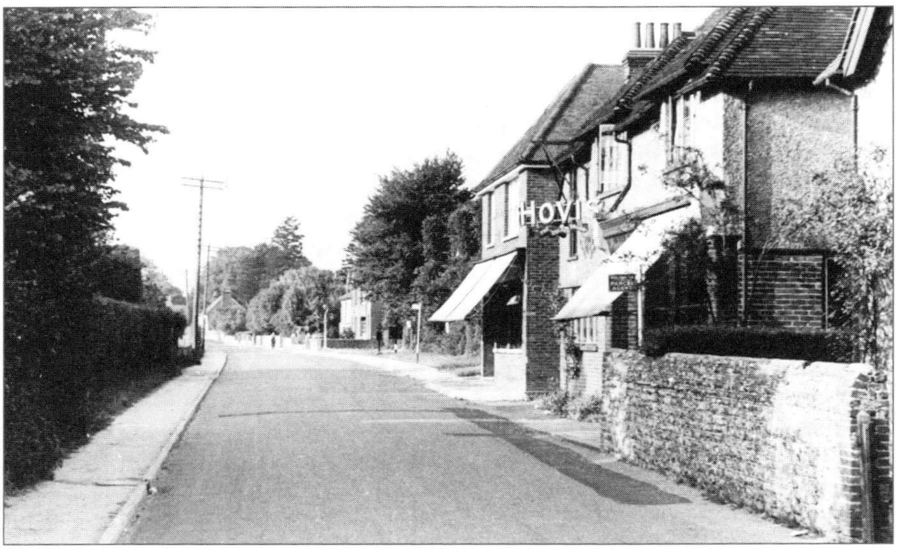

◀ **RUSTINGTON**
*The Village c1960*
R81071

All along the coastal belt, but rarely extending more than a few miles inland, rounded beach flints or cobbles were used for walls and every type of building. At Rustington, the 11th-century church and the cottages in The Street, Sea Lane and Station Road are all built of these flint boulders.

◄ **FUNTINGTON**
*Hallidays*
F160004

Nestling under the steep southern slope of the Sussex Downs, Funtington is typical of the inland villages of the coastal plain. Hallidays is built of local materials obtained within a radius of a few miles. The flints would have been collected from the fields, and the straw left over after the harvest was probably used for the thatched roof.

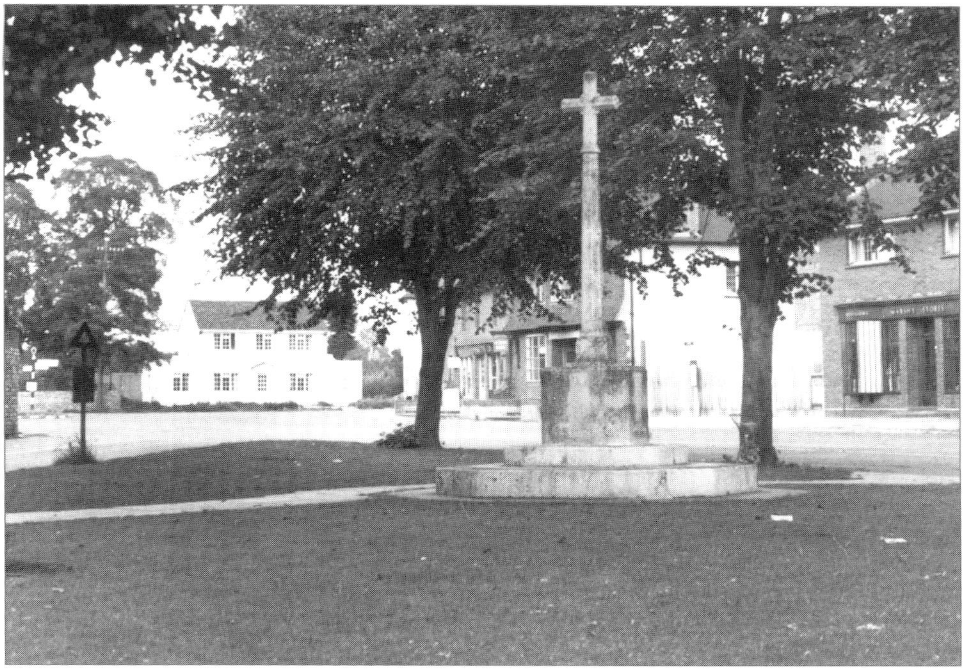

▲ **ANGMERING,** *The Village c1955* A52002

This is a tranquil scene showing Angmering Green, where lime trees were planted during the first decade of the 20th century, and a war memorial was erected in 1920. Marsh's Stores, shown on the right, is currently the village's general store and post office, while a modern building fills the gap to the left of the stores.

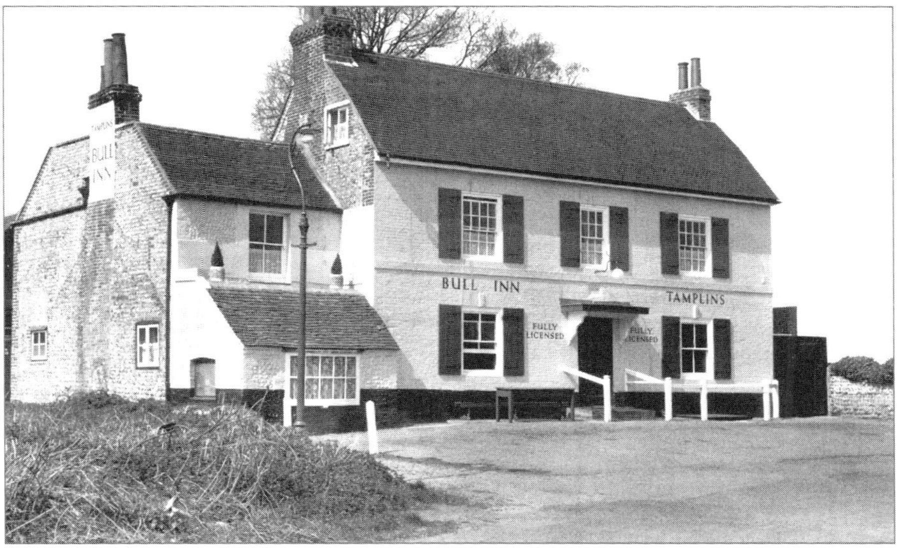


◄ **GORING-BY-SEA**
*The Bull Inn c1960*
G194018

This popular public house in Goring Street was formerly known as The Bull's Head; the old sign, which hung over the door for years, was removed by the brewery and transferred to a public house in East Sussex. Although the suggested dates for the original building range from the 17th to the 18th centuries, two Tudor windows were discovered during more recent alterations.

▼ **BROADWATER,** *The Village 1919* 68990

Large open fields surrounded many of the coastal plain settlements, and through the villages passed a solitary narrow street, often named after the village. Although Broadwater Street was picturesque, it was eventually unable to cope with the increase in modern traffic. It is regrettable that part of it had to be widened in 1932, which resulted in the demolition of several historic buildings.

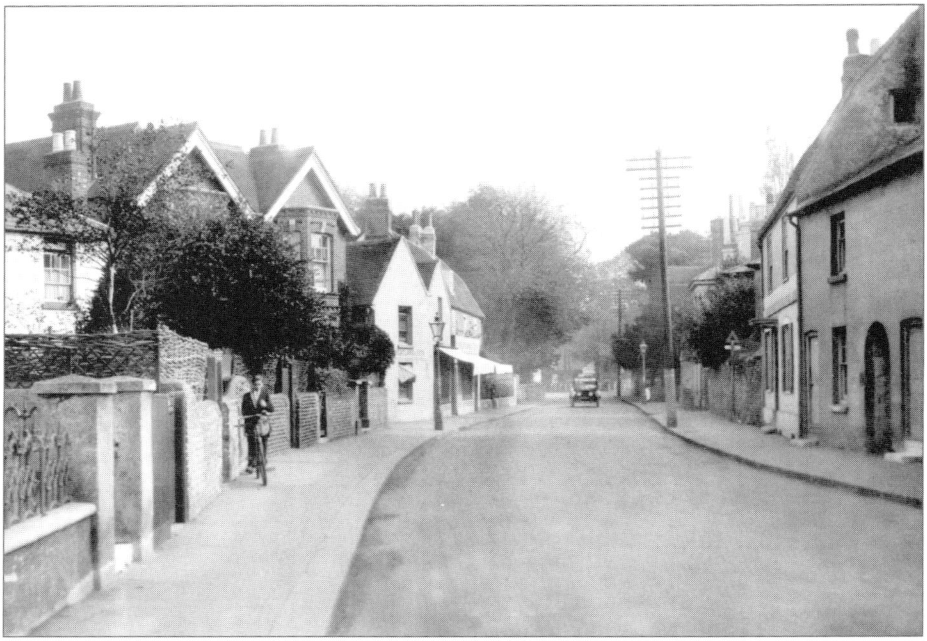

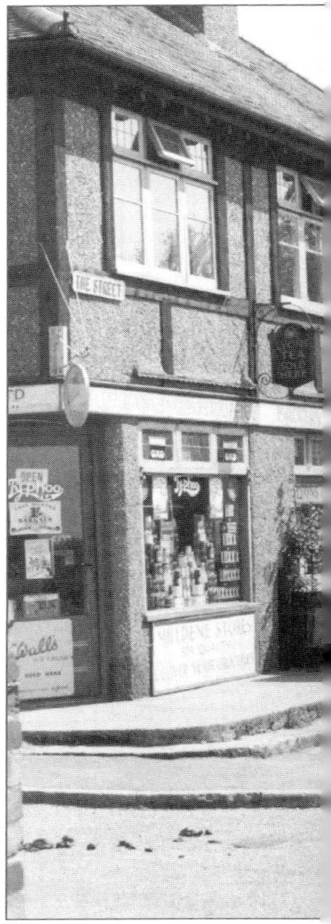


► **SOMPTING**
*West Street c1955*
S148004

West Street was originally part of the main route through Sompting, linking it to Broadwater and North Lancing. Despite modern building due to expansion, some of the older and more traditional flint-built walls and properties still survive. Opposite The Smugglers (right), which is now a restaurant, is the General Supply Store, which was one of Sompting's original shops.

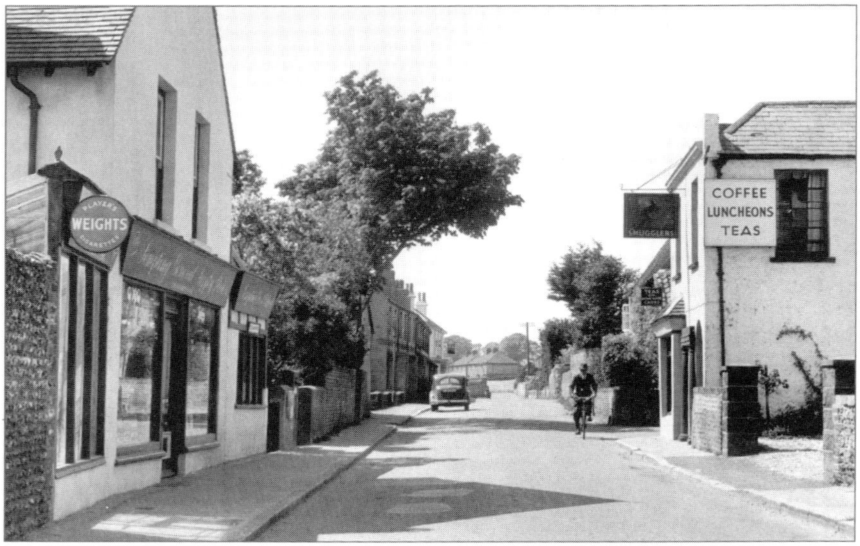

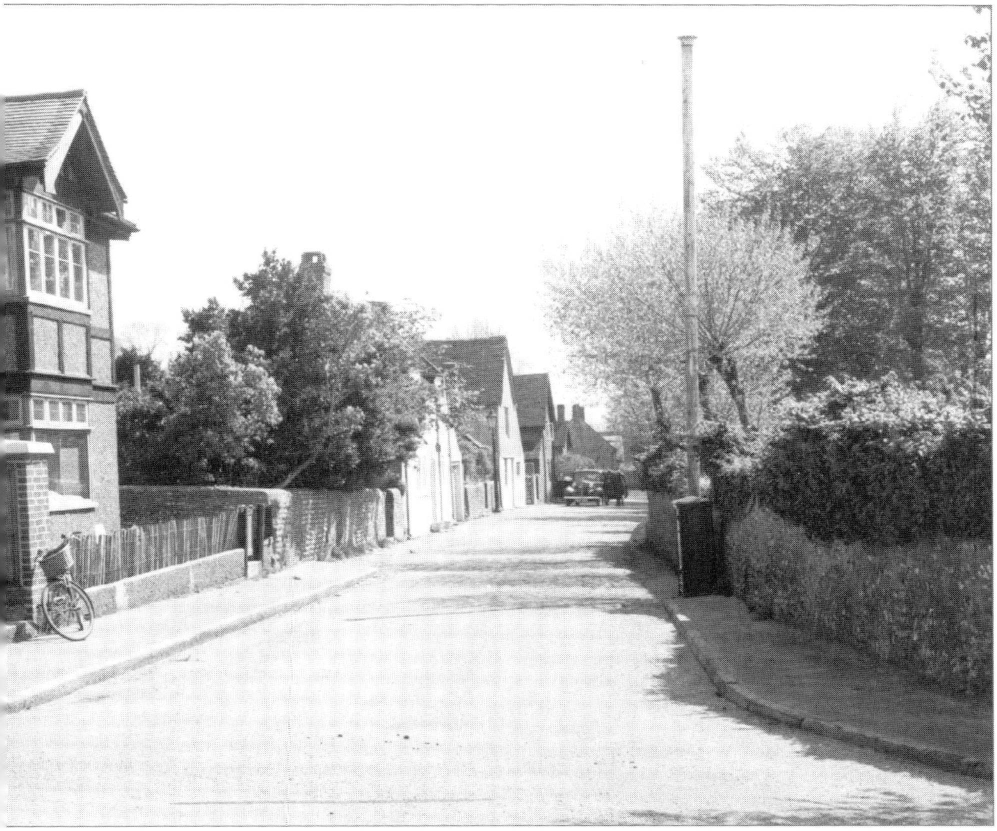

◀ **NORTH LANCING**
*The Street c1960*
N269049

The Street at Lancing was originally part of the main route through North Lancing, but it became an access road after the creation of the manor ground and a by-pass route in the early 19th century. Several old houses still survive, and the general store and post office were built in the garden of one of them.

▶ **SOUTH LANCING**
*The Church c1955*
S840007

Between 1921 and 1951 the population of Lancing nearly quadrupled, resulting in a rapid increase in the number of shops, businesses and houses in South Lancing. During this period of expansion, the church of St Michael and All Angels, consecrated in 1924, was built opposite the junction of Penhill Road and South Street.

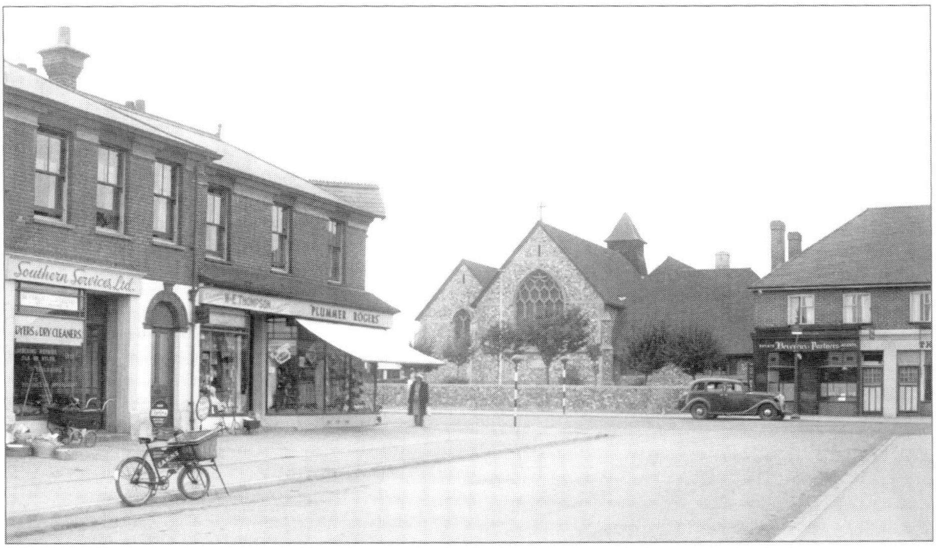

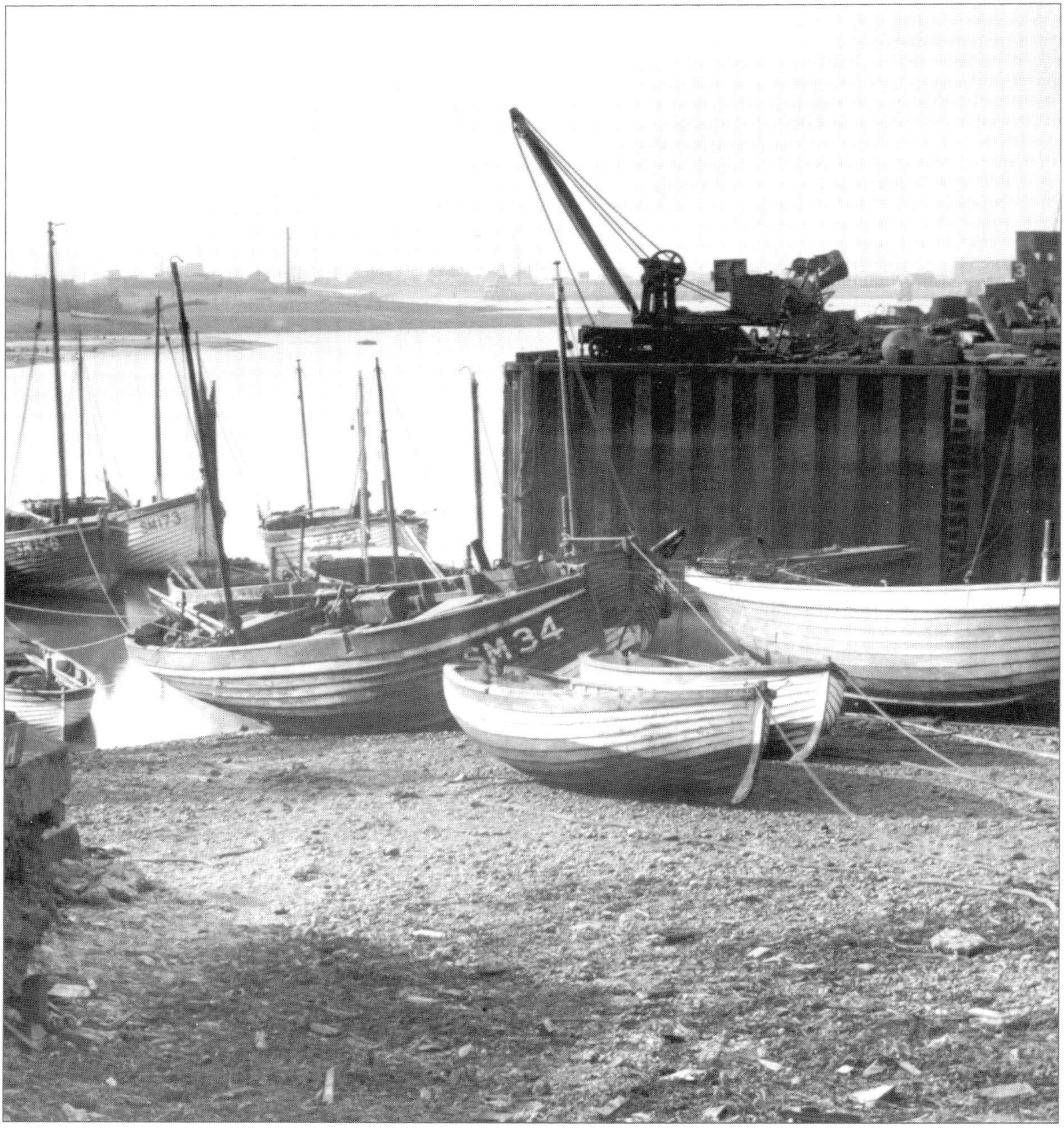


**SOUTHWICK,** *The Harbour c1955* S477018

For years the harbour and sea have provided employment for many of Southwick's inhabitants, and in 1871 the increase in population at Southwick and Fishersgate was attributed to oyster-dredgers and other seafarers who resided there. The large shingle bank on the southern side of the harbour, formerly part of the parish of Lancing, became part of Southwick in c1900.

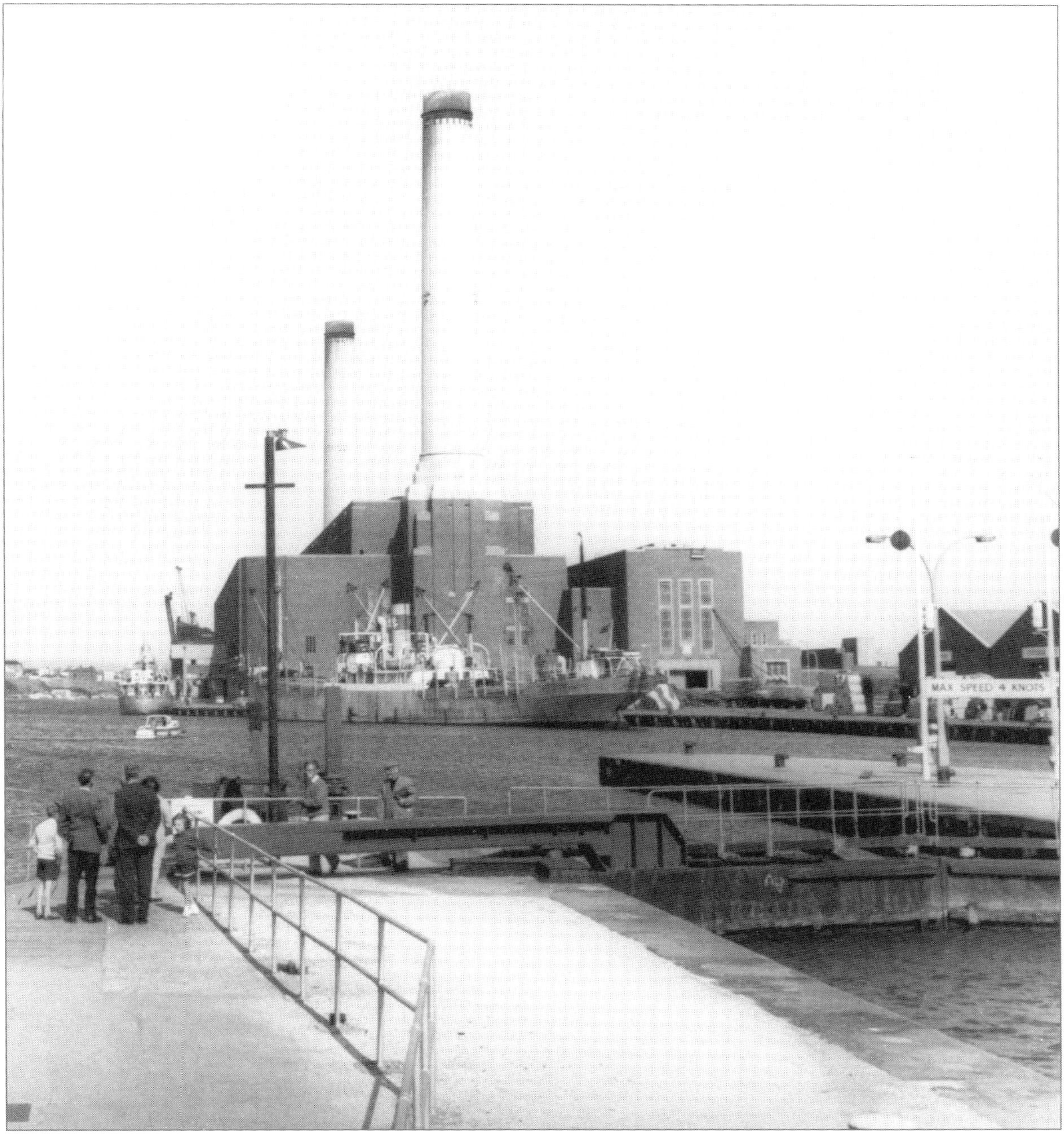


**SOUTHWICK,** *The Harbour c1965* S477072

To the south of the harbour stood the power stations and gas works, the main users of coal, which represented over half of the port's total commodities by the end of the 1950s. Following the closure of these buildings, the trade in coal significantly diminished, but an increase in other commodities, like timber imports, redressed the balance.

# THE DOWNLAND

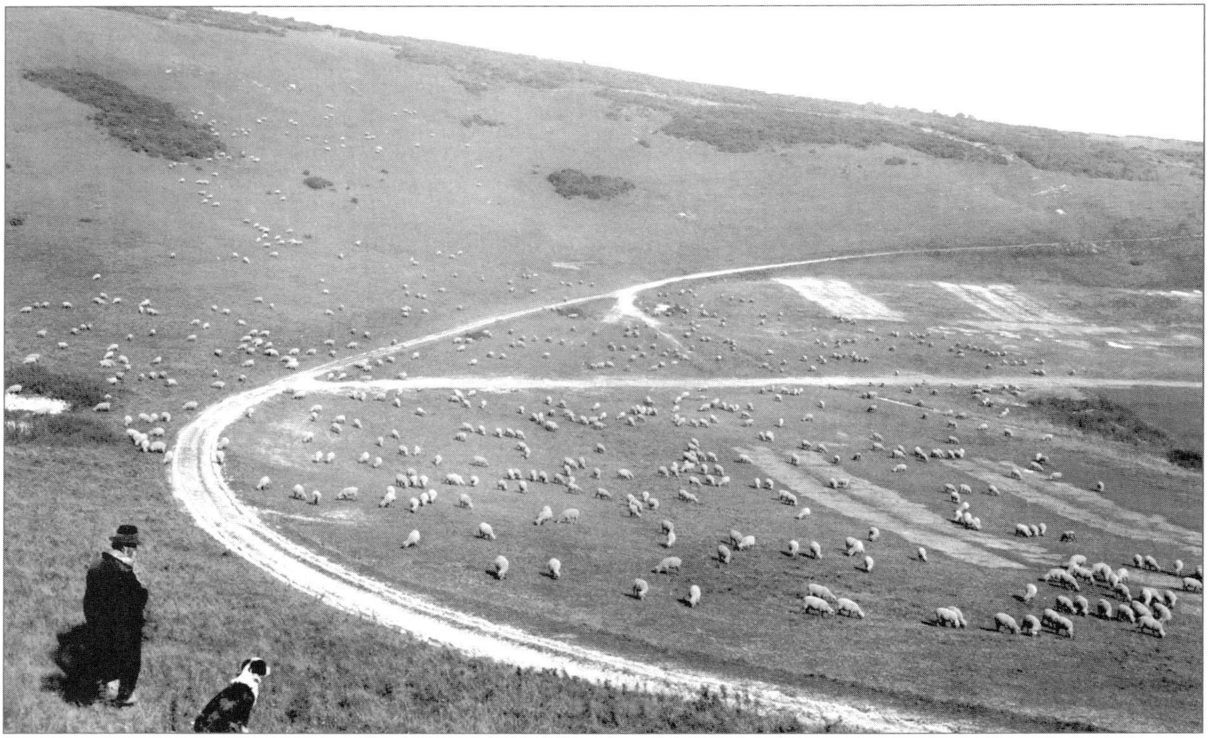

**EASTBOURNE**
*The Downs near Beachy Head 1912* 64983

In direct contrast to the over-populated coastal plain, the South Downs remained relatively deserted for centuries, for sheep require very few human guardians. The shepherd and his dog tending their flock near Beachy Head epitomise the centuries-old pastoral economy of the downland region.

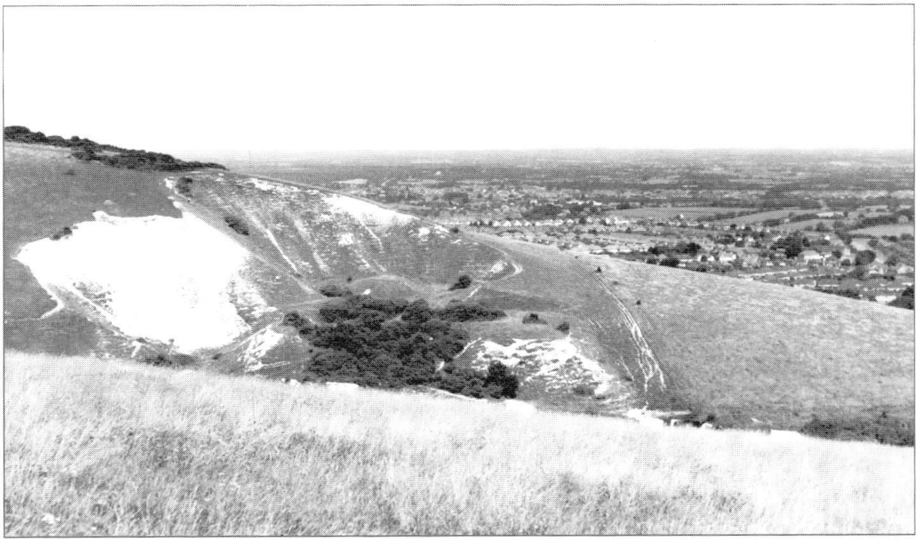

**POLEGATE**
*The Downs c1955*
P259033

Although much of the downland in Sussex was used for open sheep grazing, the clearance of the woodland at the eastern end of the South Downs by Neolithic man during the pre-historic period left the area to the north of the modern village at Polegate far too open and exposed for either sheepwalks or settlement.

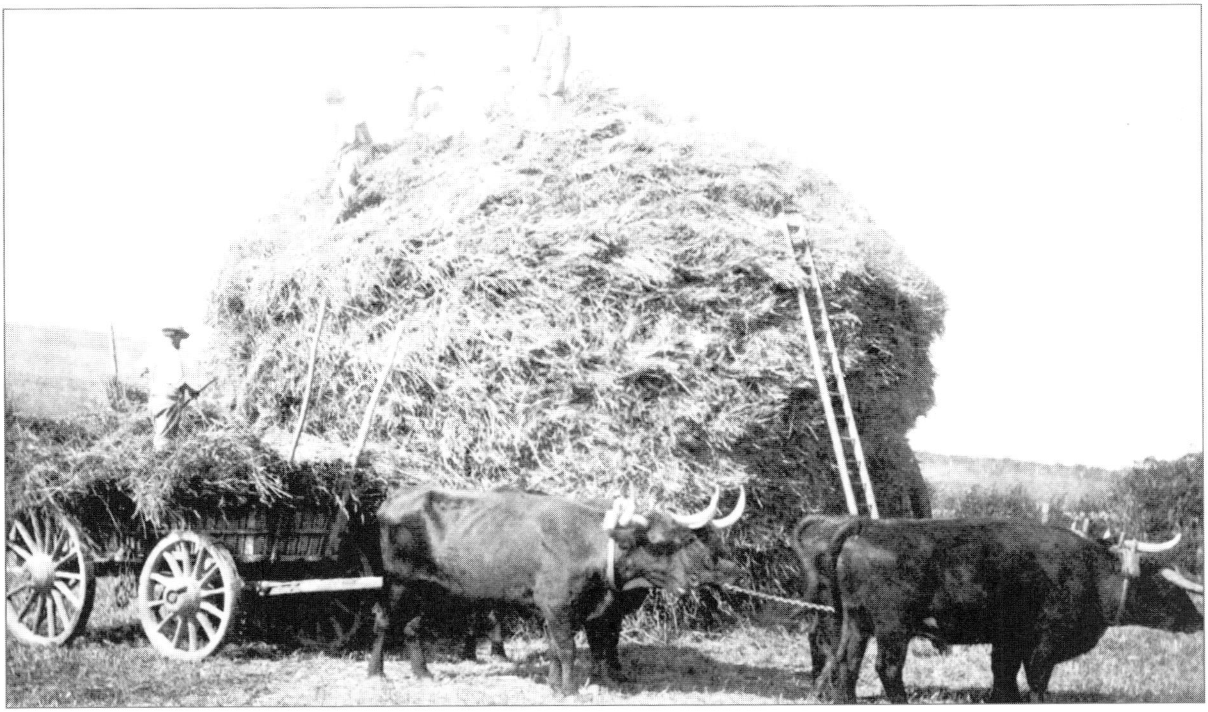

**JEVINGTON,** *Building a Haystack c1890* J13105

Helped by improved fertilisers, increased yields made farming on the Downs more profitable by the end of the Victorian period; however, arable farming on the chalky downland soils remained difficult. Note that oxen were still being used to help with the harvest here.

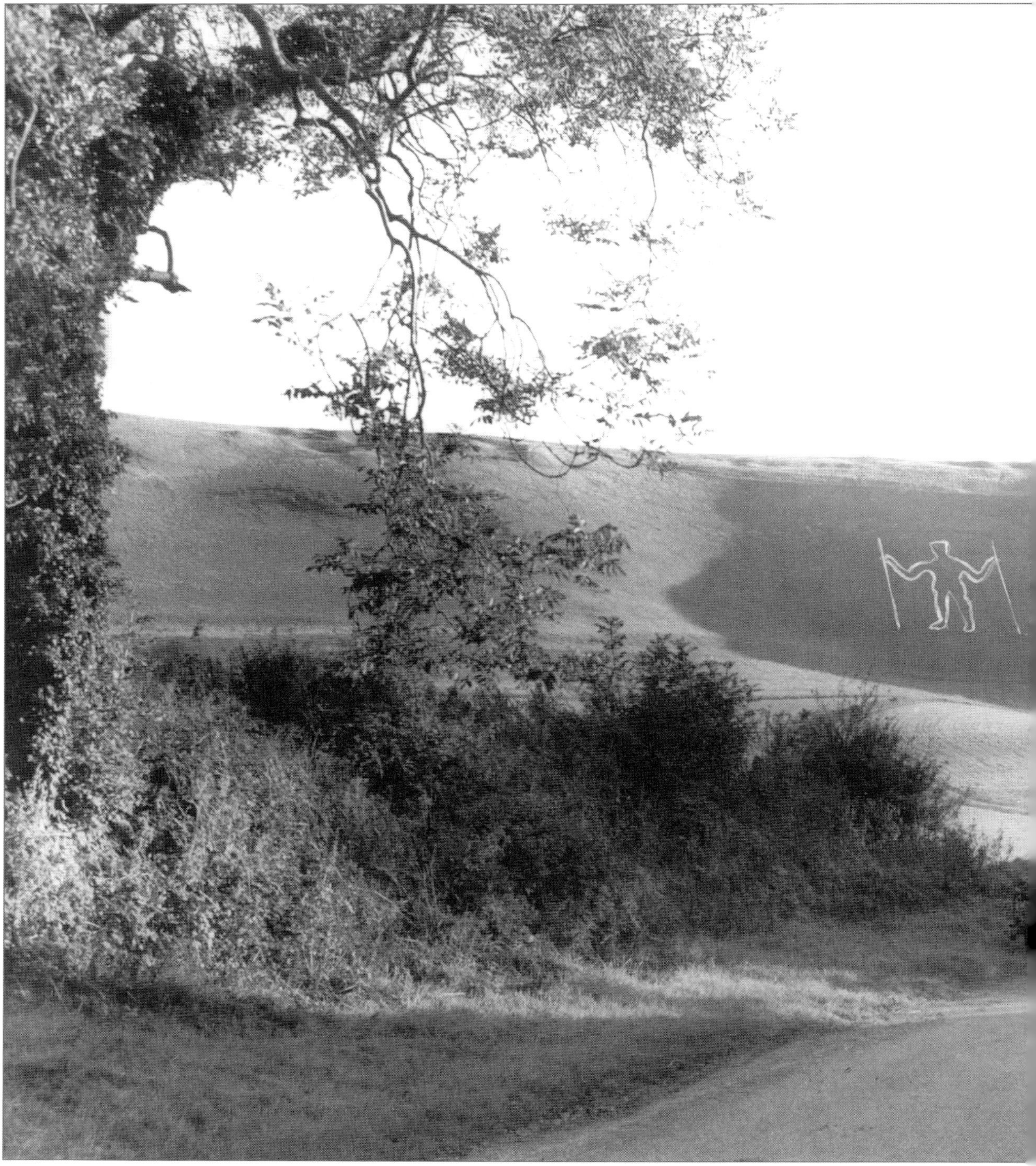

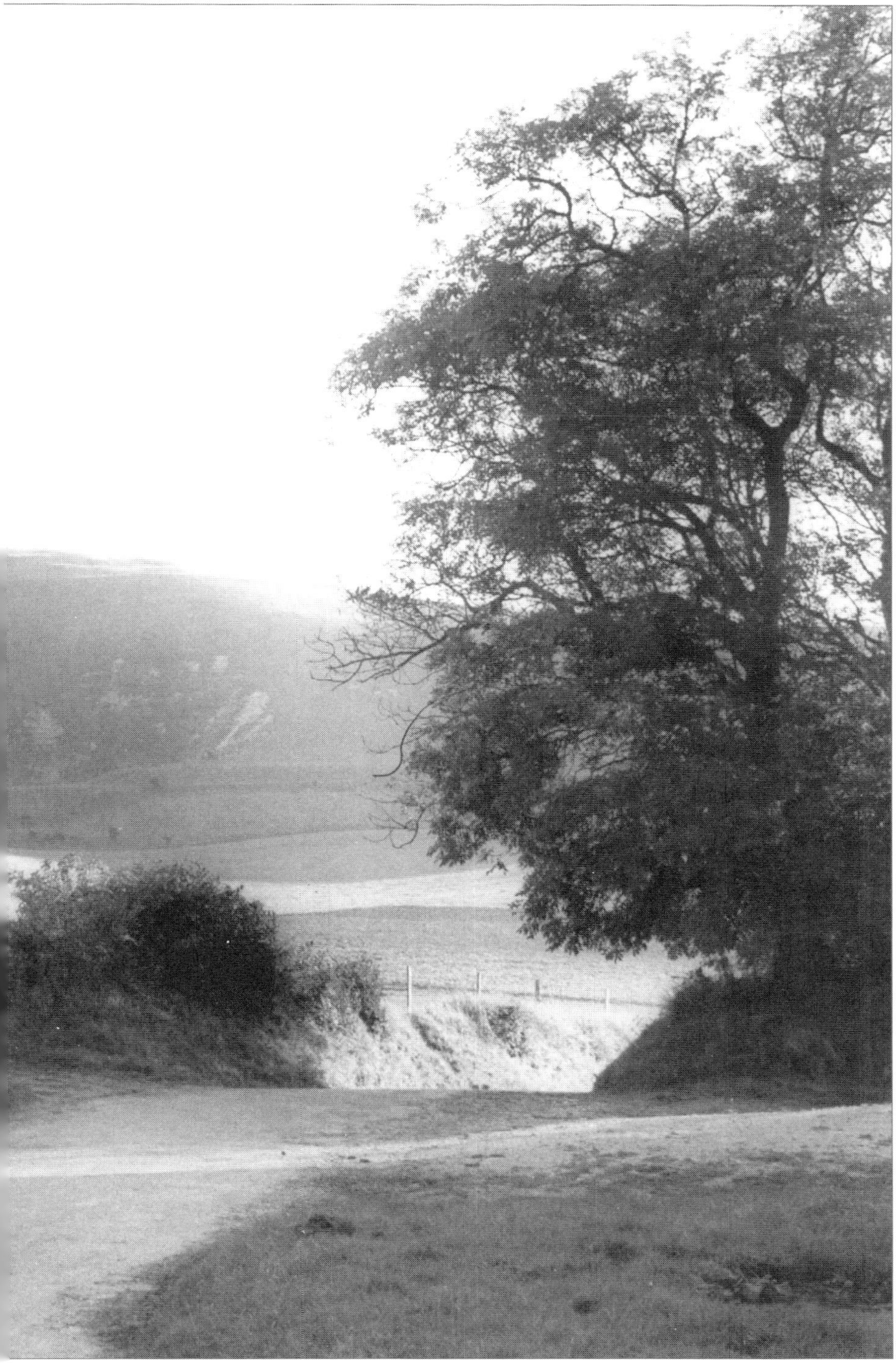

**WILMINGTON**
*The Long Man c1960*
W406004

The Long Man of Wilmington stands on the northern slope of the South Downs, today marked out in white bricks. Who he is and when he was originally cut into the downland turf is not known. Before being 'decently emasculated' in the 19th century, this imposing 70m-high chalk figure, with a longstaff in each hand, looked very similar to the pre-historic giant at Cerne Abbas in Dorset.

**WILMINGTON**
*The Priory Ruins*
W406002

Situated under the downs, very close to the Long Man, the former manorial grange at Wilmington had, by the 13th century, developed into a small priory. Its prior, as the agent of the abbey of Grestian, used its vast medieval barn to store the produce collected from the abbey's other estates, which were located in half a dozen other counties.

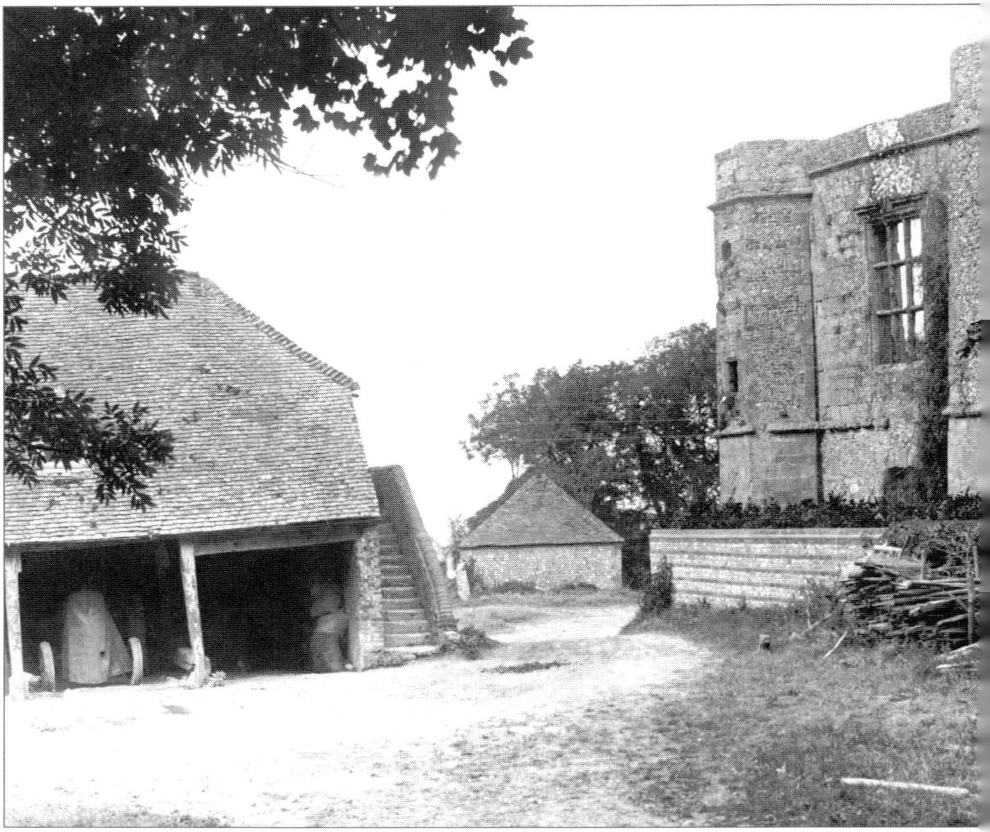

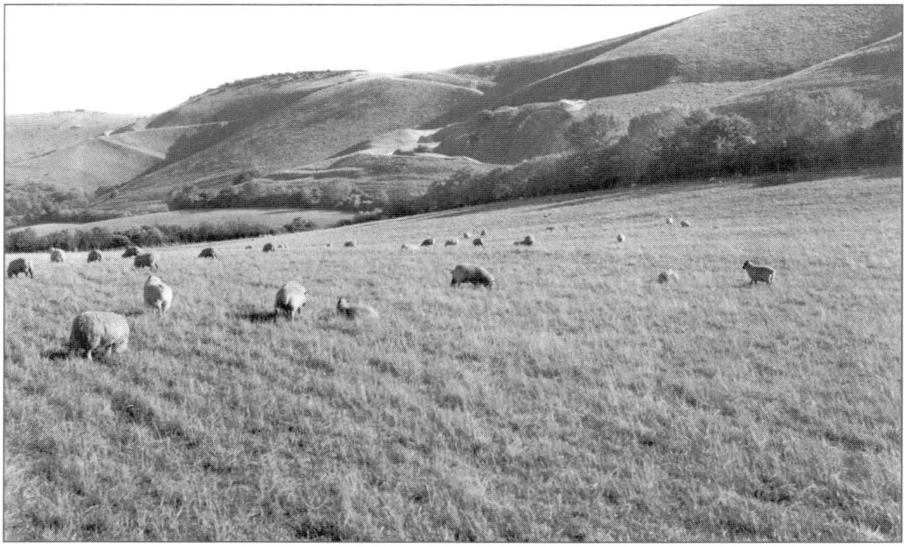

**SMALL DOLE**
*The Downs c1960*
S532004

Because the difficult alkaline downland soil yielded indifferent crops, for centuries the South Downs were vast sheepwalks; by the 18th century there were 400,000 ewes grazing between Eastbourne and Hampshire. A shortwool Southdown breed had been developed, whose meat, lightly flavoured by wild thyme, was the most delicious of all muttons.

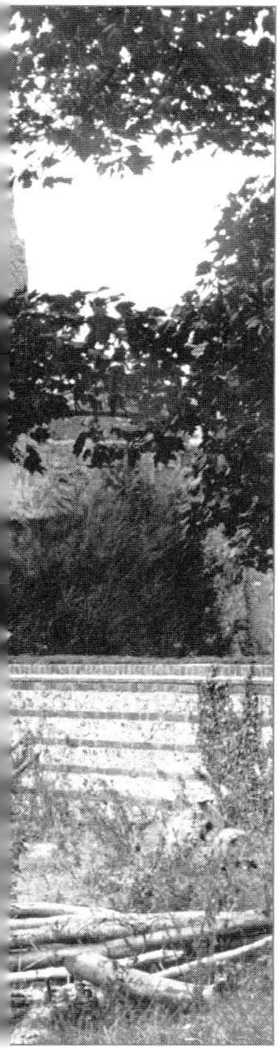

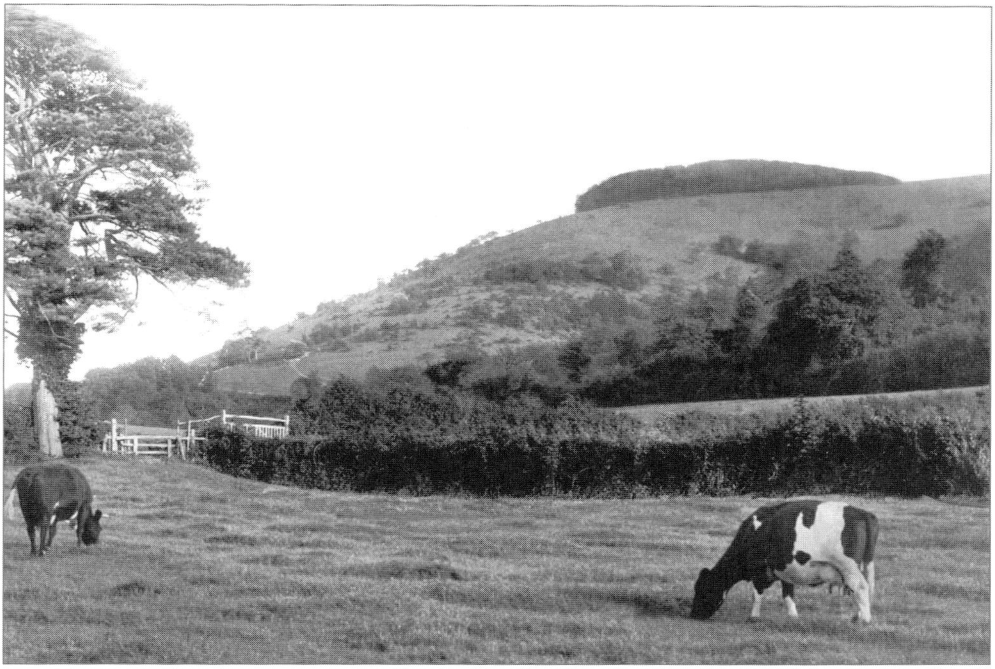

▲ **CHANCTONBURY RING,** *1894* 34416a

Standing at a height of about 260 metres above sea level is the prominent landmark of Chanctonbury Ring. Originally it was the site of an Iron Age camp, then a Roman temple, and later an Armada beacon. Before the ring of trees was damaged in the hurricane of 1987, the centre of the ring, planted in 1760 by Charles Goring of Wiston, had 'the luminous air of a temple'.

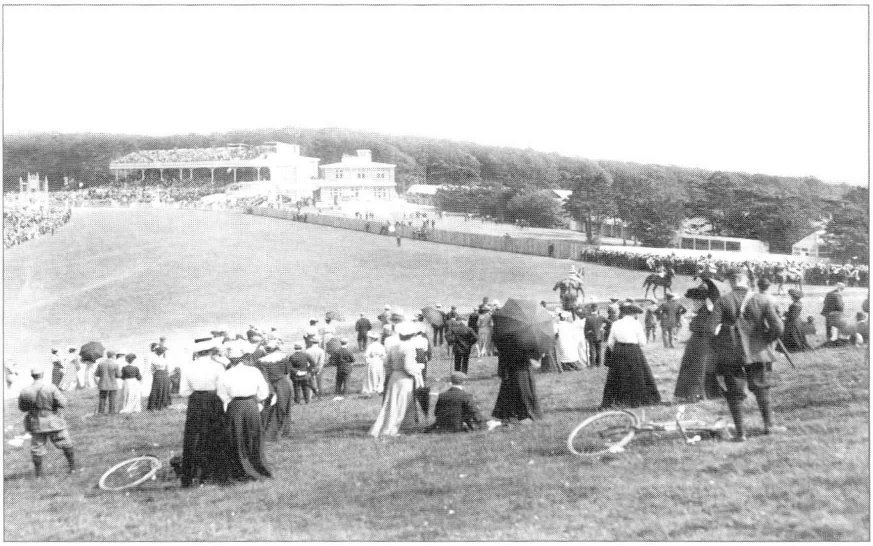

◄ **GOODWOOD HOUSE**
*The Racecourse 1904*
52292

High on the South Downs, an enthusiastic crowd, many of whom have cycled up the steep hill to the Trundle, enjoy the atmosphere of 'Glorious Goodwood', a week of racing that still begins on the last Tuesday in July. The horseshoe-shaped course was established in 1802.

▼ **GOODWOOD HOUSE,** *The Grandstand, the Royal Box 1904* 52296

When Ascot commemorated the accession of Edward VII by building a new grandstand, the Duke of Richmond responded by building an imposing two-tier grandstand to accommodate 10,000 persons at a cost of £40,000. King Edward VII was a frequent visitor to the course; he was often seen in the Royal Box at the western end of the new grandstand, which was built by 1904.

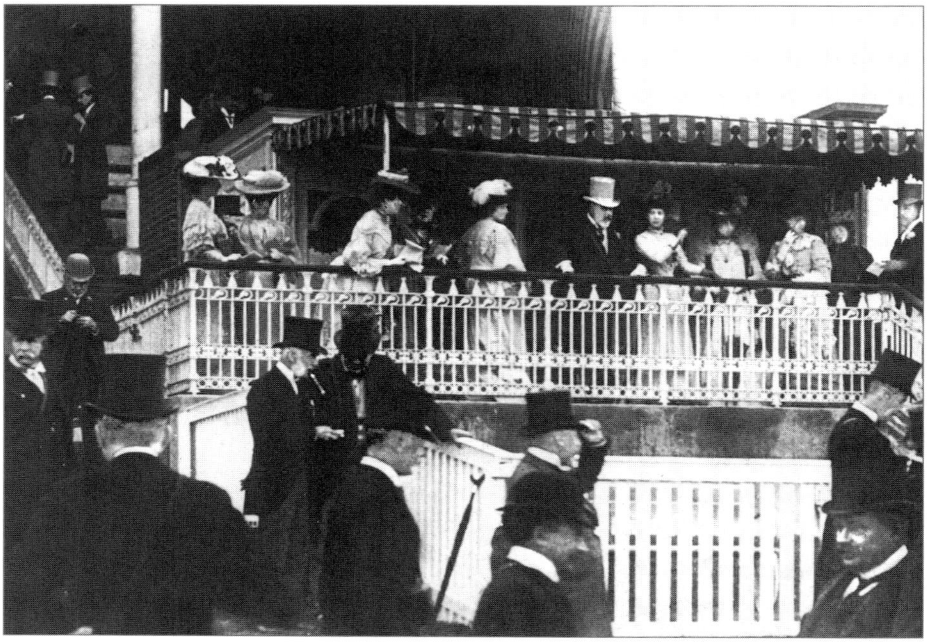

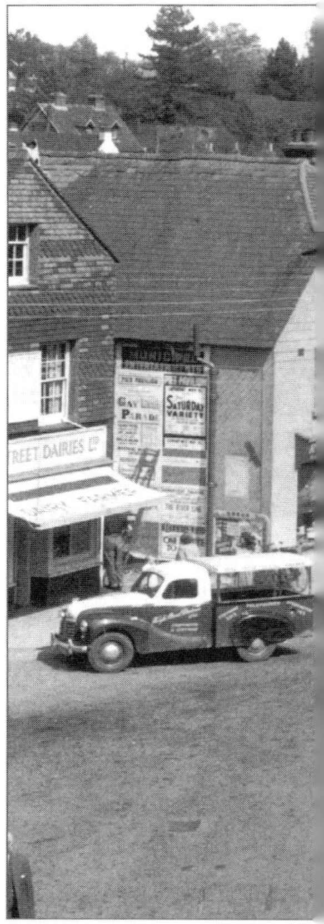


► **STORRINGTON**
*The Downs c1955*
S210018

The downs to the west of the Arun are notably more wooded than those to the east, which are remarkably open and treeless. On a clear day, we can savour an expansive view of the Weald from the South Downs overlooking Storrington.

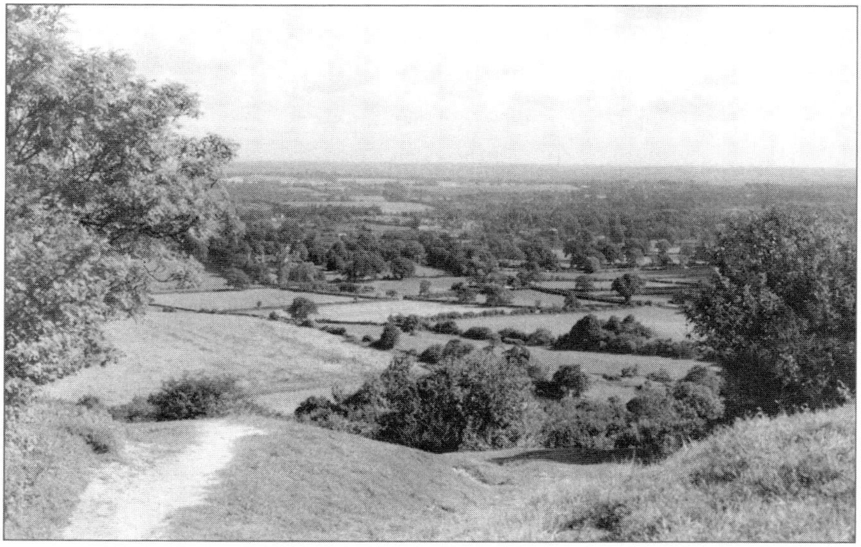

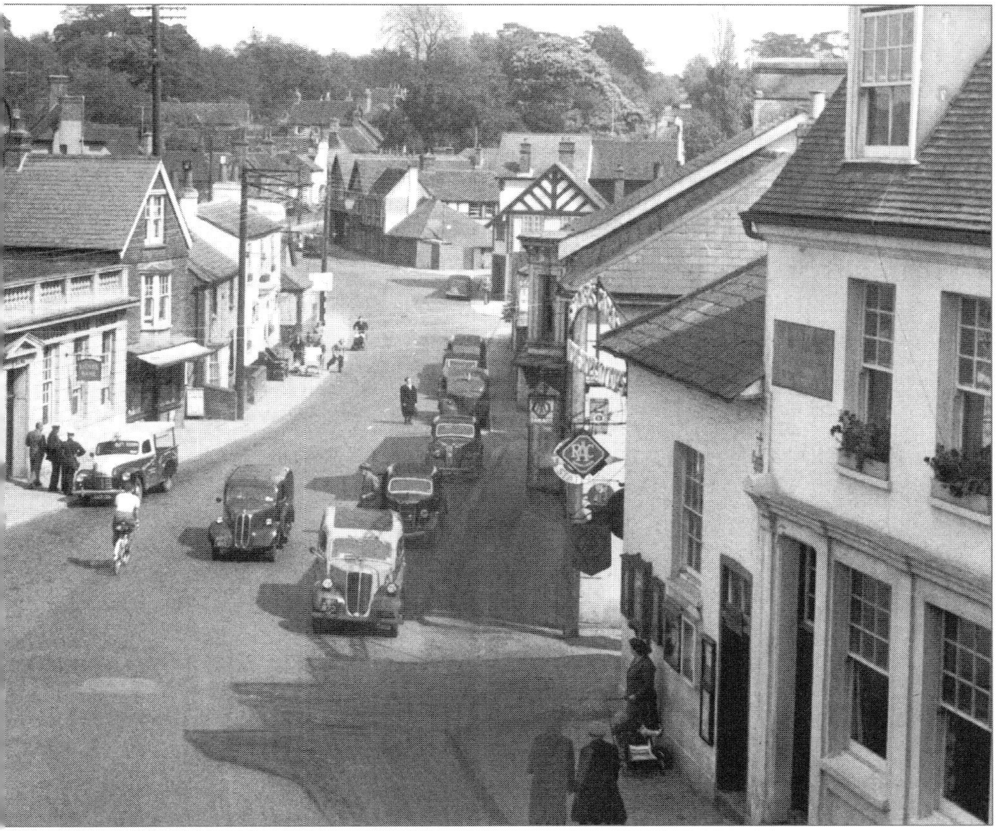

**STORRINGTON**
*High Street c1955*
S210019

Situated at the foot of the South Downs, where the River Stor flows north-west to its confluence with the Arun, Storrington is the only downland settlement that became a small market town. The High Street extends westwards from the River Stor to the triangular market place (in the foreground), which was established by 1399.

**STORRINGTON**
*West Street c1960*
S210080

Storrington never appears to have been very large, and far from being a centre of wealth, was probably no more prosperous than its neighbouring downland villages. The town centre was designated a Conservation Area in 1973. In West Street we can see the old-established retailers Farncombe, the local butcher (centre), and Greenfield's (right).

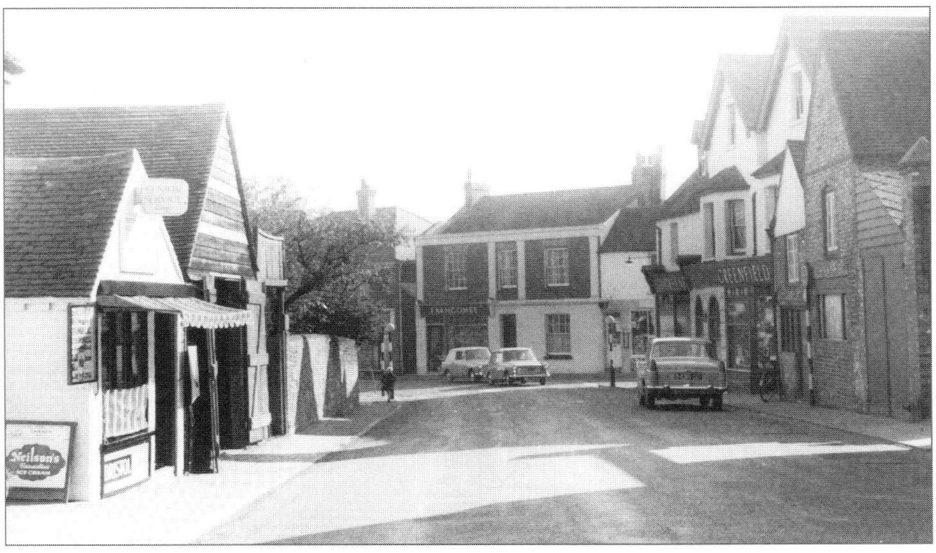

▼ **WASHINGTON,** *The Village c1960* W359025

Washington, at the crossroads of two ancient routes, lies at the northern head of a 'wind gap' in the undulating chalk downland of high ridges and dry valleys. In this relatively unspoilt village the buildings are of various materials, including brick, flint, clunch (chalk) and sandstone, which reflects its location on the border between the South Downs and the Weald.

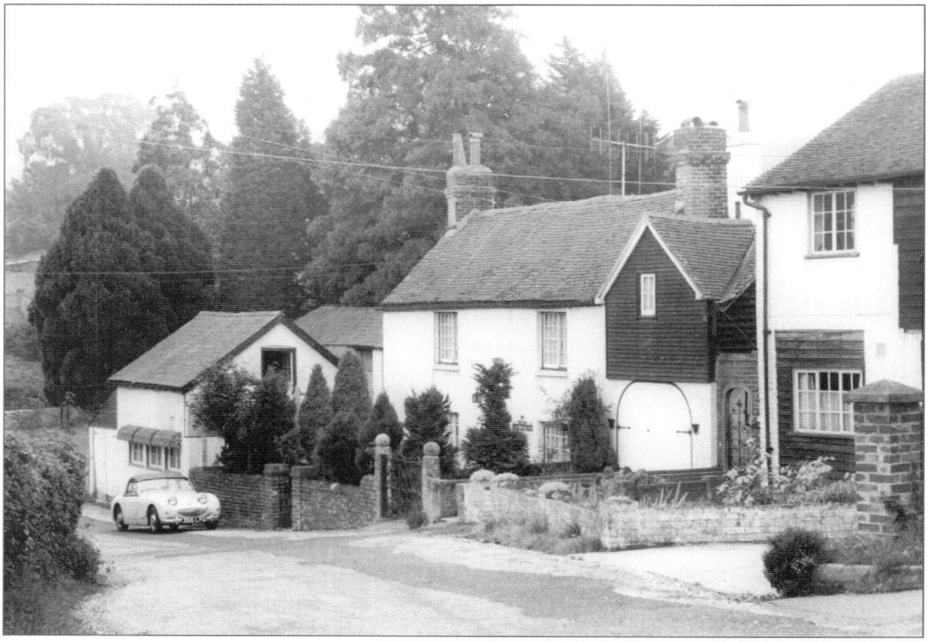

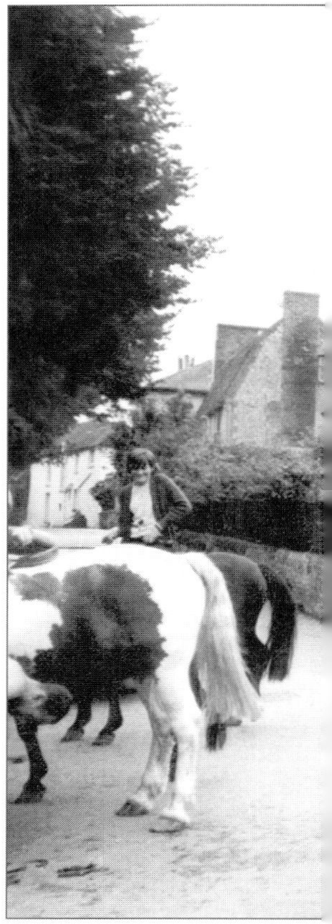

► **WASHINGTON**
*The Village Street*
*c1960* W359020

Washington's village street was formerly an ancient road that ran along the greensand ridge. The fact that the road level is significantly lower than the ground on either side confirms the antiquity of the settlement. The number of tradesmen has slowly declined, and by 1977 only two general stores and a newsagent survived.

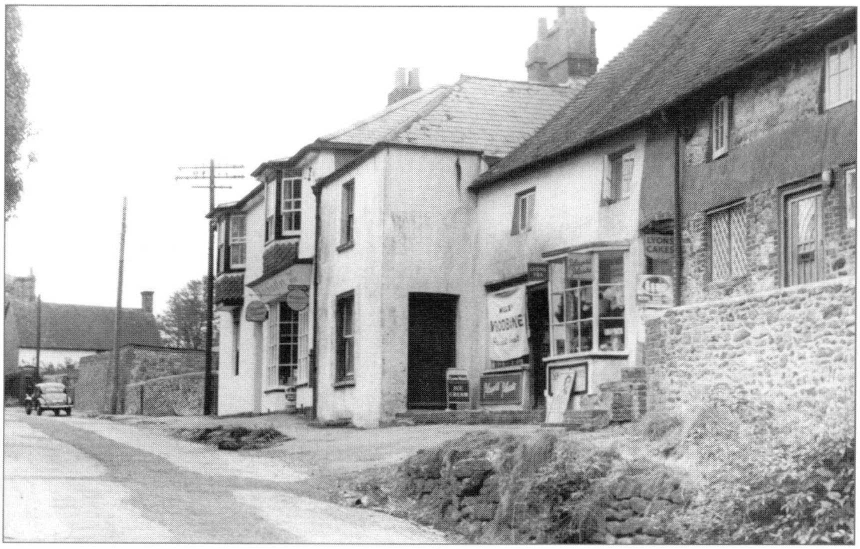

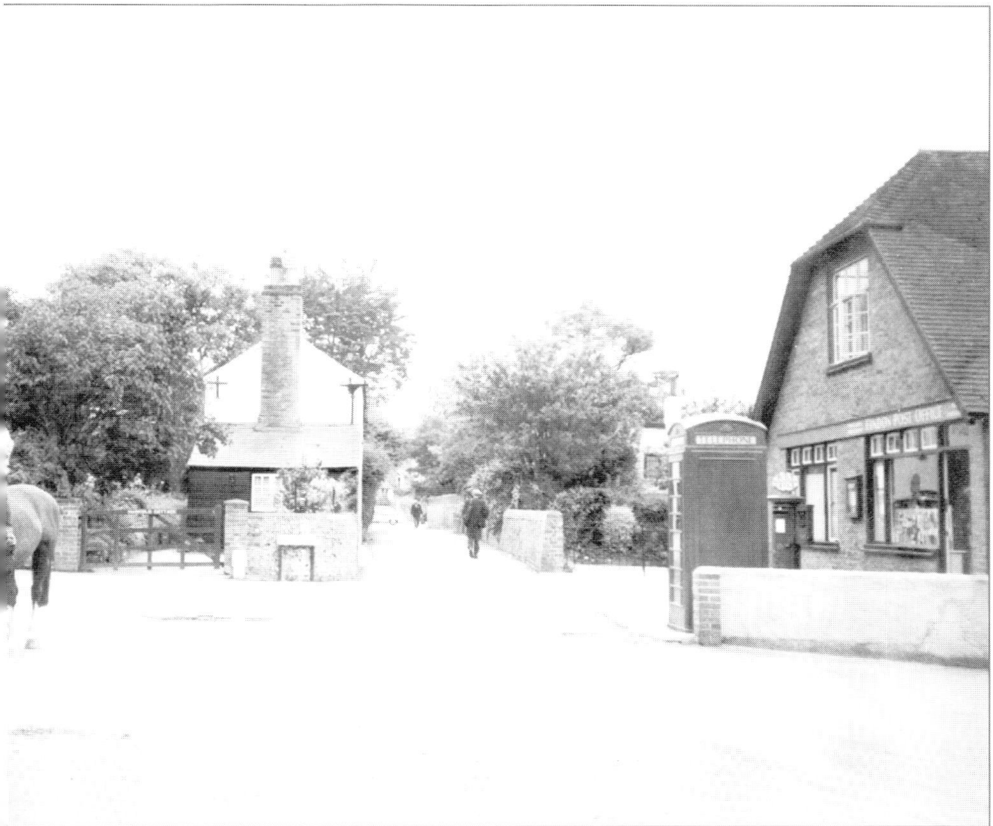


◄ **FINDON**
*Post Office Corner c1960* F131091

Much of the downland around Findon, at the southern end of the same 'wind-gap' in the South Downs, was for centuries an open sheep-walk. It is well known for its sheep fair on Nepcote Green, and for its racehorse training stables - these sustain a flourishing business for one of the few surviving blacksmiths in the area.

► **SMALL DOLE**
*The Village c1955*
S532001

Little of the early village, which was once surrounded by large areas of open sheep pasture, has survived. In 1808 a group of cottages stood on the western side of the road facing Dole Green, but only one early 19th-century building had survived by the 1990s. Its public house, The Fox and Hounds (left), dates from 1845.

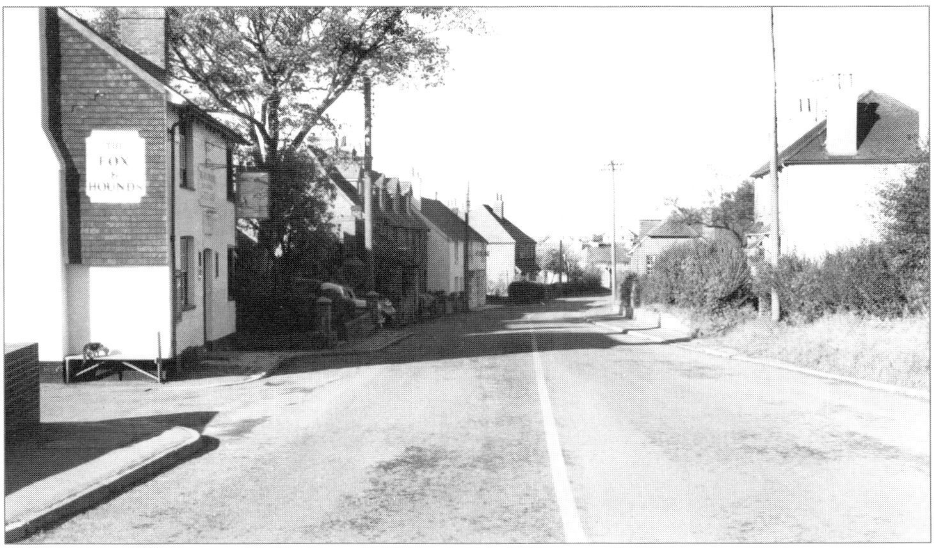

**FULKING**
*The Village c1960*
F133013

At Fulking, 16th-century cottages still lie on either side of the village street that winds its way below the South Downs. At the western end of the village, close to the popular public house aptly named the Shepherd and Dog, the Fulking stream still emerges from the downs over a small waterfall.

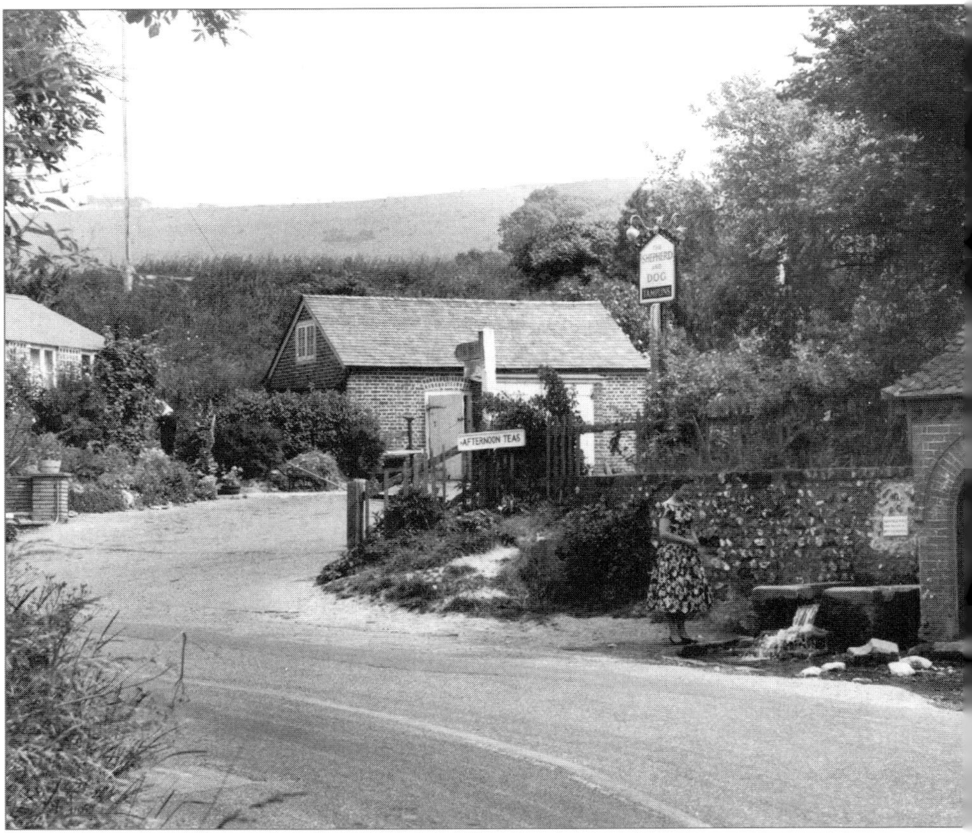


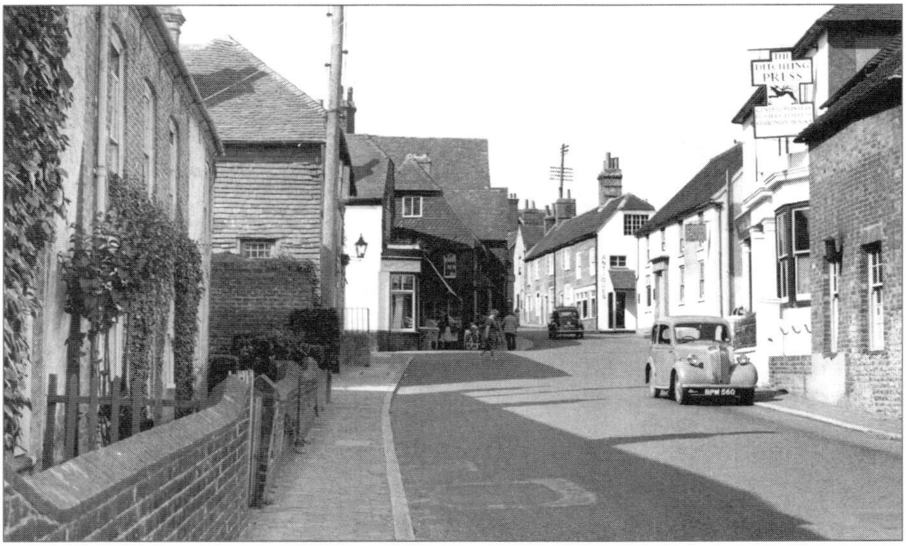

**DITCHLING**
*The Village c1955*
D158026

Lying below Ditchling Beacon, this downland village has today become a fashionable commuter village, and once-productive farmland is now used as paddocks for horses. The village is situated at the crossing of the roads from Haywards Heath to Brighton and from Hurst to Lewes. Interspersed between Georgian brick and modern shop fronts, several old flint properties still survive.

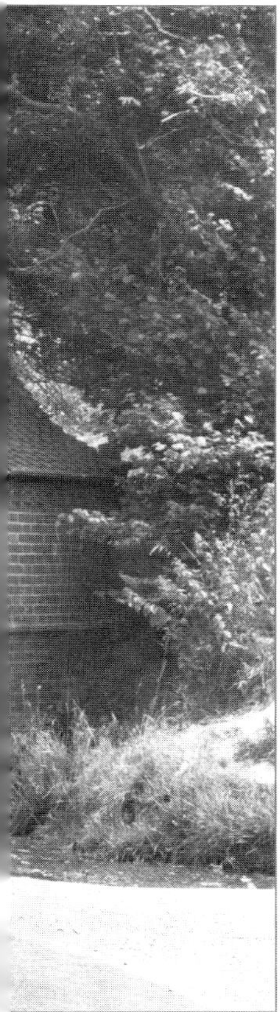

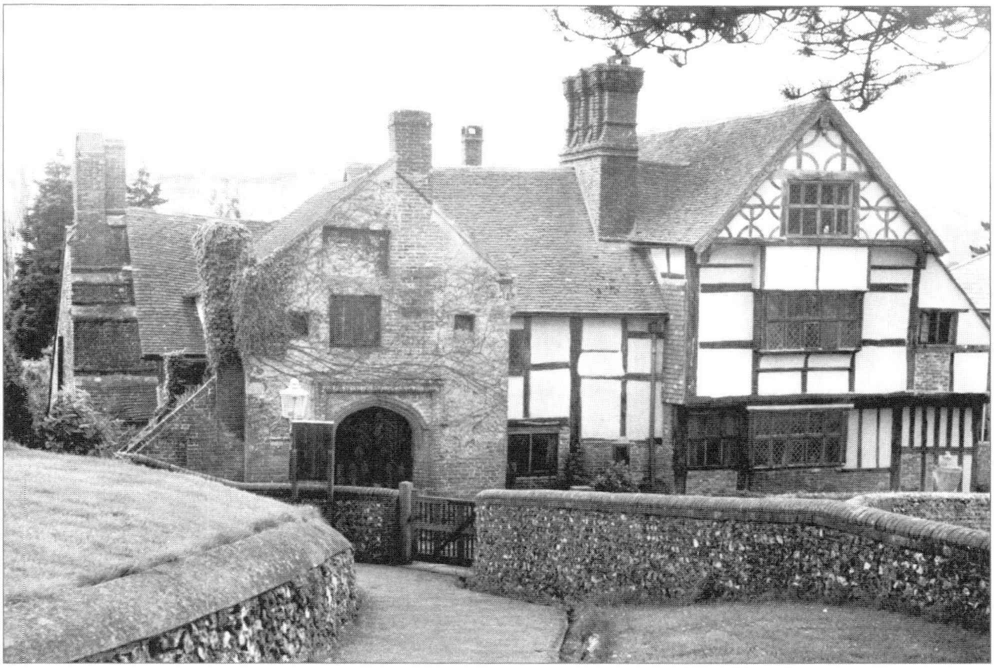

▲ **DITCHLING,** *Ann of Cleves House c1960* D158086

Ann of Cleves House is possibly the most impressive of Ditchling's 16th- and 17th-century buildings. The brick porch fronting the street was the entrance to the courtyard of an earlier Tudor house; it was retained when the Elizabethan timber-framed building was constructed.

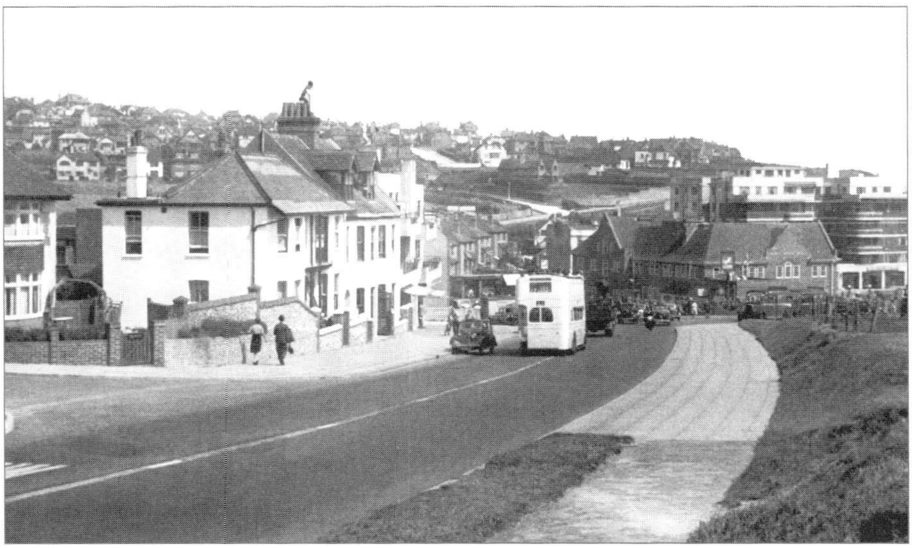

◄ **ROTTINGDEAN**
*Marine Drive c1965*
R62006

Fine sea views can be obtained from the regular summer open-top bus service which runs from Brighton to Rottingdean, a picturesque village situated in a dene, or valley in the downs. For centuries Rottingdean was a typical downland village, but its character was radically changed when modern roads and houses were constructed at the seaward end.

**ROTTINGDEAN**
*The Downs c1955* R62044

A hundred years ago, windmills were a ubiquitous feature of the downland landscape. This mill, standing proudly alongside the modern tea kiosk and ticket office for Rottingdean's pitch and putt course, is one of the many wooden smock mills erected in Sussex during the 19th century.

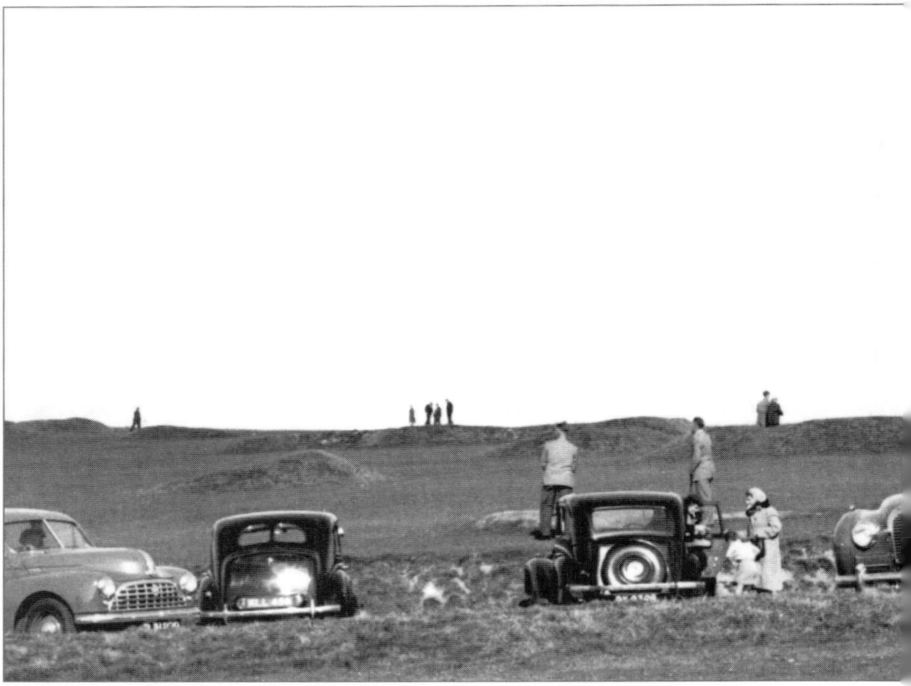

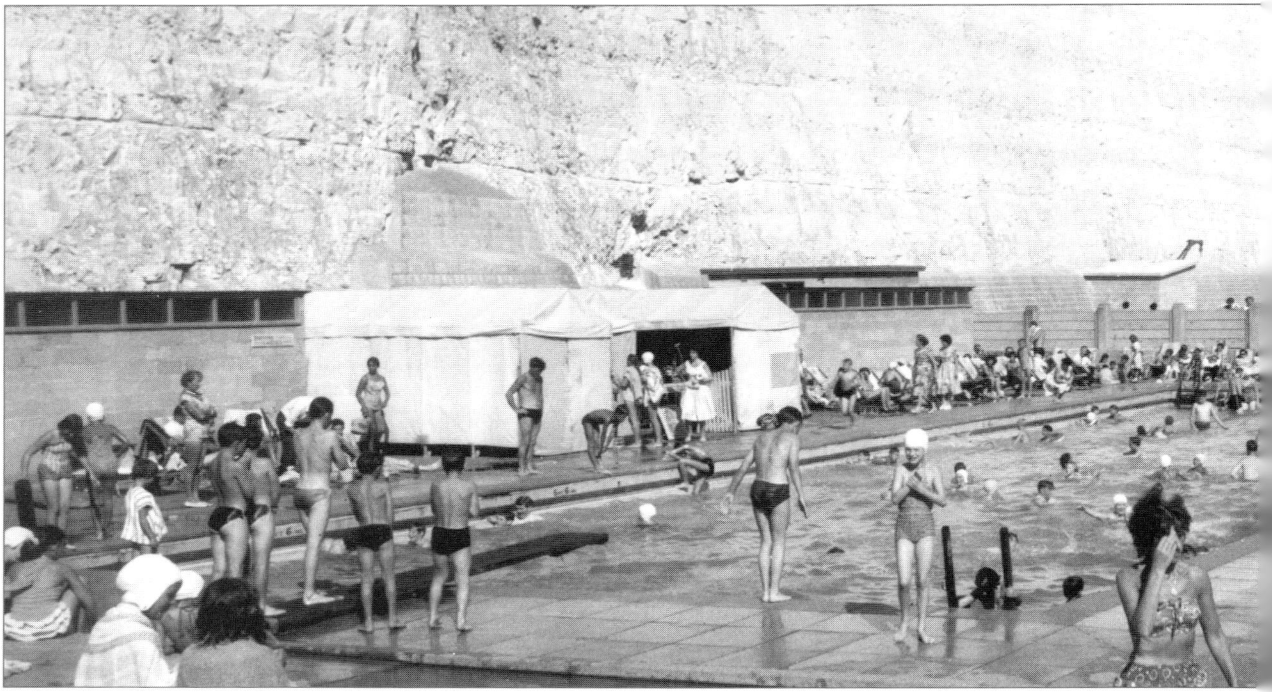

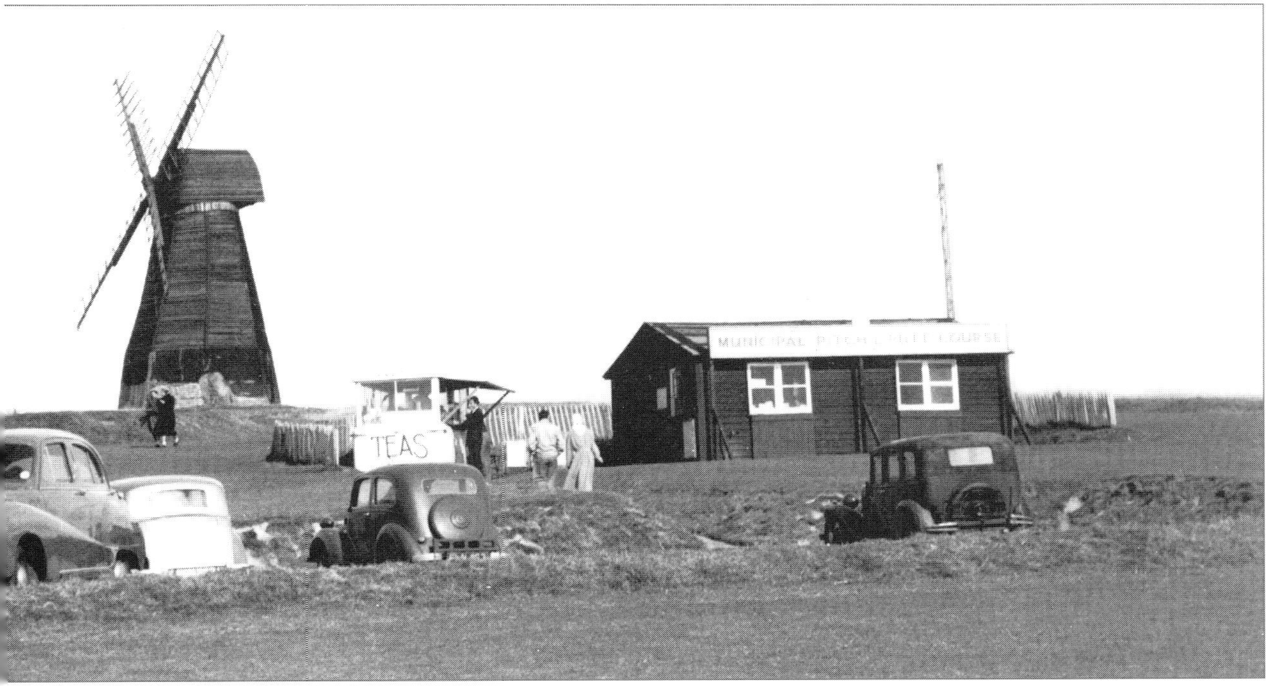


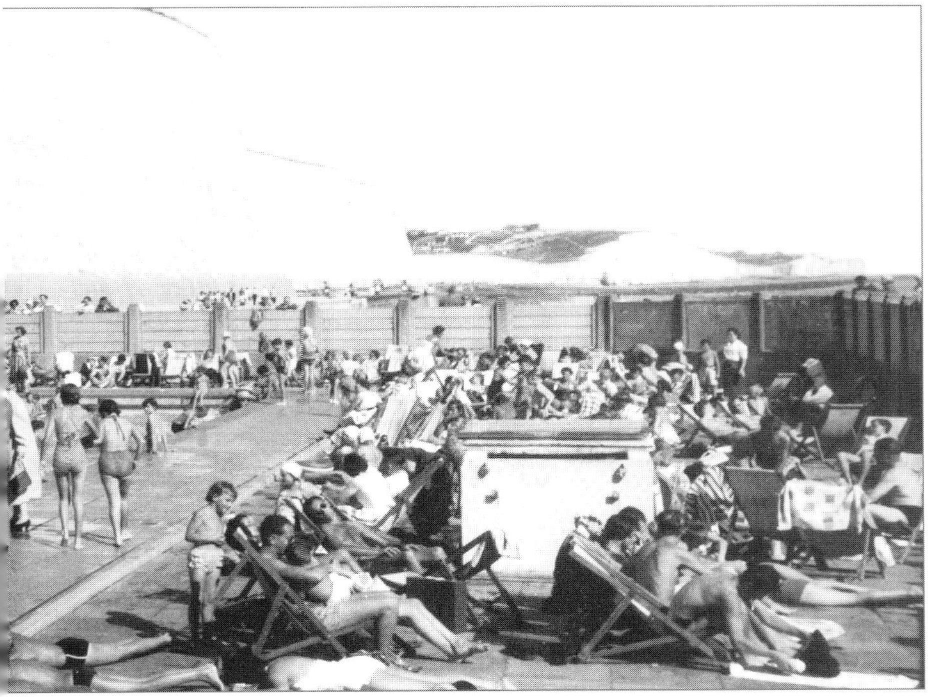

**ROTTINGDEAN**
*The Cliffs and the Swimming Pool c1965*
R62065

As a modern holiday resort and suburb of Brighton, Rottingdean benefited from an increase in holidaymakers immediately after the Second World War. The swimming pool below the retreating chalk cliffs was a popular attraction for both young and old alike.

**POLEGATE**
*The Road to Jevington c1955* P259016

Polegate, with its typical flint walls and buildings, lies just below the extreme eastern end of the South Downs. It has slowly become a dormitory village for the town of Eastbourne, whereas Jevington, hidden away in a dry valley and surrounded by trees, has retained its rural character and is possibly the most scenic of all the downland villages.

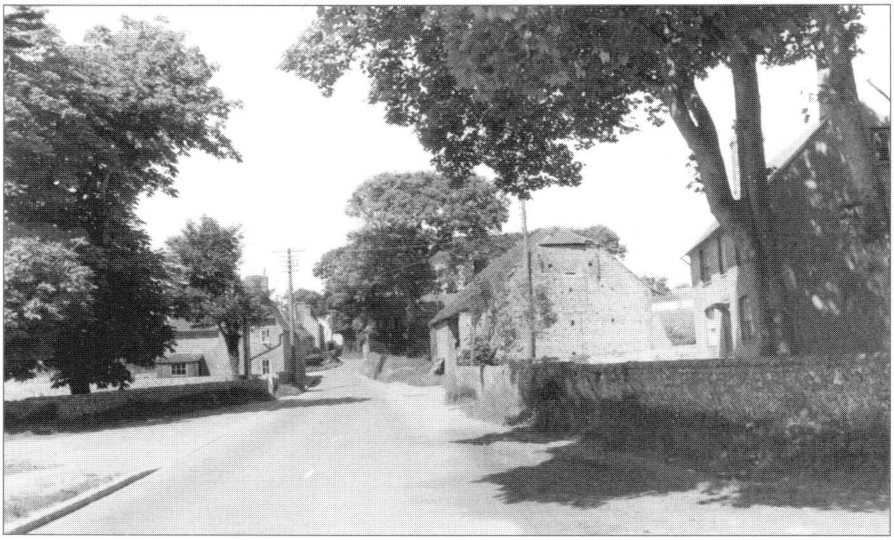

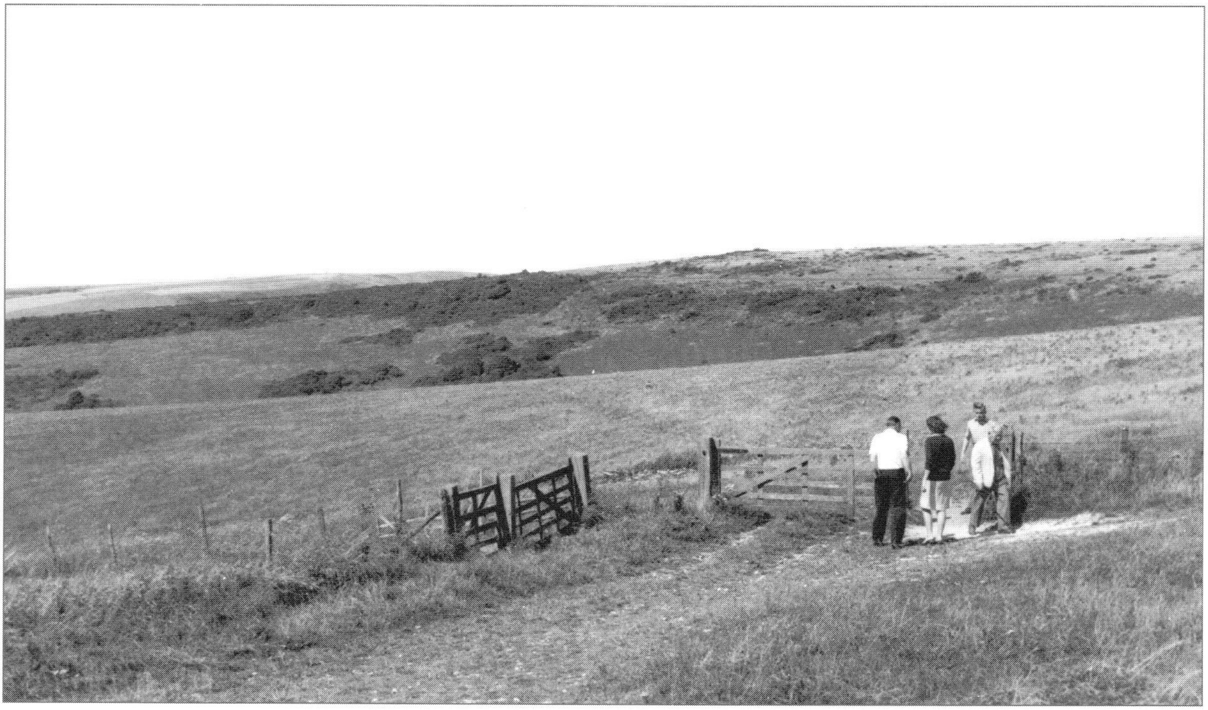

**WILLINGDON,** *The Downs c1955* W446019

Today there are fewer sheep on the downs, and visitors and residents, like the family in the picture, enjoy this rural amenity. Ramblers re-trace the steps of their prehistoric ancestors as they walk the downland paths and the ridgeway, which was used as a natural highway by Neolithic man all those centuries ago.

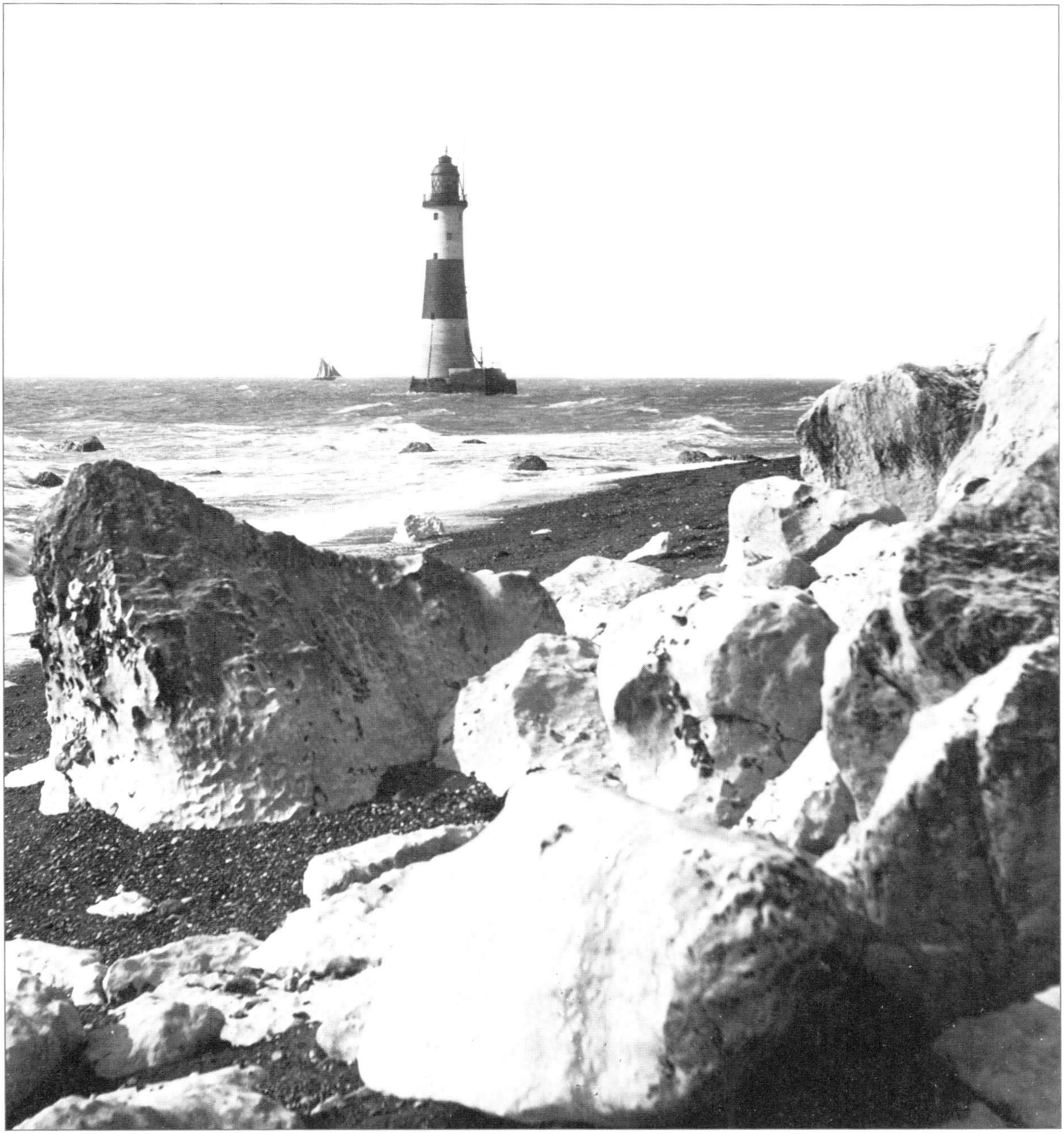

**BEACHY HEAD,** *The Lighthouse 1912* 64981

At the eastern extremity of the South Downs, the Royal Sovereign Lighthouse at the foot of Beachy Head warned shipping of the hazards of the chalk cliffs, which now lie under the sea. Built in 1901, it replaced the former Bell Tout Light on the top of the cliffs, and was itself replaced by the Sovereign Lightship anchored off-shore.

# THE WEALD

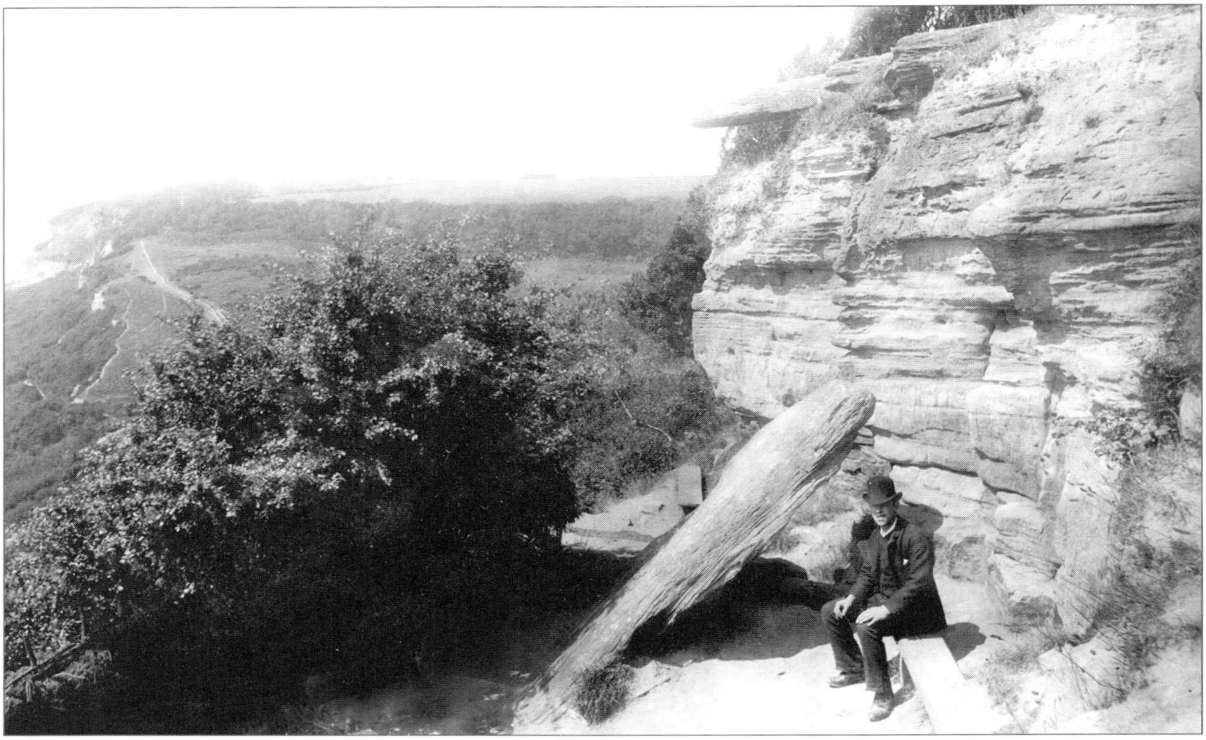

**FAIRLIGHT GLEN,** *The Lovers' Seat 1890* 22806

Some of the county's most beautiful scenery can be seen in the Wealden region of Sussex. From the Lovers' Seat, linked with a romantic legend of the 18th century, the view overlooking the sea near Hastings is possibly one of the most picturesque. It was here that two lovers secretly met. Their stolen interludes led to a clandestine marriage, just before they both tragically died.

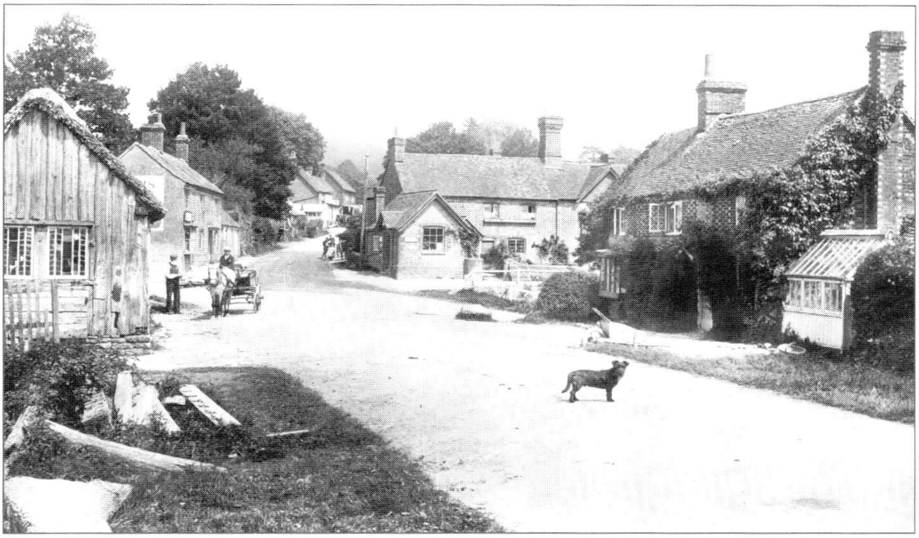

**FERNHURST**
*The Cross-Roads*
*1908* 59671

The small, relatively unspoilt village of Fernhurst lies on the Midhurst to Haslemere road in the north-west corner of Sussex. Timber from the extensive woodland surrounding Fernhurst provided fuel for the nearby ironworks at North Park during the 17th and 18th centuries.

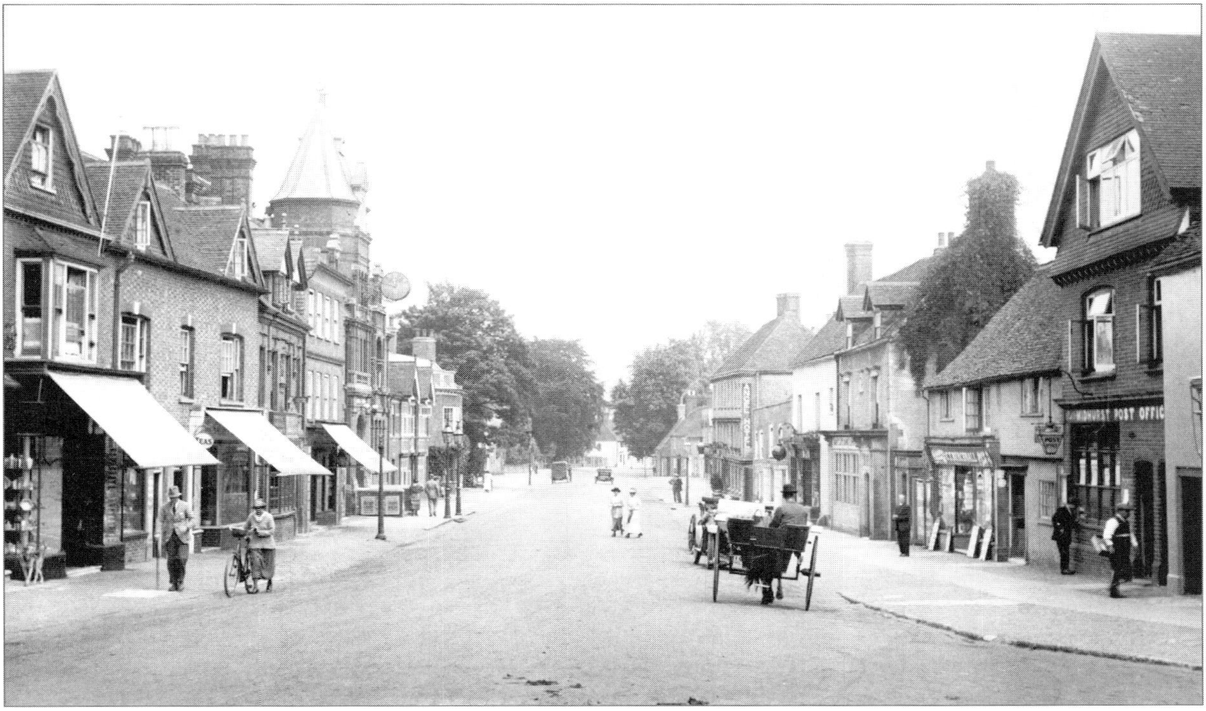

**MIDHURST,** *North Street 1921* 70085

Midhurst, where every style of architecture can be seen in perfect harmony, is possibly the most beautiful of all the medieval market towns in Sussex. It is suggested that the 16th-century Angel Inn (on the left-hand side) is where the Pilgrim Fathers paused on their way to embark on the 'Mayflower' before sailing to America.

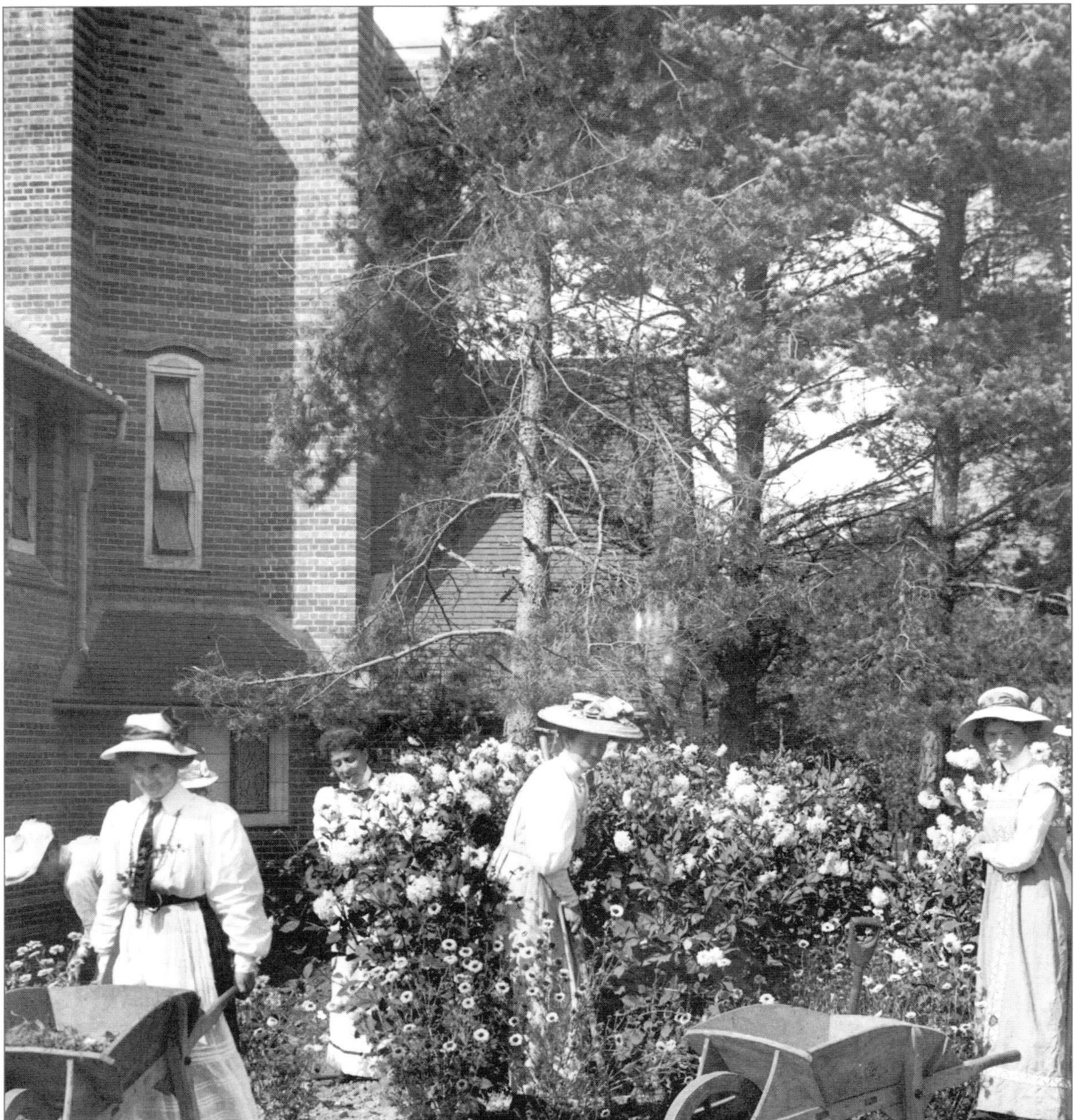

**MIDHURST,** *The King Edward Sanatorium 1907* 58337A

The ladies gardening are patients in the King Edward Sanatorium, which is situated on Great Common about two miles north of Midhurst. King Edward VII laid the foundation stone on 3 November 1903, and the sanatorium was completed nearly two years later. Its balconies were designed so that patients could enjoy fresh air while sheltered from the wind.

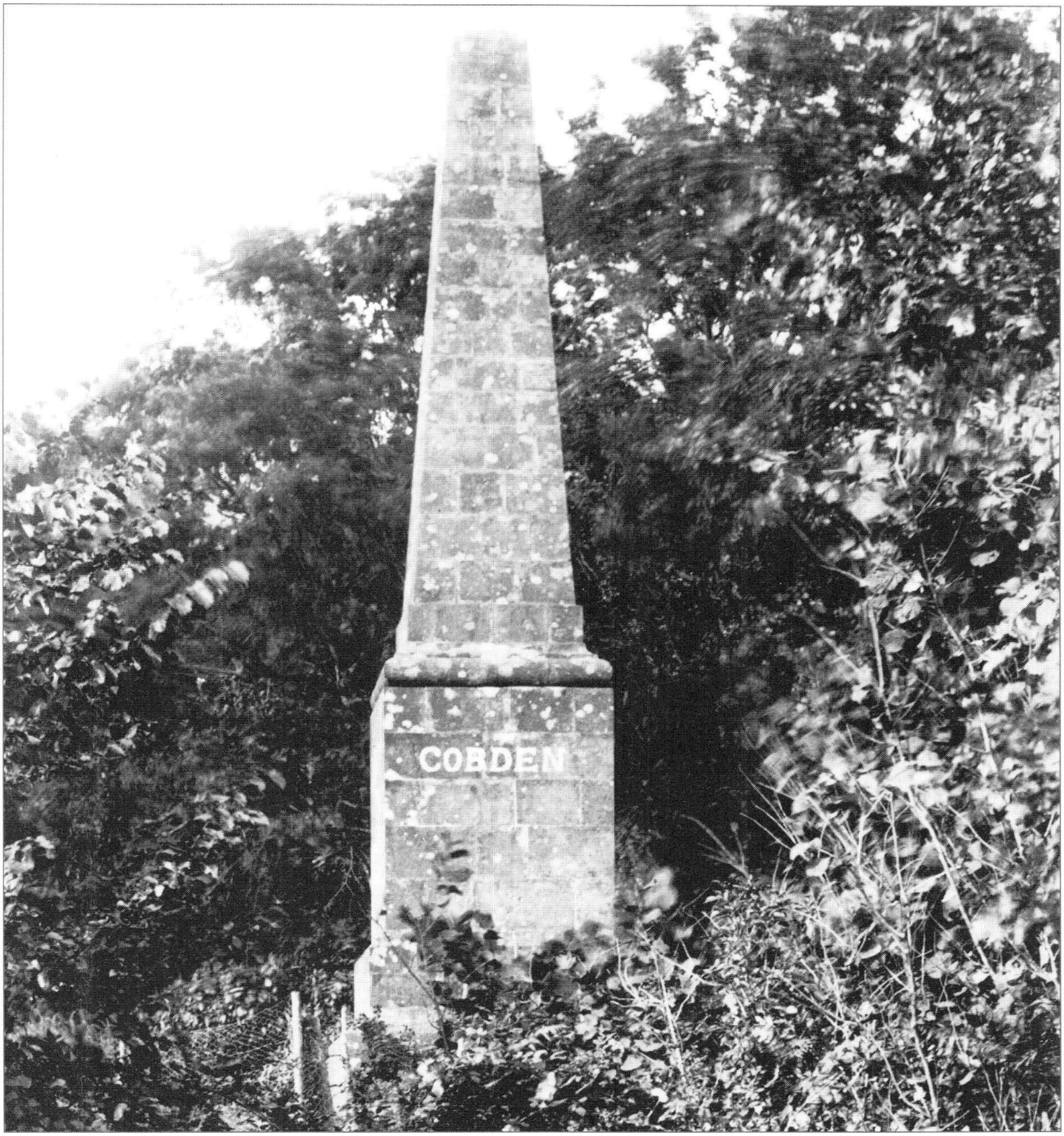


**HEYSHOTT,** *The Cobden Monument 1906* 54390

Situated in woodland near the Midhurst to Cocking road, the Cobden Monument was erected in memory of Richard Cobden MP, an advocate of free trade and an anti-Corn Law agitator. With the funds of the National Testimonial to him, he purchased and re-built Dunsford House, his birthplace, which was presented to the Liberal Party in 1924 by his daughter.

▼ **PETWORTH,** *The House 1898* 42840A

Petworth House was re-built at the end of the 17th century; it incorporated a 13th-century chapel and undercroft that was already on the site. The west side, with its balanced Renaissance design, overlooks the lake, which with its meandering curves and seemingly natural islands forms part of the adjoining walled park, landscaped by Capability Brown in the late 1750s.

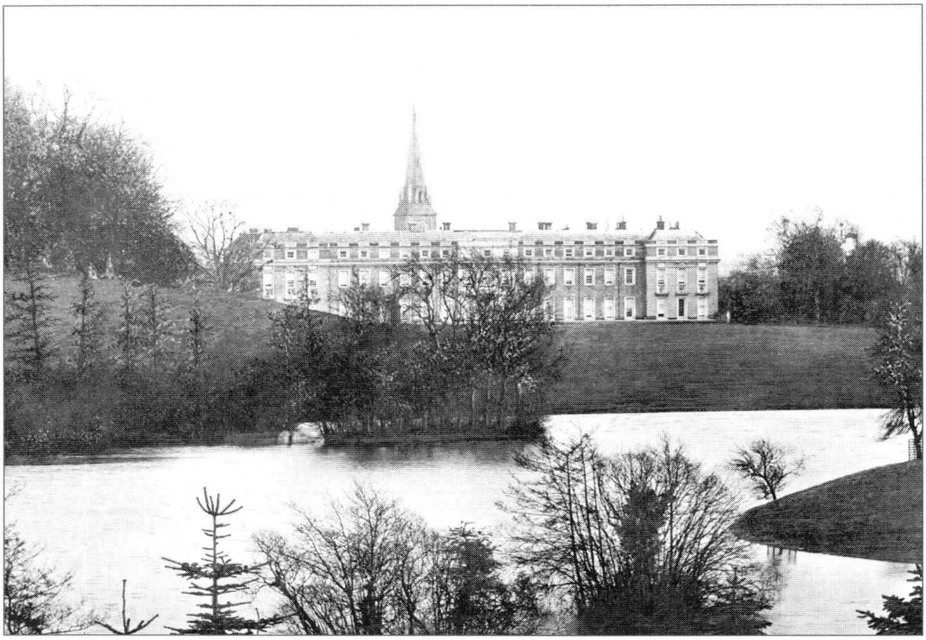

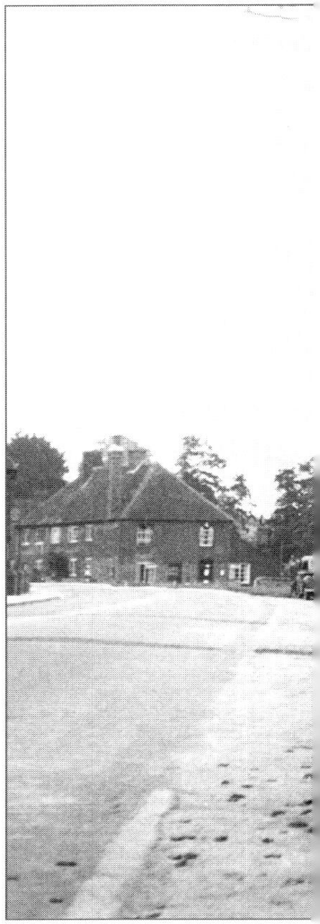

► **PETWORTH**
*Near the Church 1912*
64899X

Petworth is one of the oldest and most unusual of the Sussex towns. In the shadow of the 13th-century church of St Mary, to the south of Petworth House, the two young girls and the driver of the horse and cart pose for the camera in one of the innumerable nooks and crannies that lead off Petworth's narrow circuitous roads.

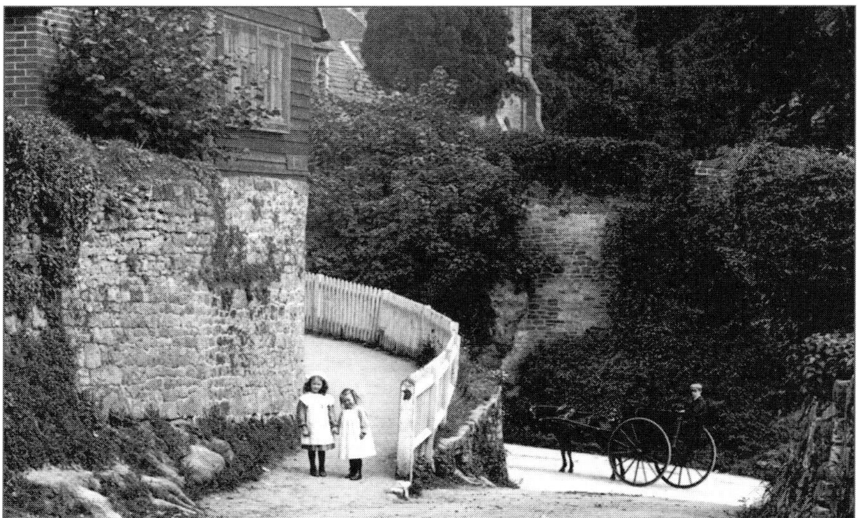

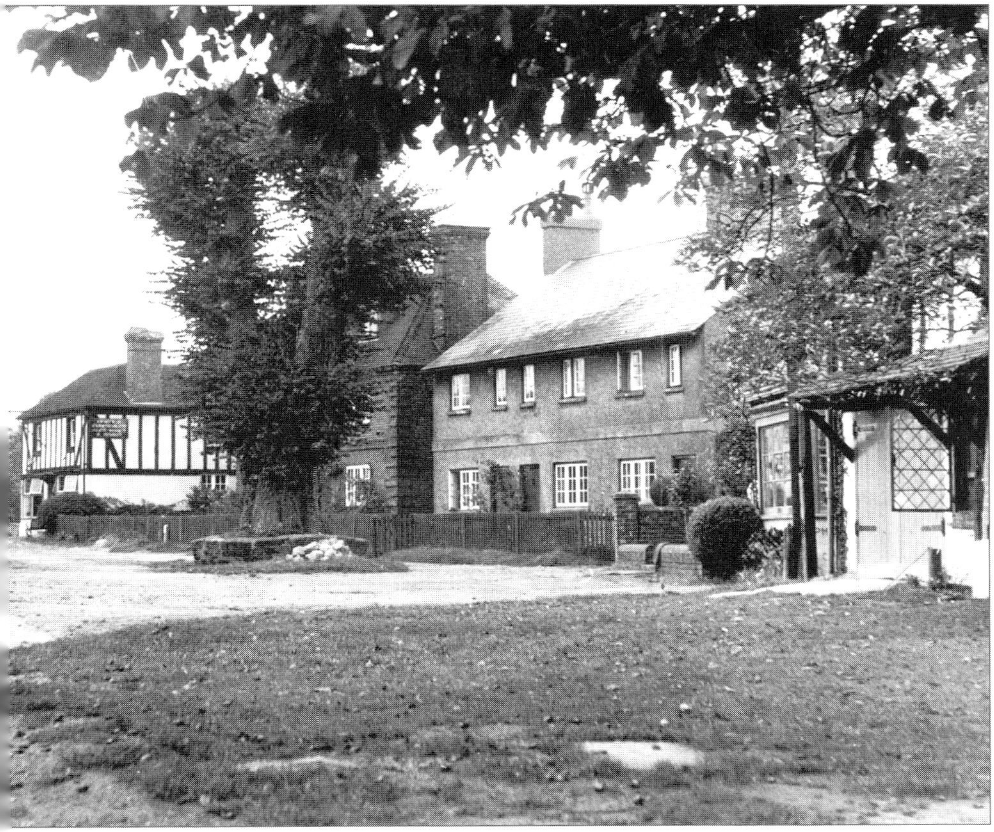

◄ **NORTHCHAPEL**
*The Village c1955*
N160005

The village of Northchapel, which is situated 5 miles north of Petworth, was formerly a chapelry of Petworth, and only became a parish in its own right after an Act of Parliament in 1693. The old half-timbered Swan Inn (centre left) has now been renamed the Deepwell Inn. On the right is Old Forge Cottage, which adjoined the blacksmith's shop.

► **BILLINGSHURST**
*The Village 1928* 81440

The Roman road of Stane Street bisects the village of Billingshurst. The shop of W J Barnes (on the left) stands on the causeway; it was formerly the old family shop of Joseph Luxford, a carrier. The dormer windows and shop front were added between c1892 and 1906. The middle property is Tithe Cottage. Causeway Cottages, once a late medieval Wealden hall house, are in the background.

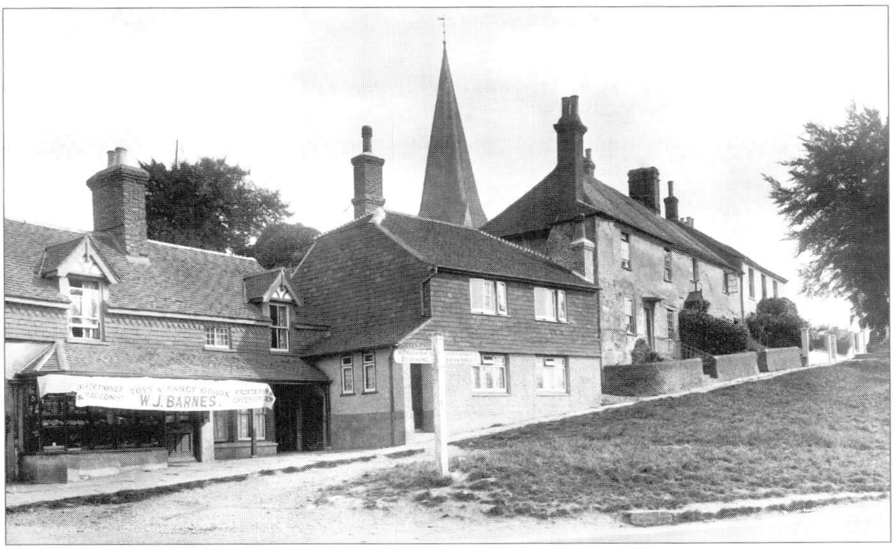

**BARNS GREEN**
*The Village c1960*
B504027

Initially a hamlet, the village of Barns Green dates from the Middle Ages, but grew rapidly during the 18th and 19th centuries following the opening of the Mid-Sussex railway line. Parker's shop opposite the green is one of two shops recorded in the village in the 1960s. In more recent years the village has been the annual venue for a very popular half-marathon road race.

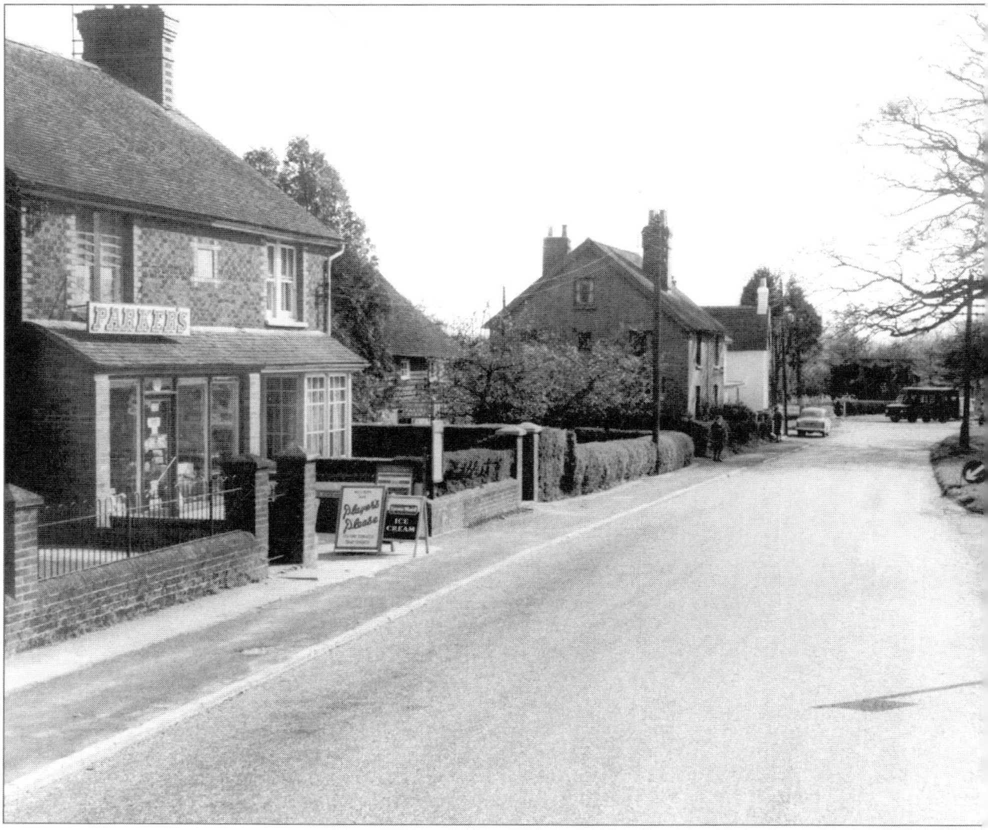


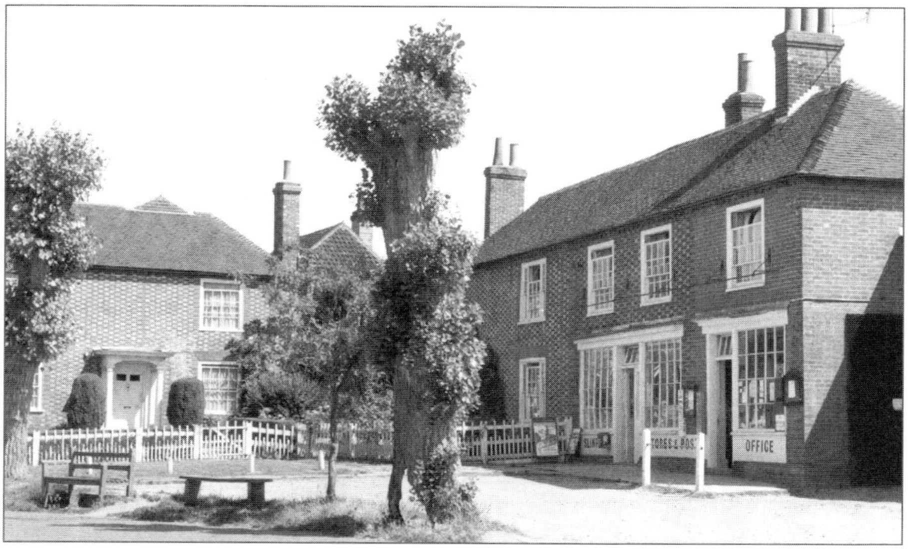


**SLINFOLD**
*The Post Office c1955* S591038

To the east of Stane Street, and four miles north of Billingshurst, is the village of Slinfold. Both Slinfold House (on the left) and Slinfold's stores and post office are clad in an attractive pattern of mathematical tiles, which were very popular in the 18th century. The historian James Dalloway was rector of the parish between 1803 and 1834.

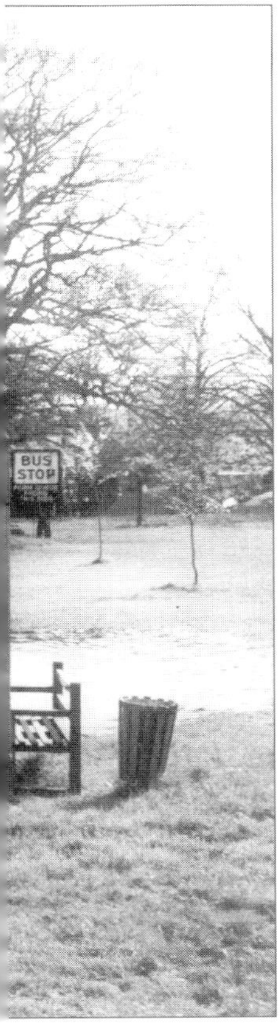


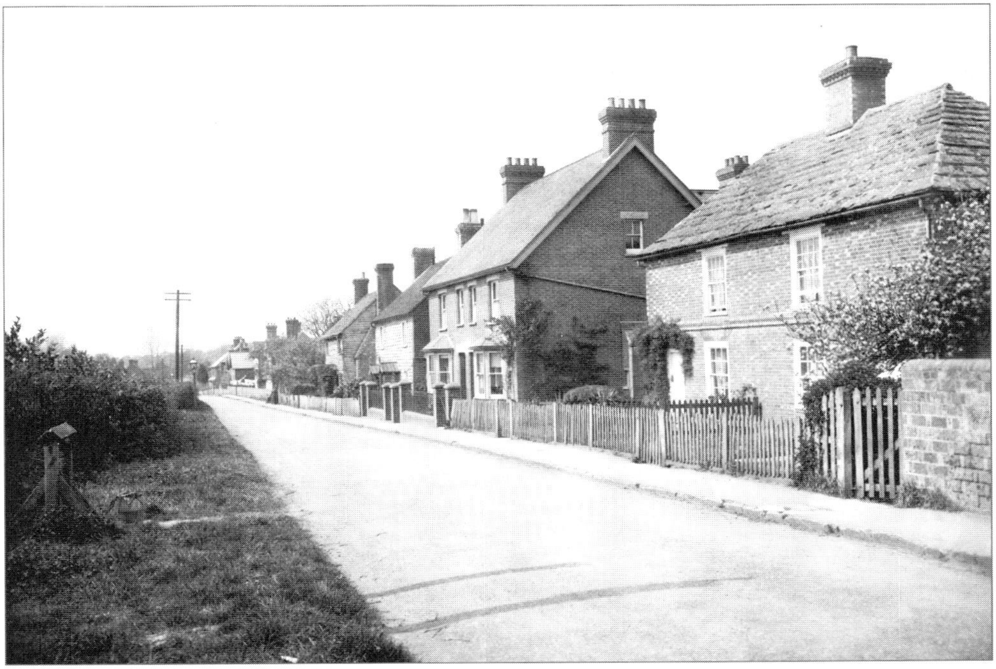

▲ **WARNHAM,** *Friday Street 1921* 69974

Warnham parish lies mainly on Wealden clay about 2 miles north-west of Horsham. During the medieval period it was undoubtedly extensively wooded, and its name possibly means 'the grazing place of feral stallions'. It is thought that the name 'Friday Street' may record a distinct area of settlement. Note the old well to the left.

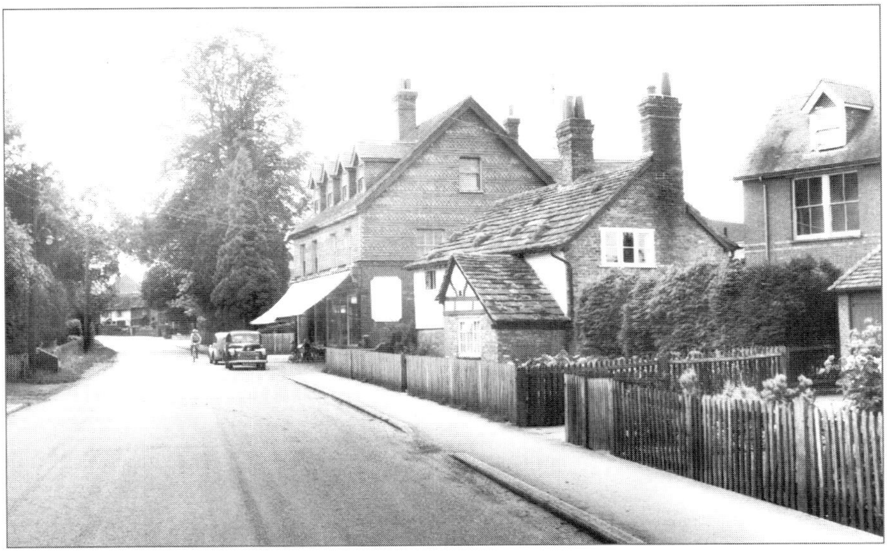

◄ **WARNHAM**
*Church Street c1960*
W28016

The large building in the centre was erected in 1879 on the site of an earlier small shop. Known as Warnham Stores, it operated until 1948, selling groceries, china, drapery, furniture, and products from its own bakery at the rear. To the right is an old house, formerly occupied by the village boot and shoe repairer.

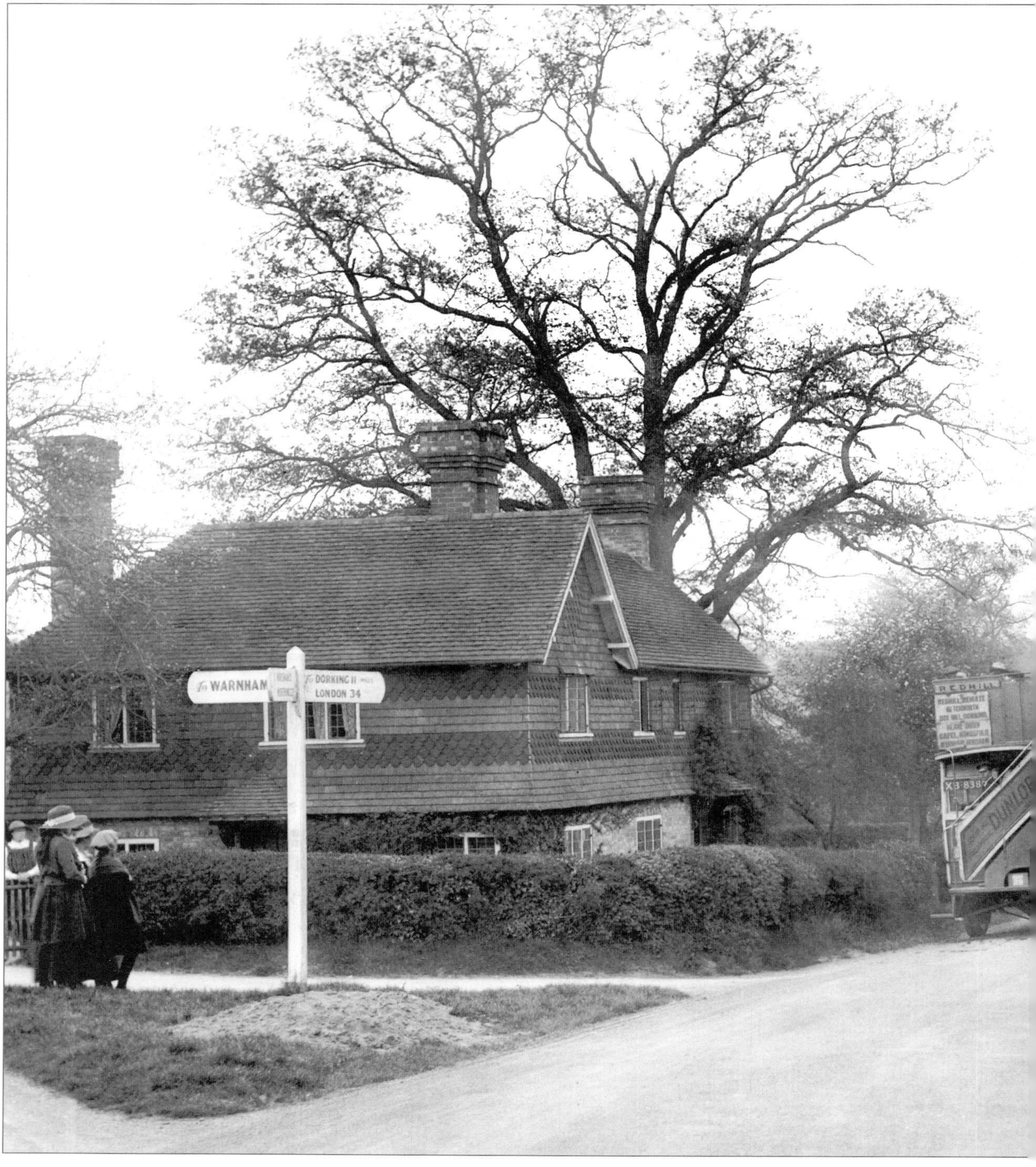
To WARNHAM
To DORKING 11 MILES
LONDON 34
REDHILL
DUNLOP

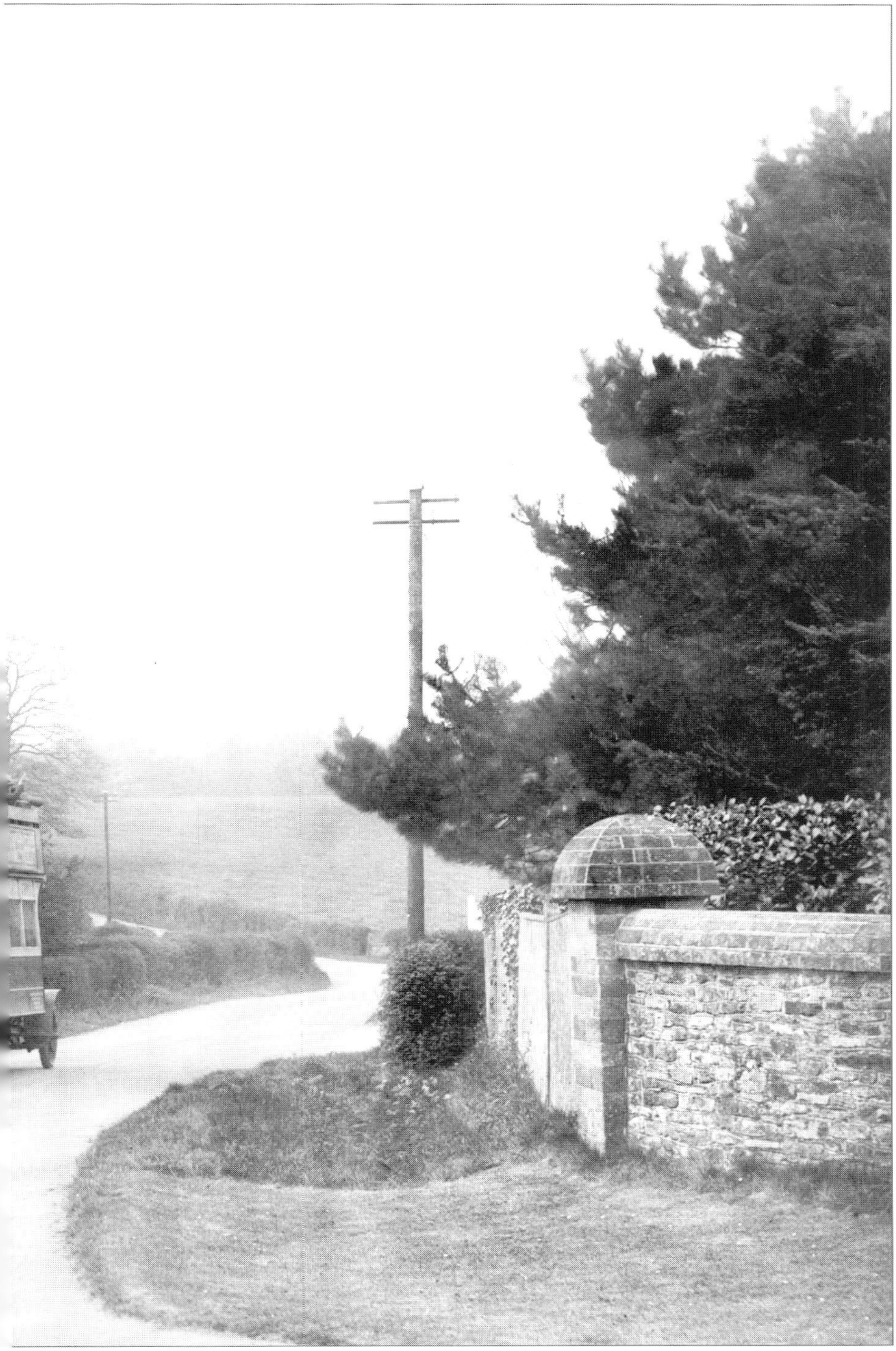

**WARNHAM**
*Corner House 1921*
69980

The open-topped bus receiving a great deal of attention from the people on the left is travelling along part of the old coaching route. After the horses had been changed at Kingsfold, the stagecoaches ran through Warnham down Little London Hill, past Warnham Corner at the junction of Station Road.

▼ **WARNHAM,** *Field Place 1923* 74922

The poet Percy Bysshe Shelley, eldest son of Sir Timothy Shelley MP, was born on 4 August 1792 at Field Place in Warnham, where he spent his childhood. Parts of the house date from the medieval period, but it has been greatly altered over the years, and was restored in the 1920s. There was parkland on the estate by 1795, which by 1813 contained three lakes.

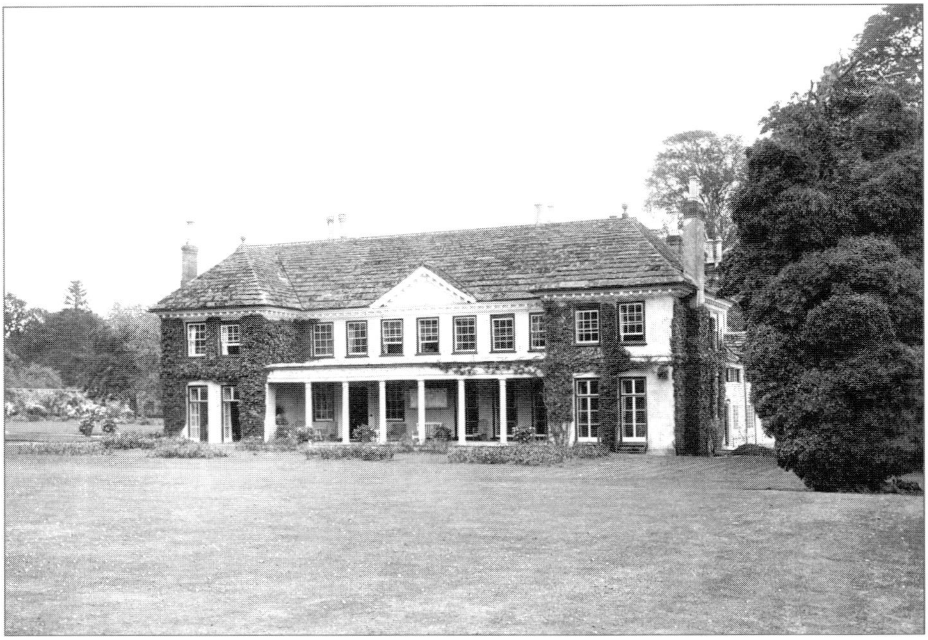

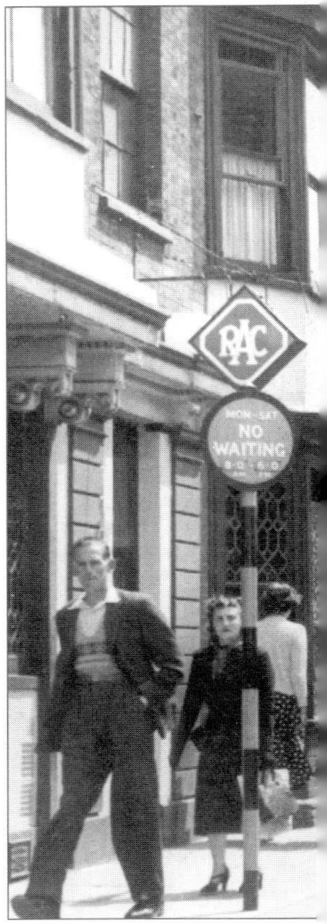


► **HORSHAM**
*Queen Street 1924* 75334

Horsham was described as a borough in the early 13th century, and it had become one of the chief towns in the county by the 17th and 18th centuries. In 1775 the town's new gaol was built in Queen Street, but this was demolished in 1845, one year after Horsham's last public execution on the special gallows erected outside.

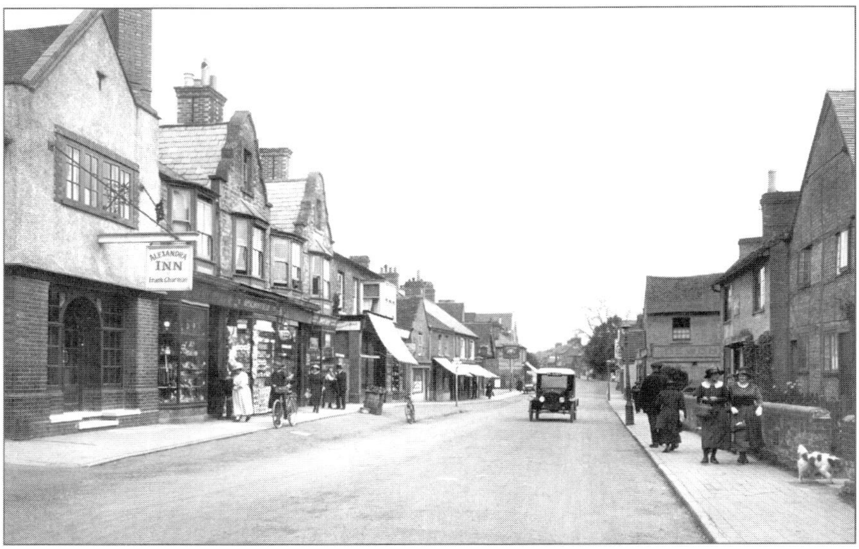

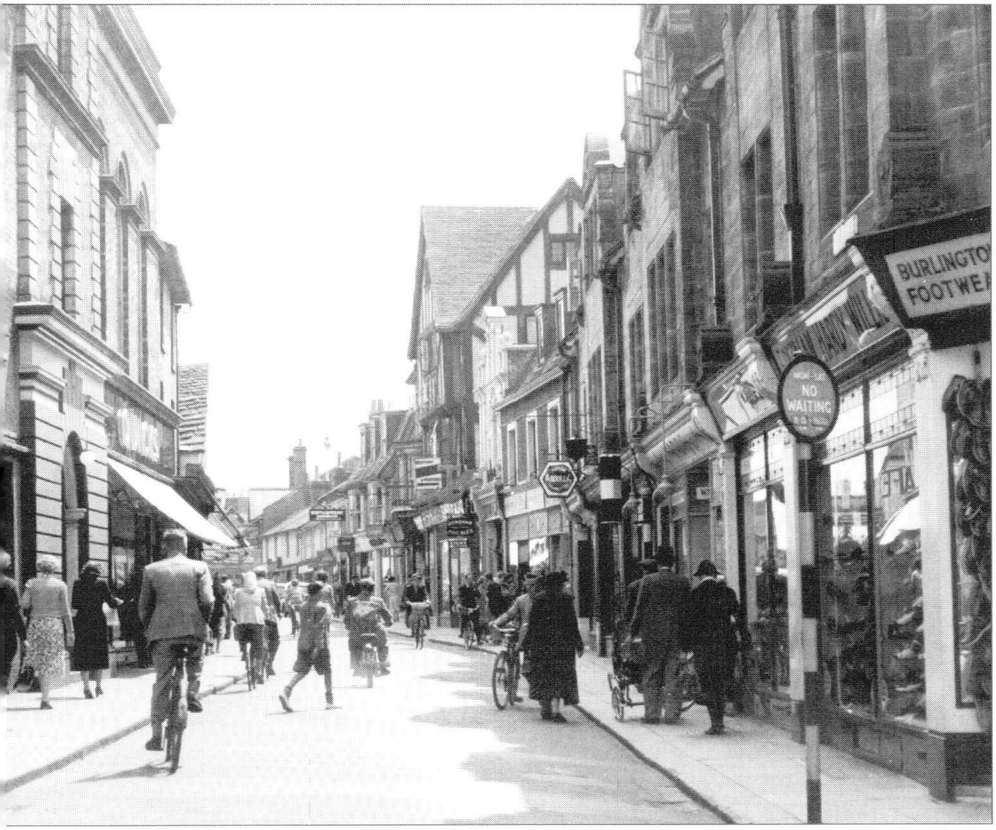


**HORSHAM**
*East Street c1955*
H119068

East Street, recorded from 1457, contains some early buildings. On the far left (displaying the RAC sign) is the Kings Head Hotel, which was in existence by 1669; the main entrance to this former coaching inn was in the Carfax. It was improved in the late 18th century, and had become the principal inn at Horsham by the 1830s.

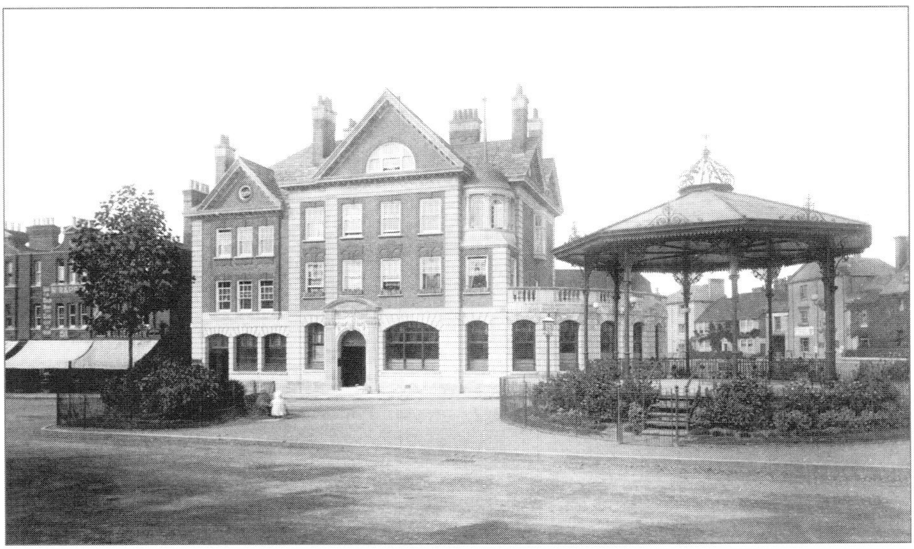

**HORSHAM**
*The Carfax and the Bank 1899* 42852

Between the 16th and 17th centuries, Horsham's July fair was held in the Carfax. By 1877, it had become almost entirely a pleasure fair and a nuisance to the inhabitants, and was abolished. Music was also popular in Horsham, and a bandstand was erected in the Carfax in 1891from money collected by subscription.

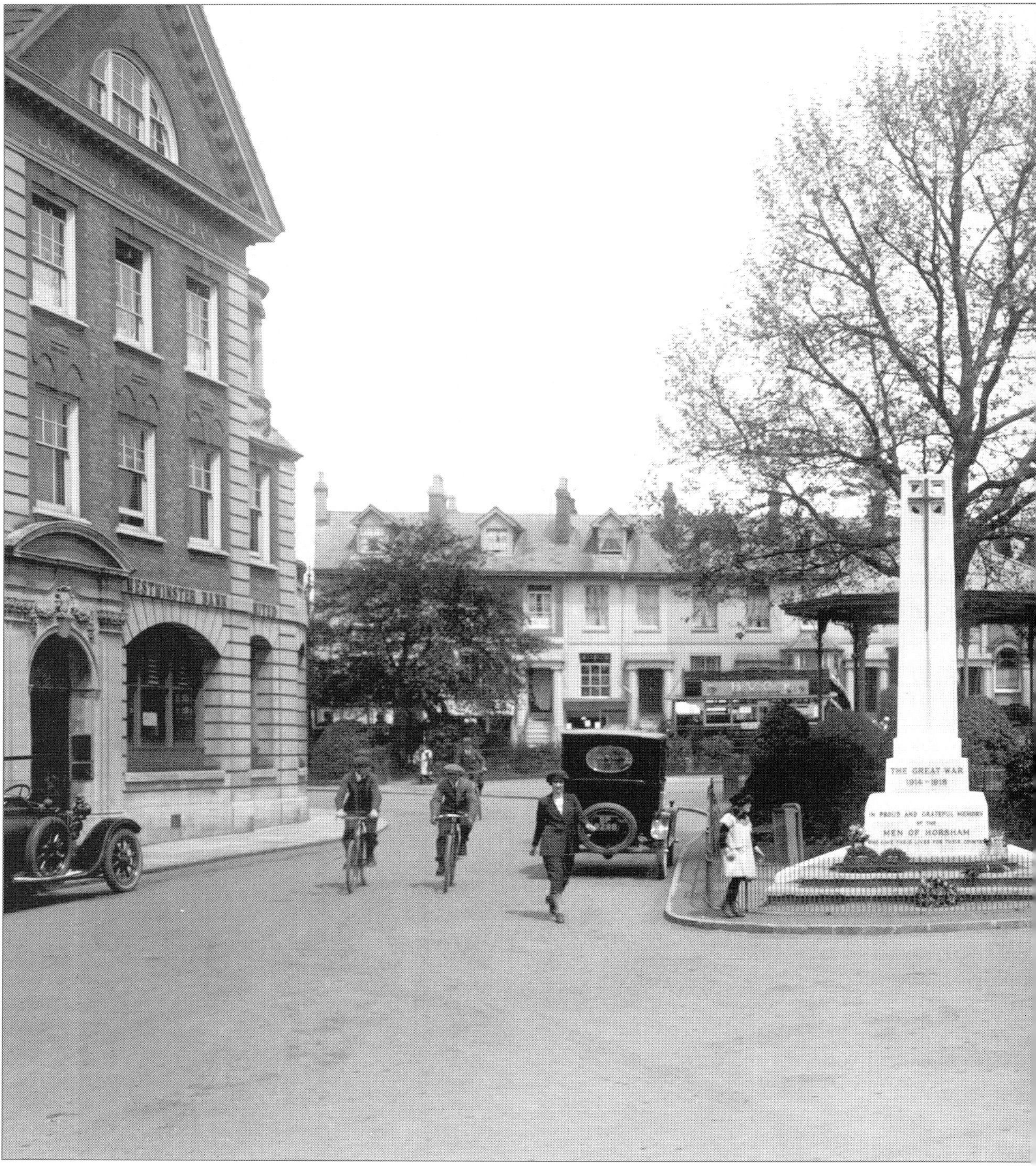
THE GREAT WAR
1914-1918
IN PROUD AND GRATEFUL MEMORY
MEN OF HORSHAM

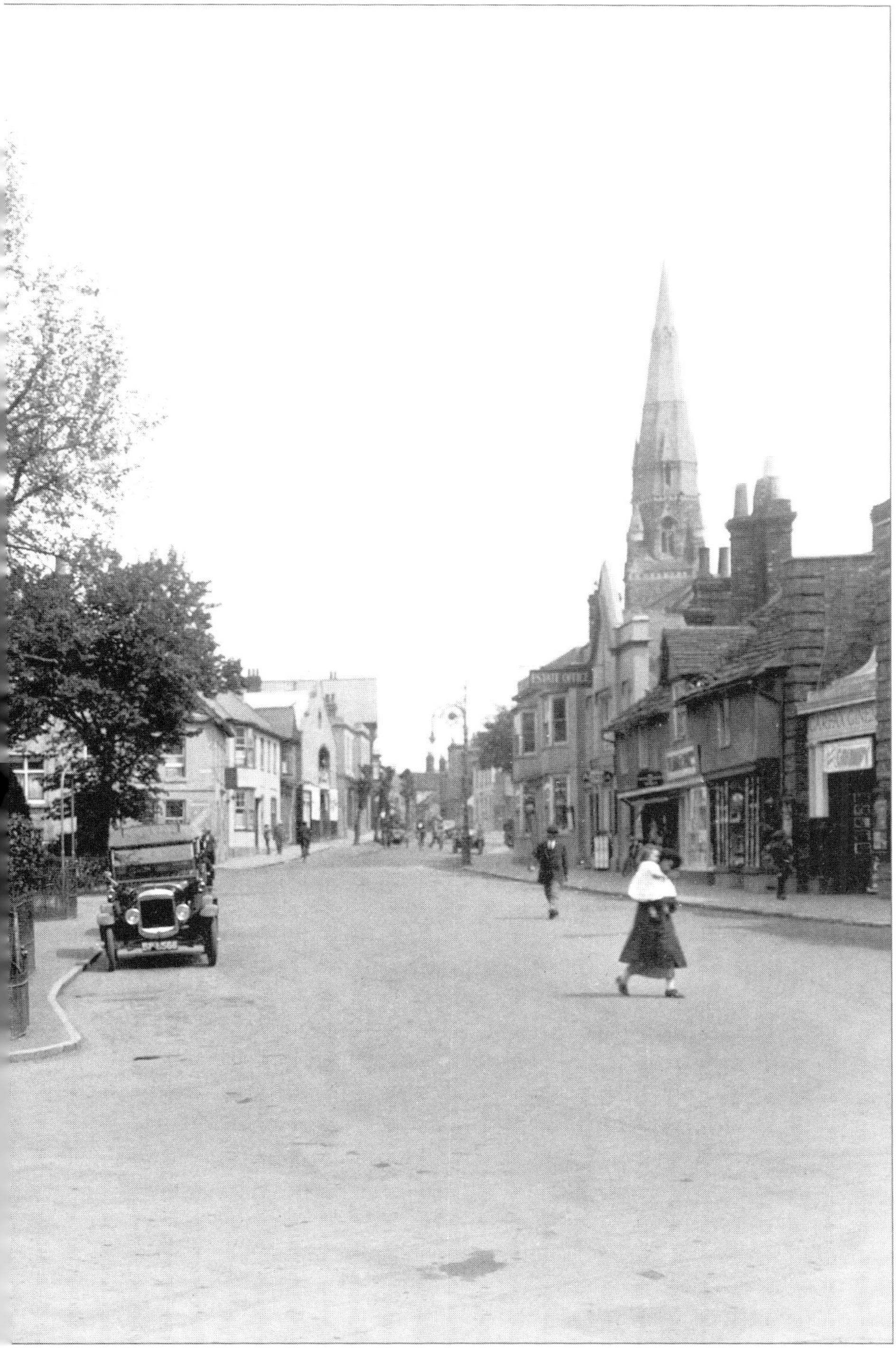

**HORSHAM**
*The Carfax, East Side*
*1924* 75330

Originally the open central area in Horsham was known as the market place, but by the later 19th century the northern part was called the Carfax, a name possibly derived from 'Skarfolkes', used in 1524 for taxation purposes, or from the street called 'Skarfax' mentioned in 1548. The war memorial was erected in 1921, but it has since been re-sited.

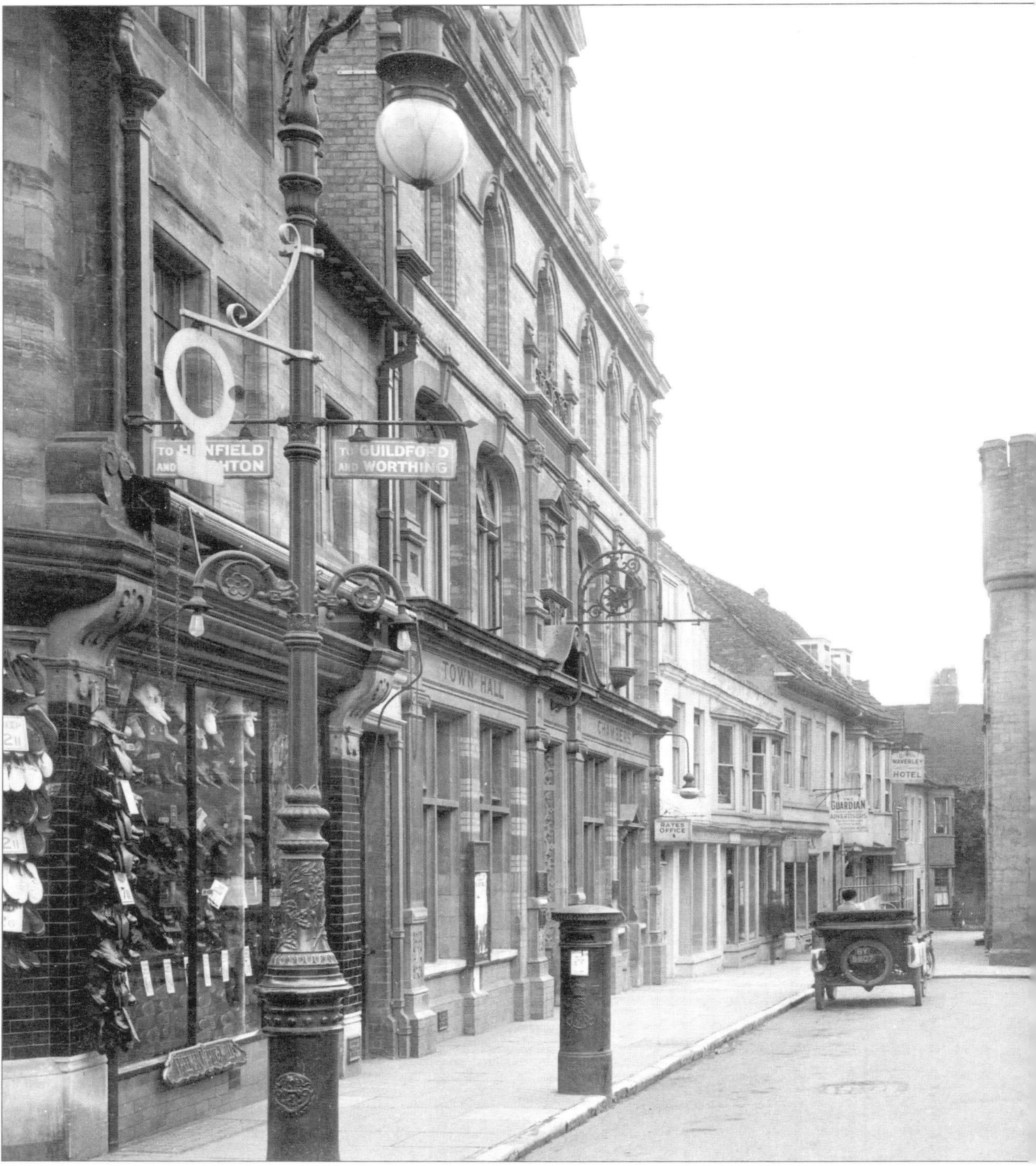
TO GUILDFORD AND WORTHING
TOWN HALL
CHAMBERS
RATES OFFICE
GUARDIAN
WAVERLEY HOTEL

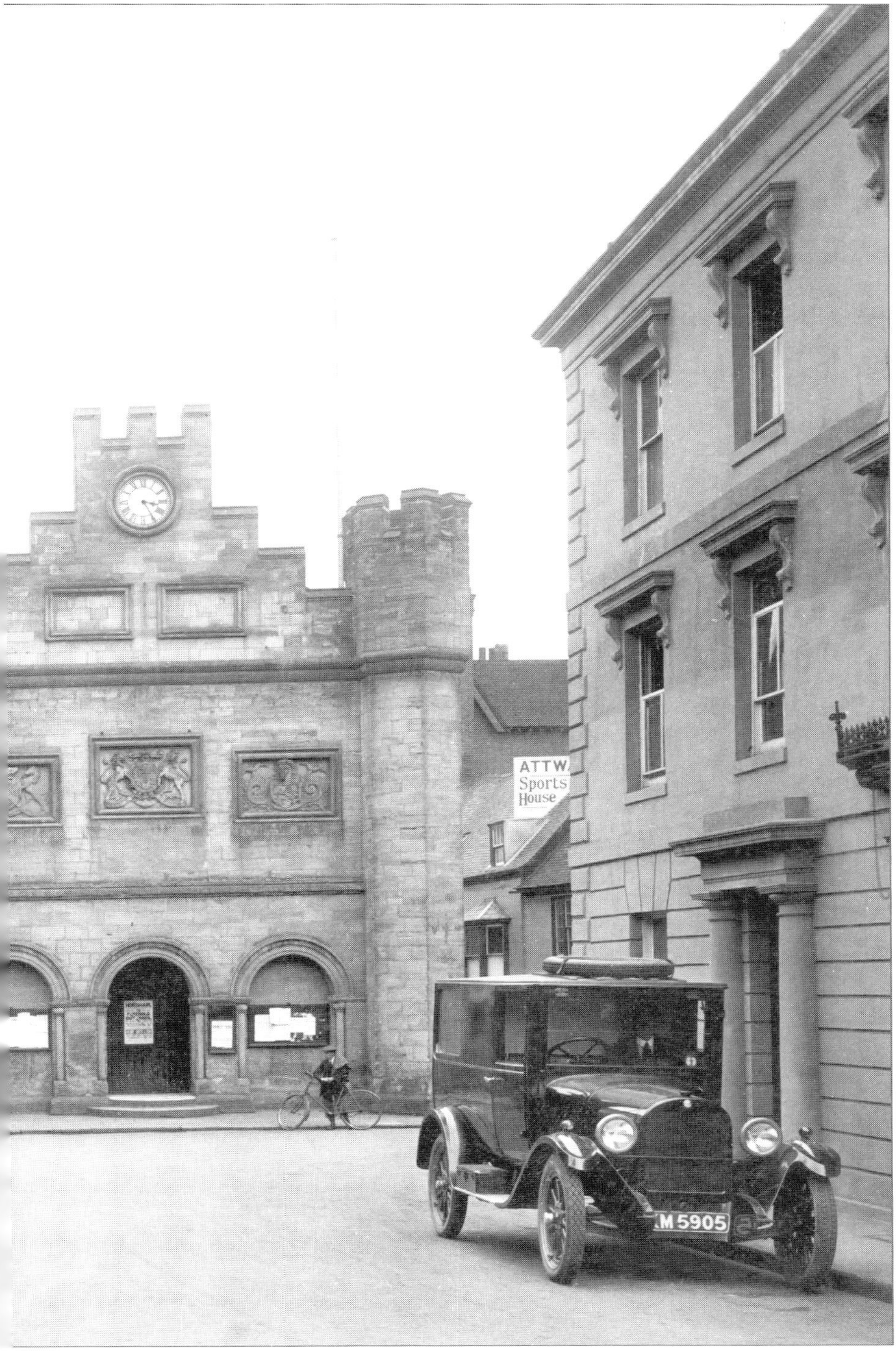


**HORSHAM**
*The Town Hall 1923*
73406

On the southern part of the market is the old Town Hall or Market House; the original open arcade on the ground floor was used as a butter and poultry market. The former 18th-century building was completely rebuilt in 1888, and was used for council meetings and legal administration.

▼ **BURGESS HILL,** *Station Road c1955* B284002

Burgess Hill is one of the mid 19th-century settlements created on enclosed Wealden commons. It developed around the railway station when houses were built for middle-class Victorian families who chose to live surrounded by beautiful woodland scenery. The Railway Hotel on the right is a fitting reminder of the railway's influence on the town's subsequent growth.

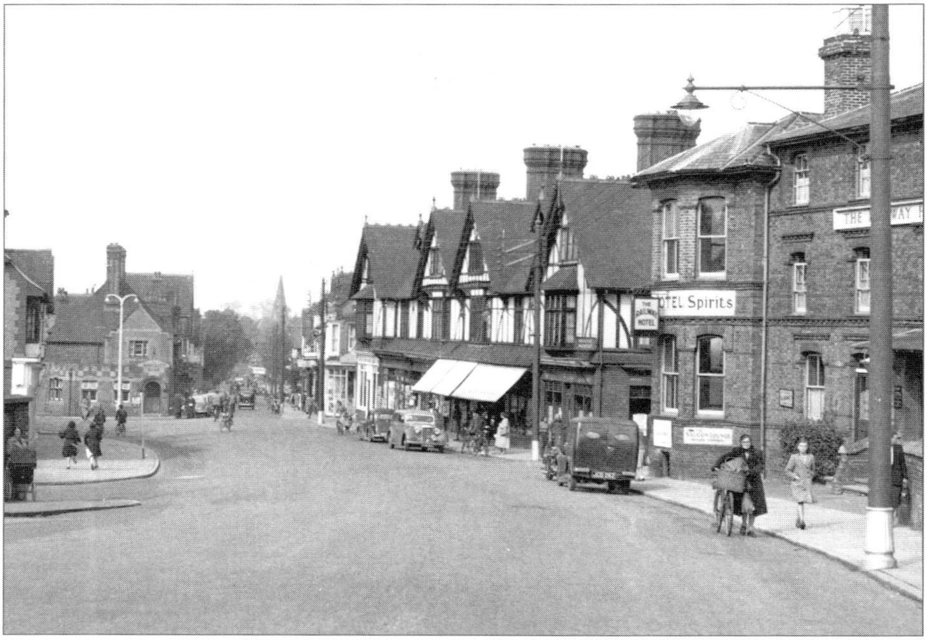


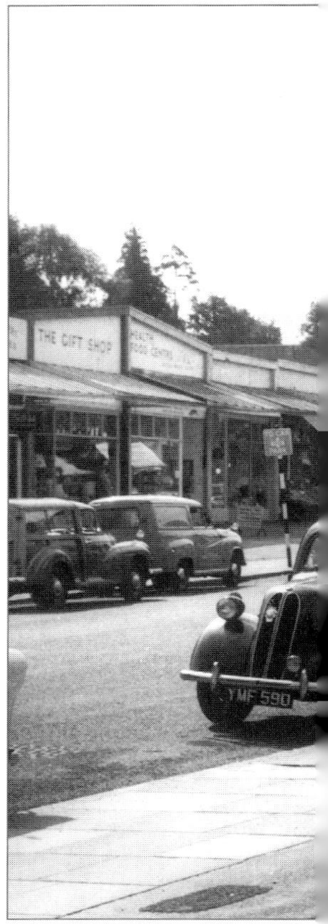


► **BURGESS HILL**
*Church Road c1960*
B284035

By the end of the 19th century, Church Road was Burgess Hill's main shopping centre. The corner building on the right, partly occupied by the Farm Shop Dairy, was once known as Terry's Corner after Mr Edward Terry, a draper from Brighton. Owing to his policy of 'good value for cash', his enterprise eventually expanded from a single shop, built in 1887, into six shops.

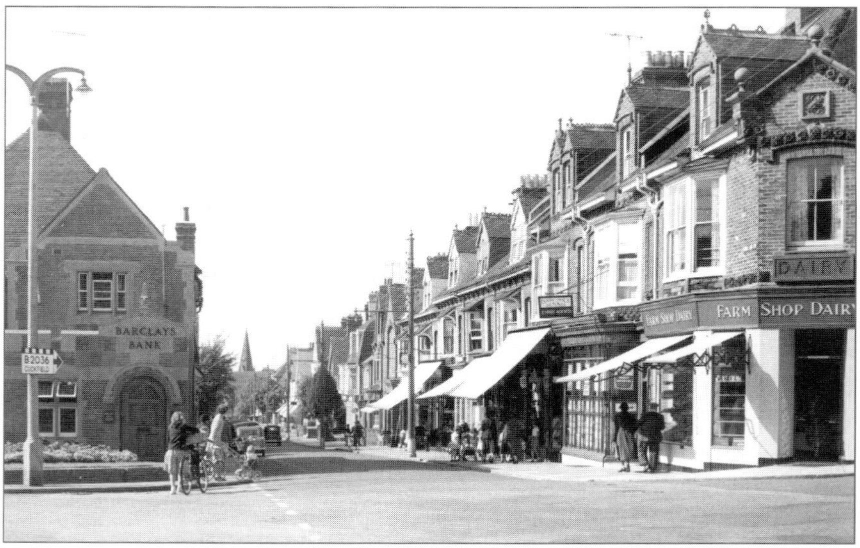

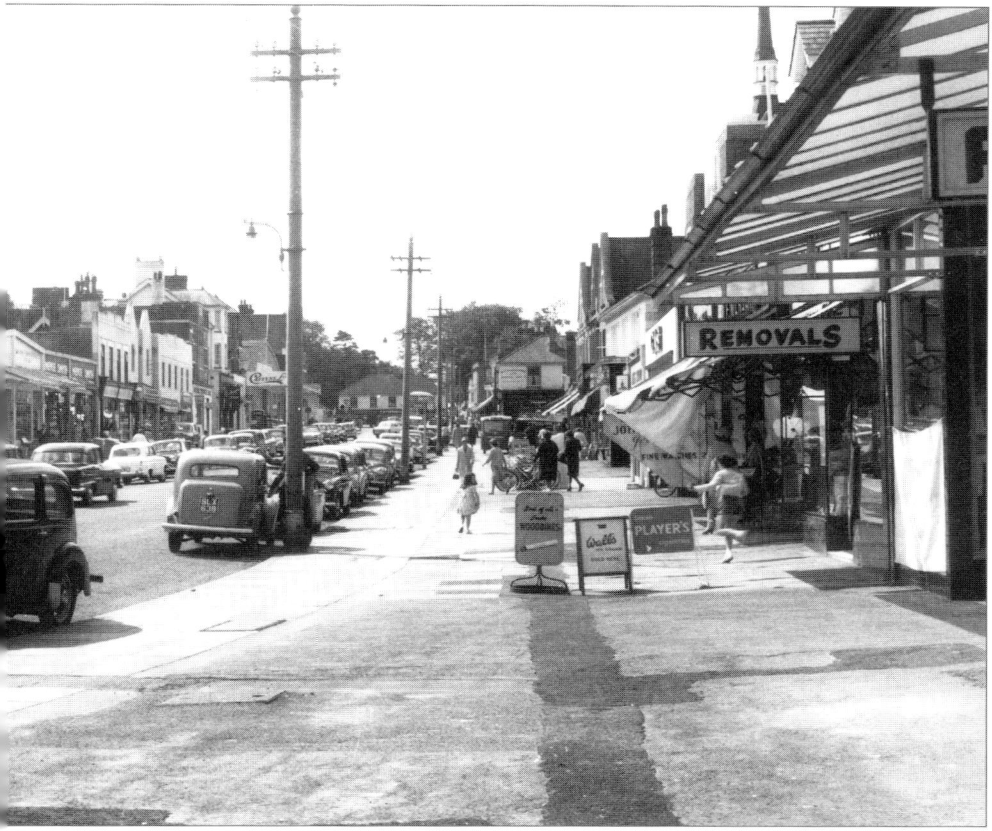


**HAYWARDS HEATH**
*The Broadway c1955* H252030

In 1830 Haywards Heath was described as 'a byword for the wilderness of its aspect, the rusticity of its few and scattered cottages, and the miryness of its roads'. Once the railway arrived this all changed, and Haywards Heath developed rapidly on an enclosed common. Little of the original common survives, and the Broadway is typical of the unstructured development during the Victorian and Edwardian era.

**CRAWLEY**
*The George Hotel 1903* 50758

The medieval settlement of Crawley, situated half way along the London to Brighton Road, was ideally located to become an 18th-century coaching town. The George Hotel, with its gallows inn sign straddling the road, dates from the 16th century, and still retains part of the original timber-framed building.

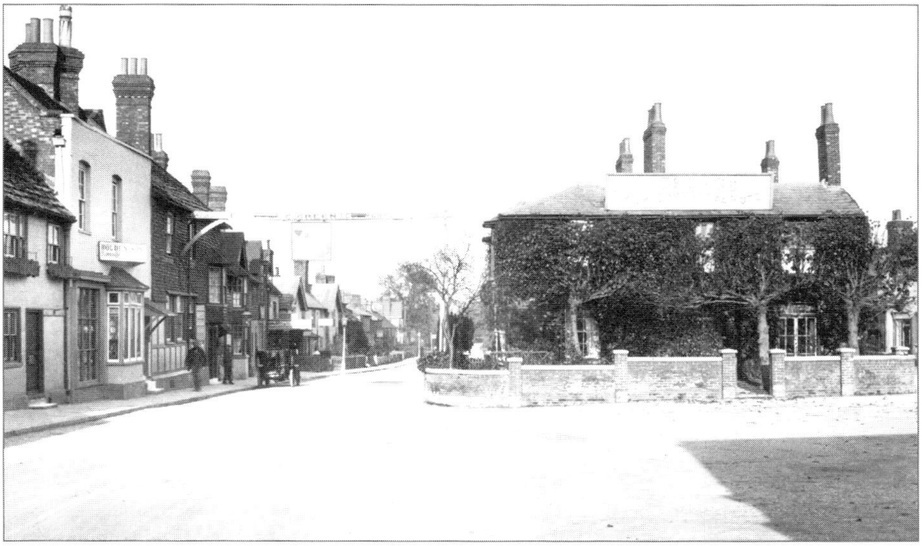

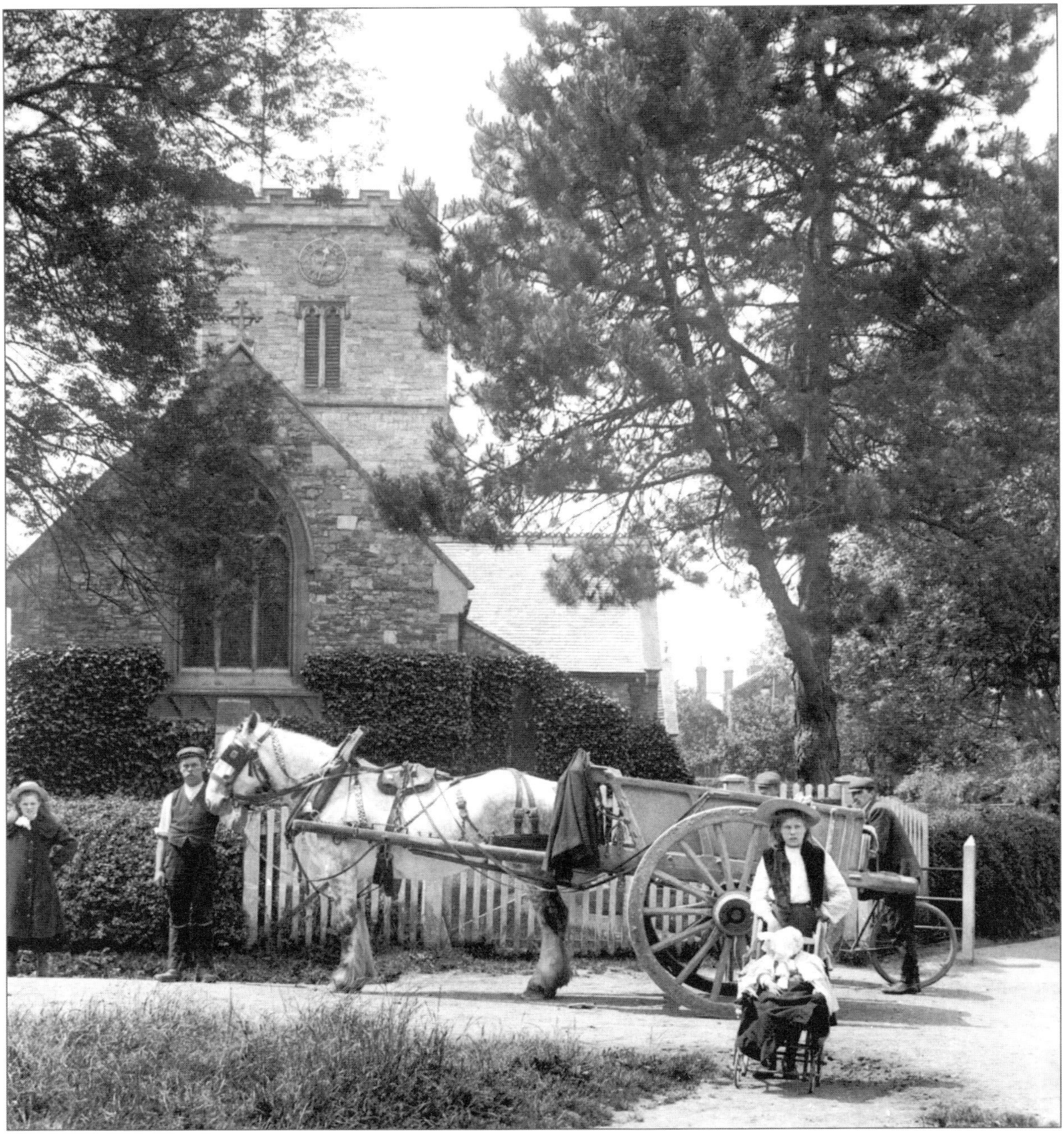

**CRAWLEY,** *The Church 1907* 57773

This peaceful and idyllic rural scene, with the horse and cart behind a small girl pushing a pram outside the church of St John the Baptist, belies Crawley's mid 19th-century expansion into a railway town, following the construction of the line from Three Bridges to Horsham.

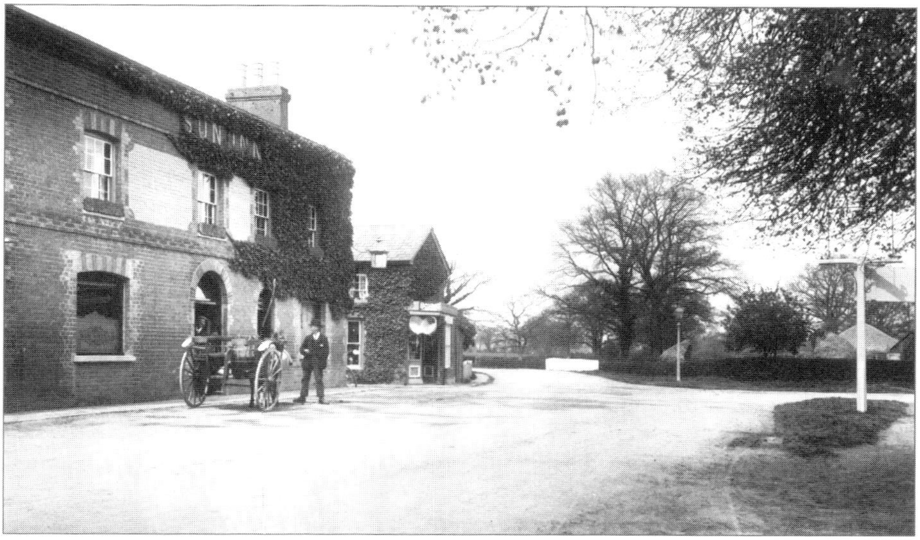

**CRAWLEY**
*The Sun Inn 1905*
53315

By 1870 the 'New Town' not only covered the small parish of Crawley, but also parts of its neighbours, Ifield and Worth. The Swan Inn, built in 1874, was one of the many new Victorian properties built on the western side of the High Street. At the date of this photograph, the street appears to have been devoid of any vehicles other than a solitary horse and cart.

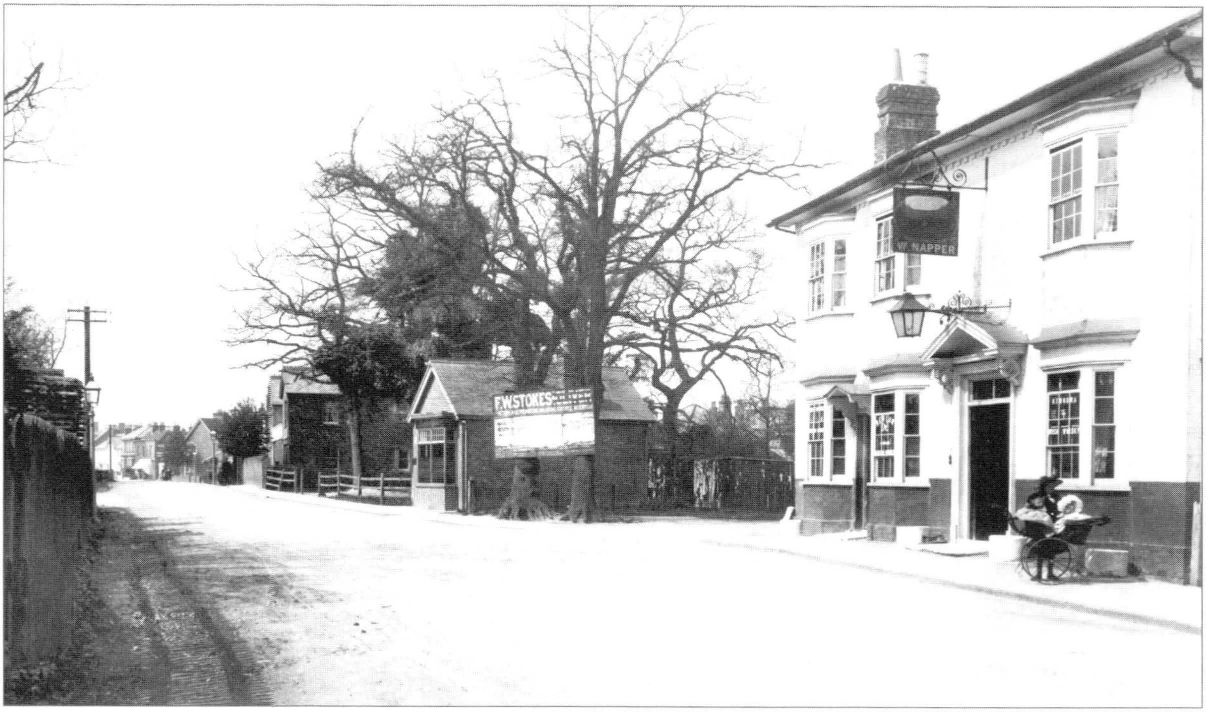


**THREE BRIDGES,** *The Fox 1905* 53311

Three Bridges derives its name from its bridges over the River Mole. Before the arrival of the railway in 1841 it was a small settlement, but it grew around a station and busy junction on the London to Brighton line. By 1841 the Fox Railway Inn (on the right) had been opened by the railway company. It was demolished in 1989.

**THREE BRIDGES**
*The Bridge off the Mill Path 1906*
55386

Before the development of Crawley New Town, the Hazlewick Mill path and bridge was a renowned beauty spot. Hazlewick Mill dated from the 17th or 18th century; it was closed in the 1890s, but was not demolished until many years later.

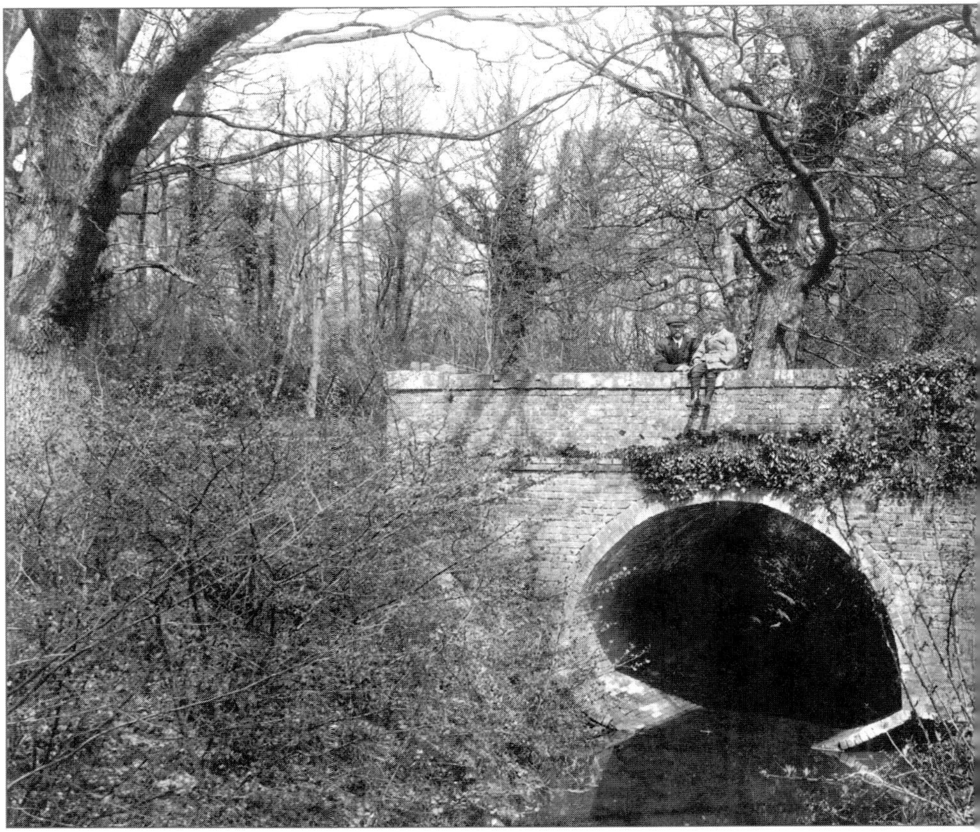

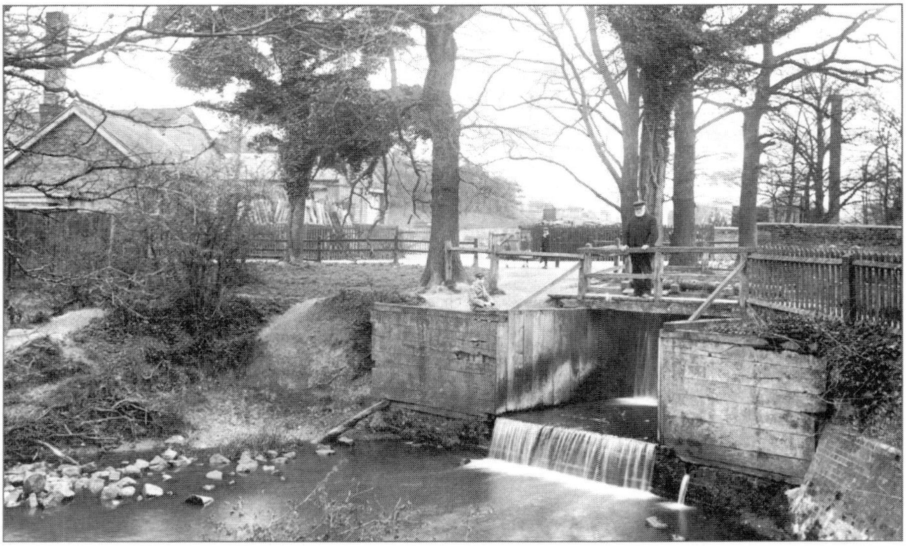

**THREE BRIDGES**
*The Flood Gates 1906* 55384

The millpond for the old Hazlewick mill was fed by the River Mole, which flowed close to Three Bridges railway station (on the left through the trees). Flooding in the area still occurred despite the provision of flood gates to control the water levels. The old water mill may have closed as a result of the new steam mill, which opened near the station.

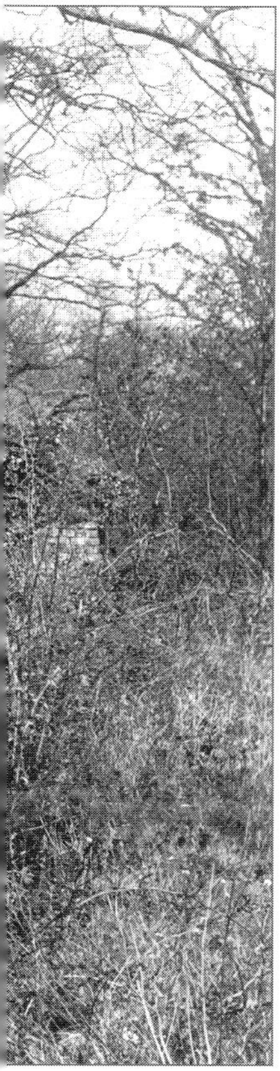

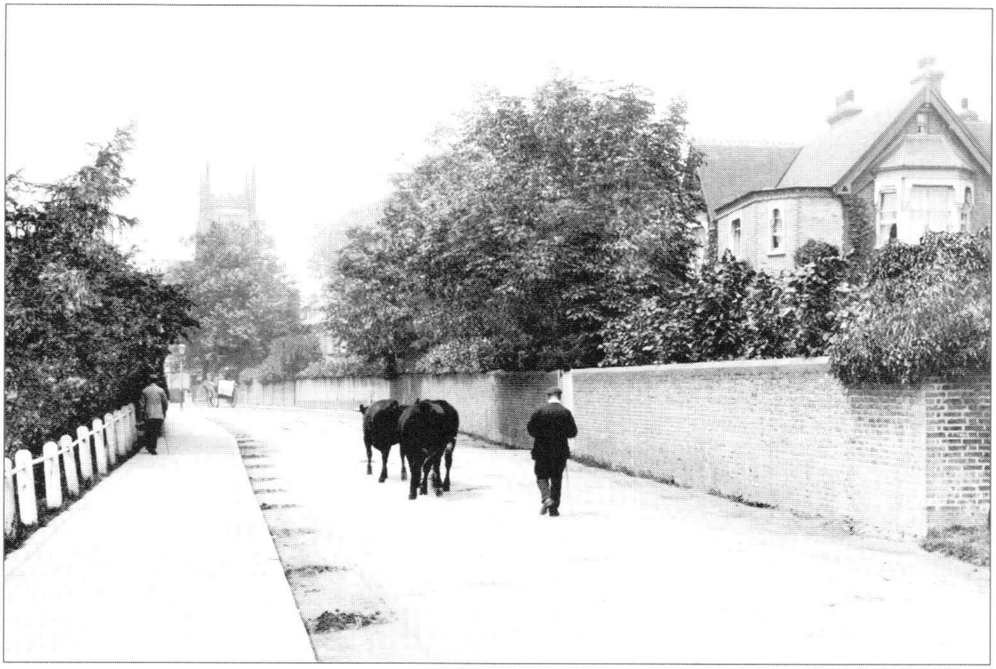

▲ **EAST GRINSTEAD,** *Lewes Road 1907* 57947

East Grinstead, a Wealden market town founded during the early 13th-century woodland clearances, was recorded as a borough by 1235. For centuries the town's High Street and the area in front of the church was used for markets and fairs. These cattle walking down the Lewes Road were probably heading for the weekly cattle market.

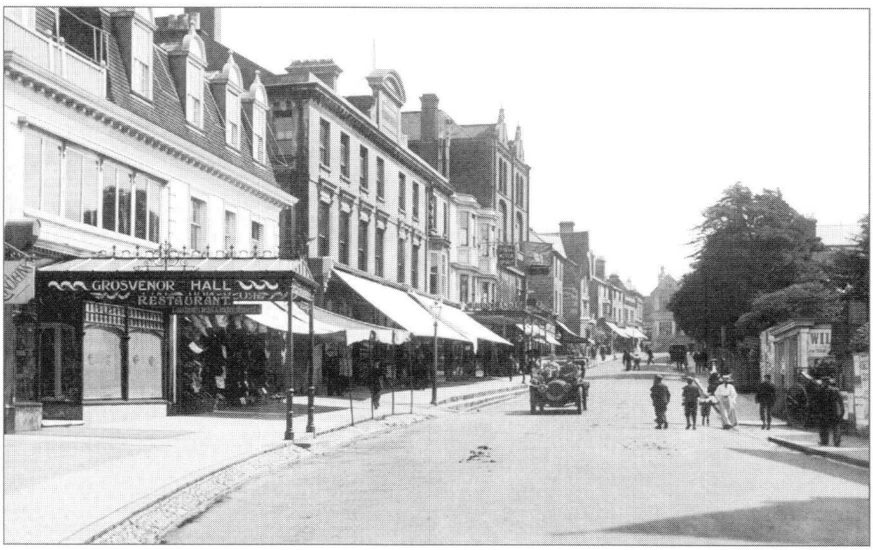


◄ **EAST GRINSTEAD**
*London Road 1910*
62801

London Road is part of the medieval route through East Grinstead. By 1910 the latest mode of transport, the motor car, could be seen on this and many other roads. Grosvenor Hall (left) was built in 1883. It was later acquired by Letherby & Christopher, and was re-opened as the Whitehall in 1910. The extended building contained a skating rink, a restaurant and a theatre, which showed early films and newsreels.

**EAST GRINSTEAD**
*Tooth's Shop 1927*
79594

This interior of a 15th-century Tudor house is part of Tooth's stationery shop, located on the south side of the High Street. Comparison with a similar photograph of c1905 shows few changes in the shop's stock of books, postcards, artist's materials and stationery over the years, although the shop's name, F & E Tooth, changed to E Tooth in 1923.

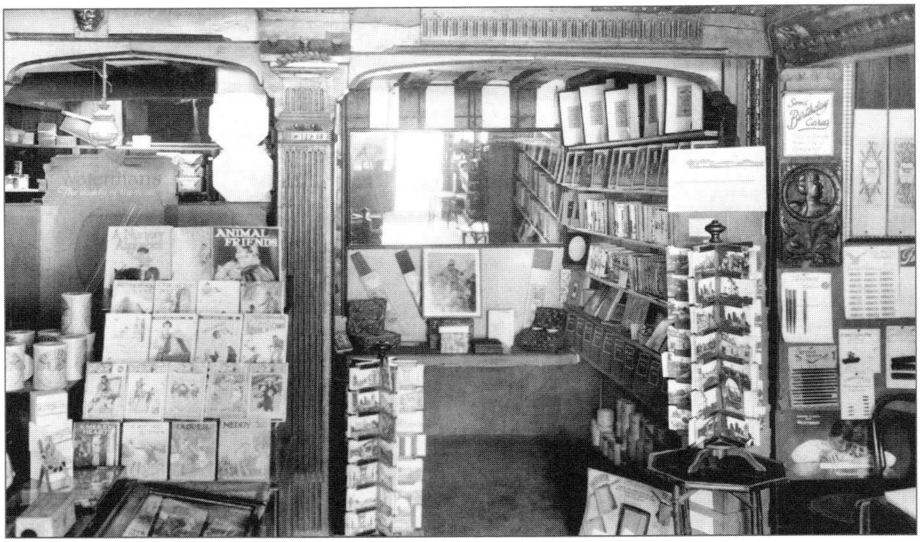

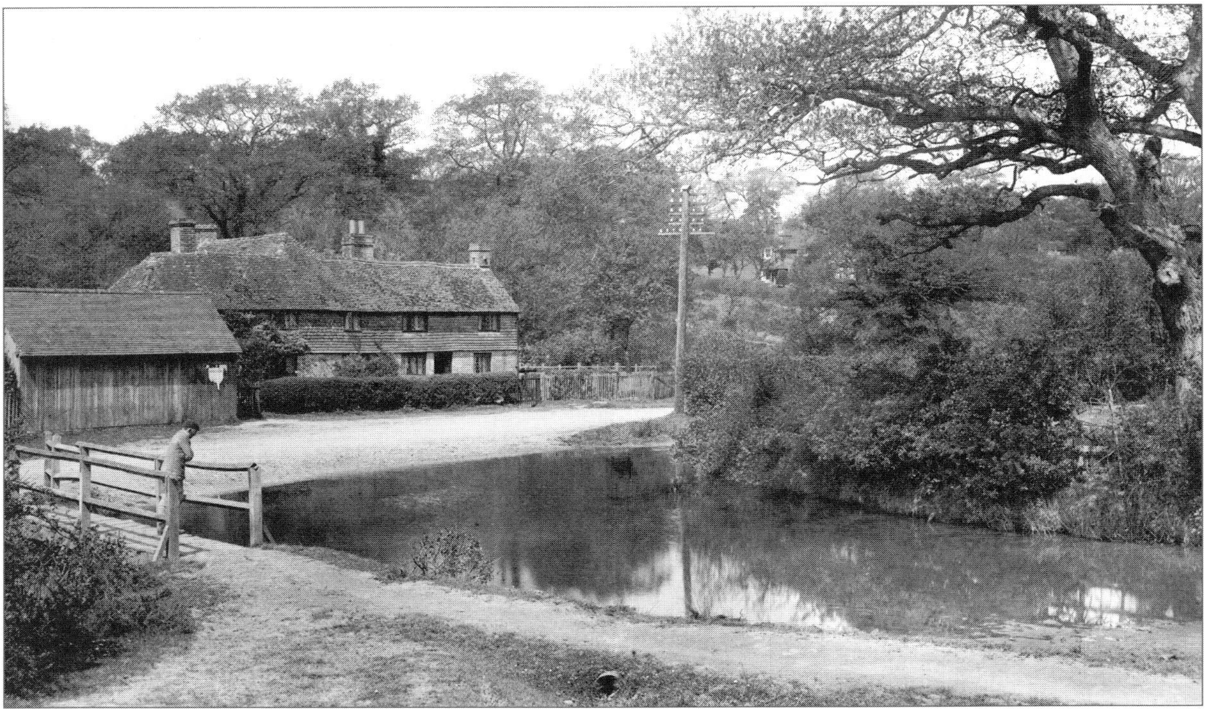

**COLEMANS HATCH,** *The River 1928* 80771

Colemans Hatch is a good example of one of the 14th-century settlements that developed along the edges of the forest and waste; its name implies an old entrance into the forested area. It slowly developed into a shapeless hamlet, with dispersed cottages situated at various springs and river crossings. Several of these have survived in this idyllic rural setting.

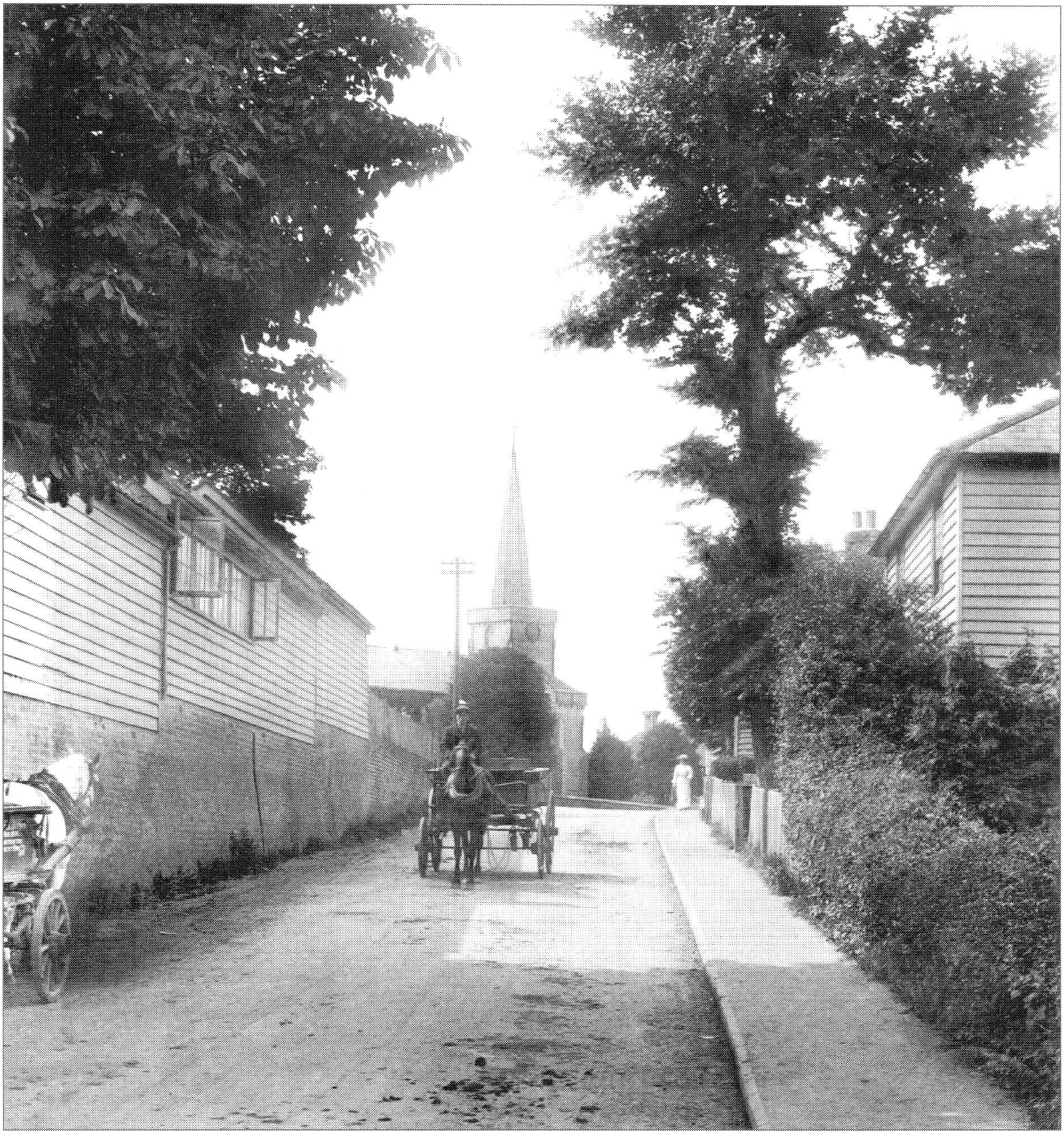

**FOREST ROW,** *Hartfield Road 1907* 57959

Forest Row, recorded in the early 14th century, lies three miles south-west of East Grinstead on the verge of Ashdown Forest. As its name implies, it was originally a single row of houses, but it developed rapidly after the opening of its own railway station in 1866. Its surrounding beauty and cheap land attracted wealthy people seeking second homes or retirement.

**CHELWOOD GATE**
*From Beaconsfield Road 1930* 83558

Chelwood Gate, a hamlet on the western side of Ashdown Forest, lies between East Grinstead and Lewes. Today it is centred on a long main street. By the time of this photograph, the view from the Beaconsfield Road had changed very little over the previous twenty years or so, except for the addition of the garage next to the parked vehicle (right).

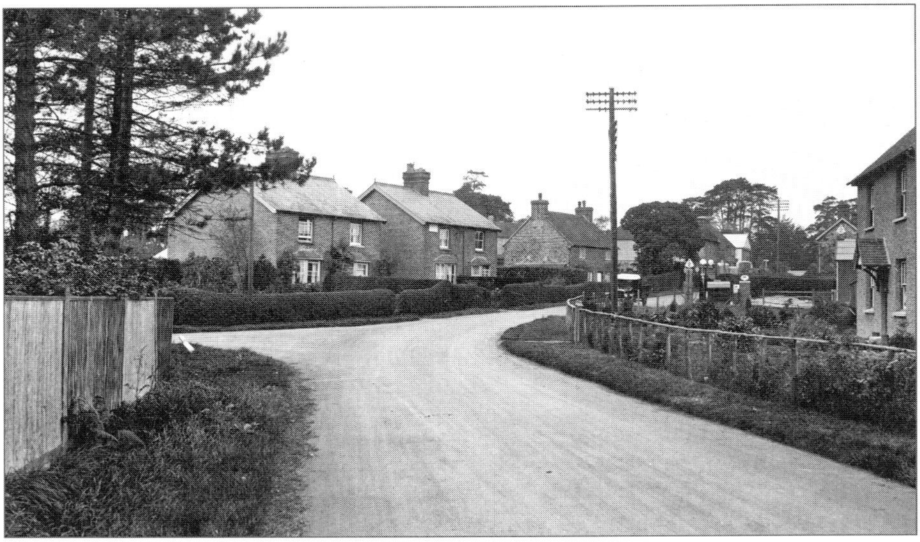

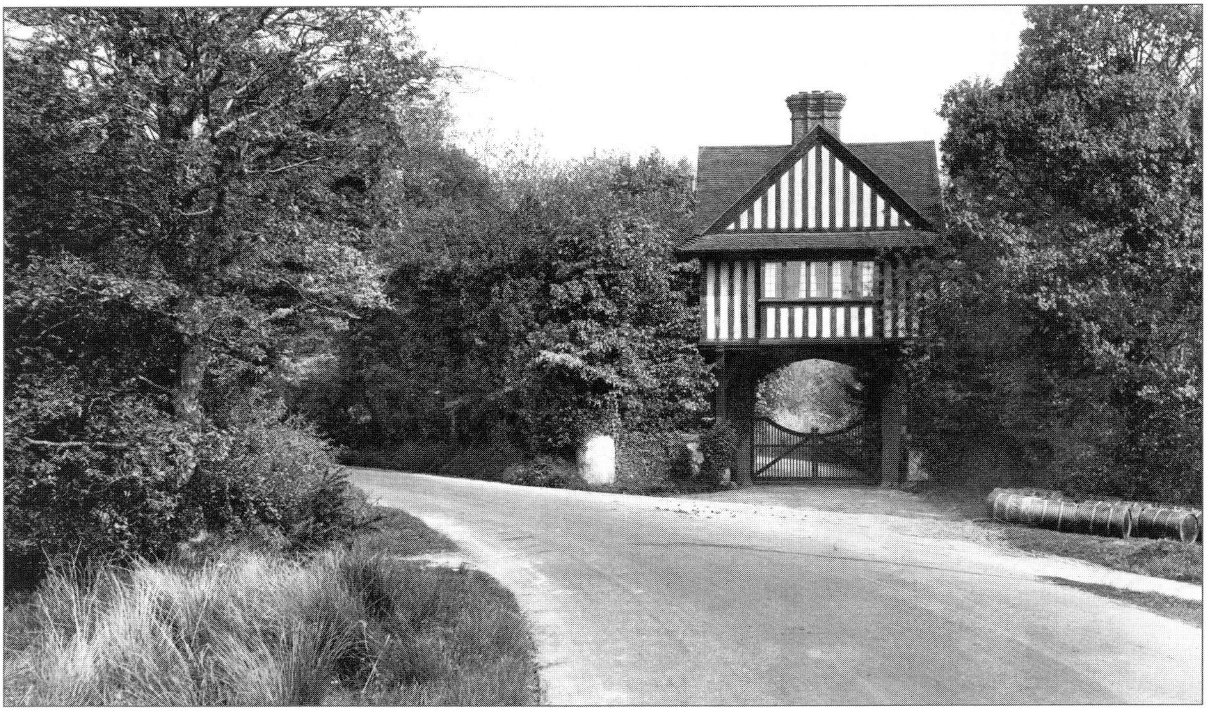

**CHELWOOD GATE,** *The Gateway 1928* 80743

Ashdown Forest, the great forest of Anderida, once stretched between the rivers Medway and Ouse. The building in the photograph, which is known as Chelwood Gate, stands as an entrance into Ashdown Forest; a map of the area dated 1693 has Chelwood Gate clearly marked.

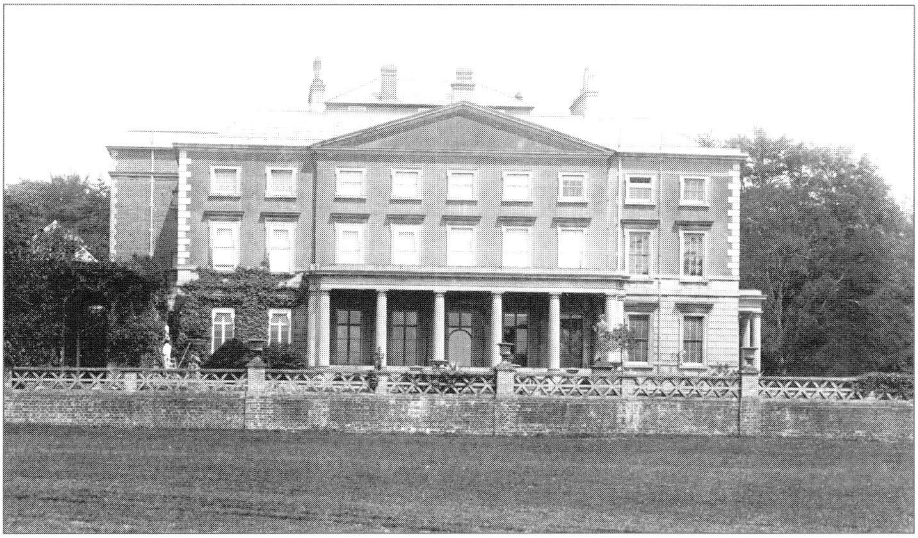

**BUXTED**
*Buxted Park House 1902* 48210

This house was built by the three Medley brothers in c1750 in the grounds of Buxted Park, situated about two miles north of Uckfield. In 1831 the Earl of Liverpool removed the old village of Buxted when he enlarged the park to make it more secluded. The house is recorded in 1910 as being in 'a well wooded park of 300 acres'.

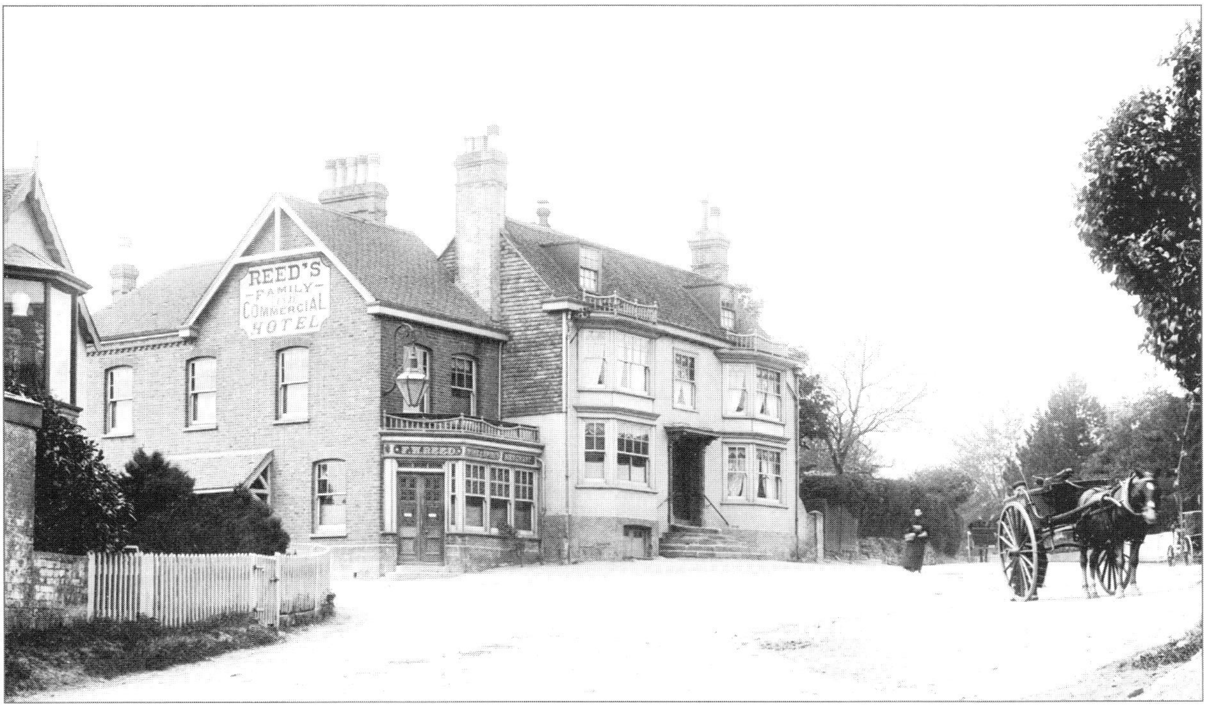


**CROWBOROUGH,** *The Red Cross Hotel 1900* 44949

Crowborough Cross, the intersection of four roads, is situated nearly 245 metres above sea level in Crowborough. Nearby is the Red Cross Hotel (now the Crowborough Cross Hotel). This former inn dates from the mid 17th century, and its name probably originates from the small red cross placed on coaching maps to denote Crowborough Cross for illiterate coachmen.

**FRANT**
*The Post Office c1955* F173001

The parish of Frant lies on the forest-ridge approximately 180 metres above sea level, and overlooks landscapes in both Kent and Sussex. The origin of its name suggests a former wilderness or desert. The houses on the left are typical of the Wealden style, and H Kemp's Stores and Post Office still exist.

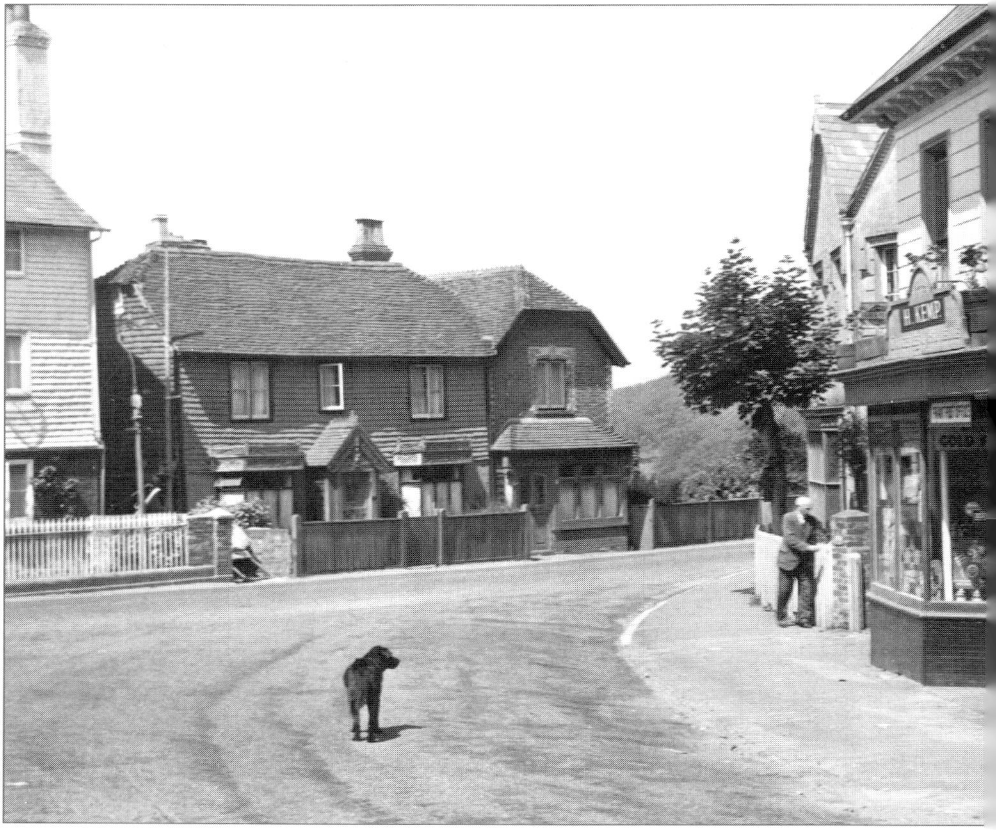


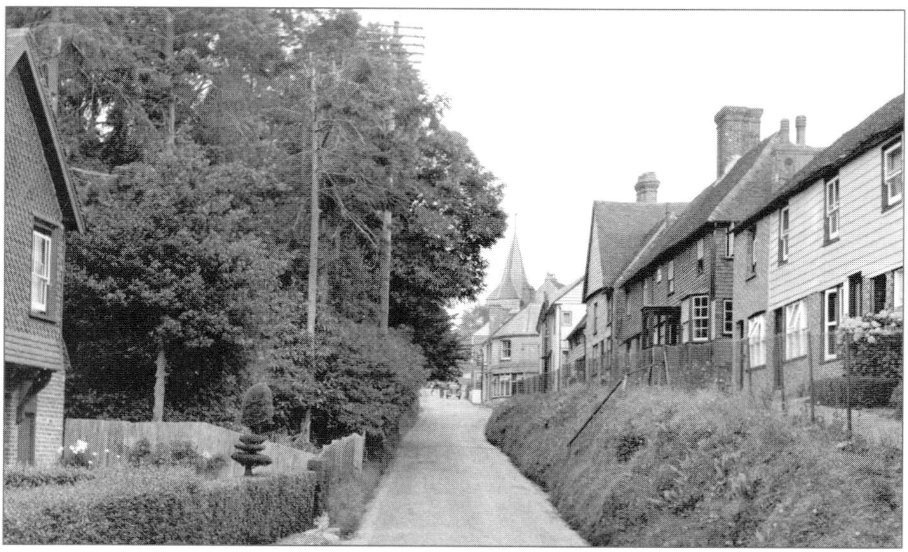

**MAYFIELD**
*West Street c1955*
M242028

A Sussex legend recalls how St Dunstan, Archbishop of Canterbury, met with the Devil at Mayfield. The wooden church built by St Dunstan was destroyed in a disastrous fire in 1389, along with most of the other buildings in the surrounding village. The spire of the present church can be seen at the top of West Street.

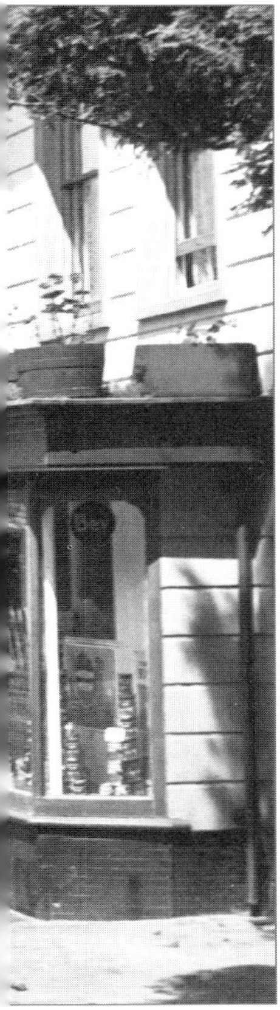

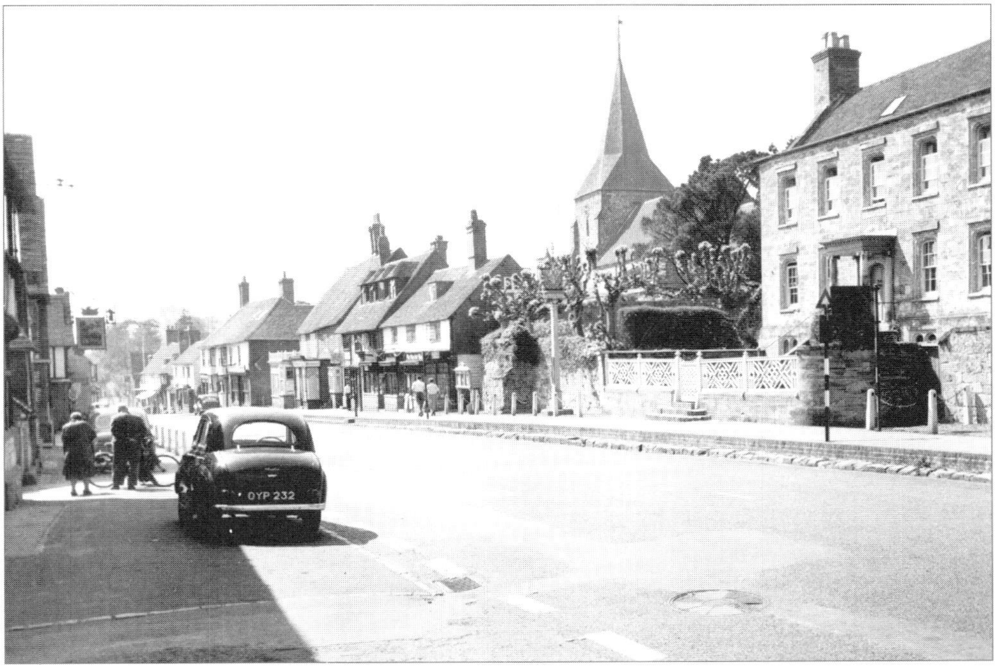


▲ **MAYFIELD,** *High Street c1955* M242071

Mayfield stands on the summit of a hill, and has one of the most picturesque long streets in the county. Middle House and Walnut Tree Cottage, just visible on the left of the parked car, are two timber-framed buildings which have survived from the period when Mayfield gained its prosperity from iron working.

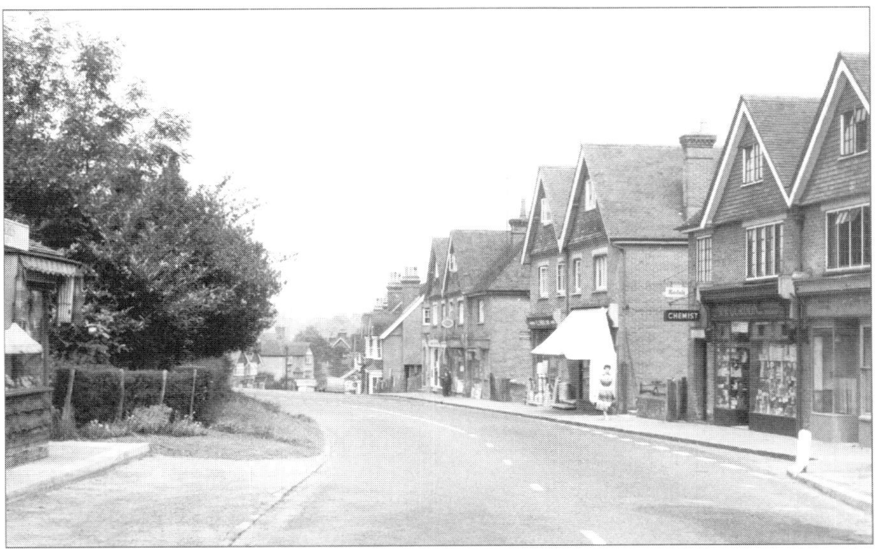


◄ **HORAM**
*Main Road c1955*
H329026

The village of Horam, two miles south of Heathfield, is famous for its Merrydown vintage cider. Until 1925 the settlement was known as Horeham Road, but following a ballot of the villagers the name was changed to Horam. Its church was not built until 1890, and the village has become primarily a modern residential district.

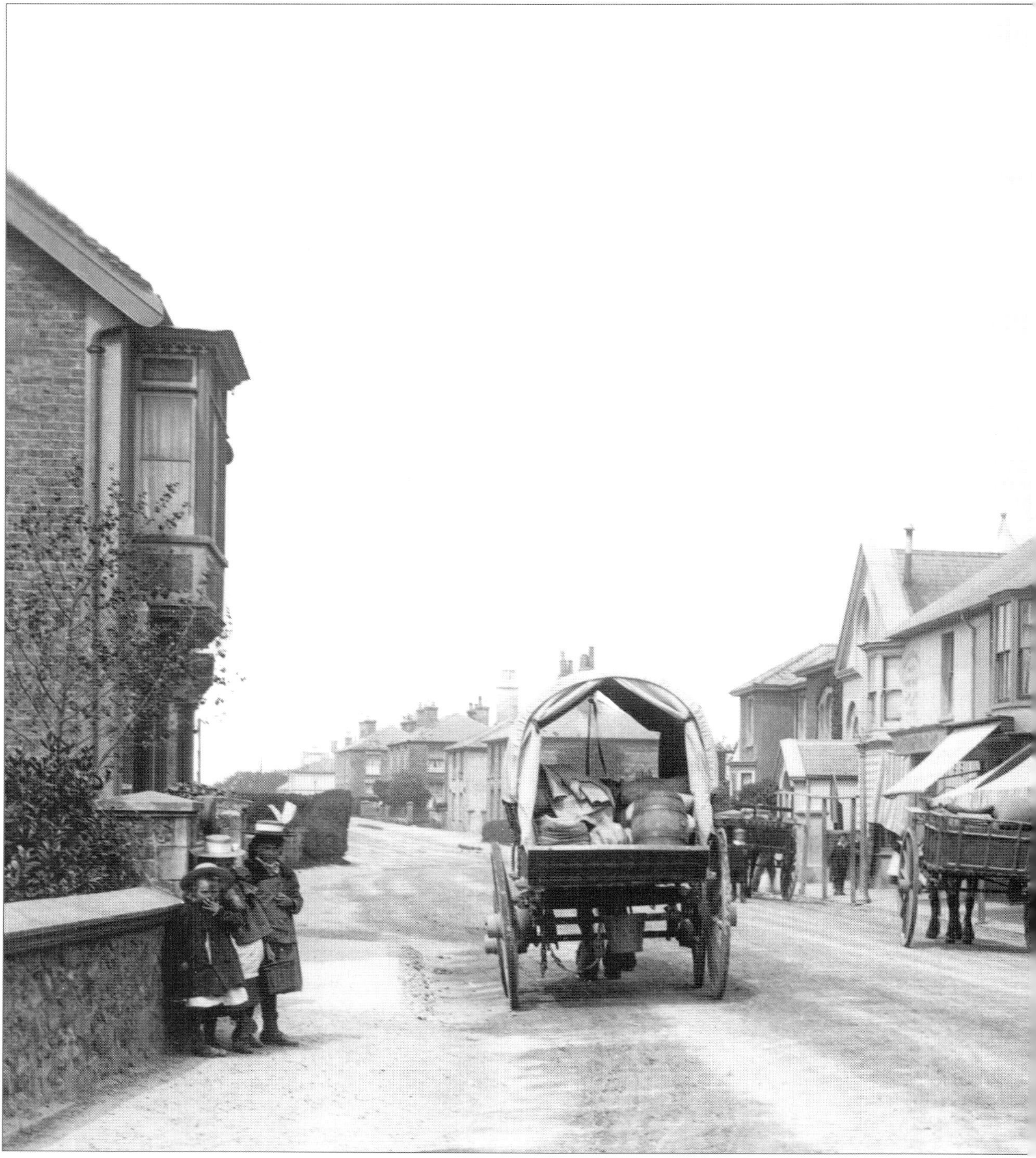

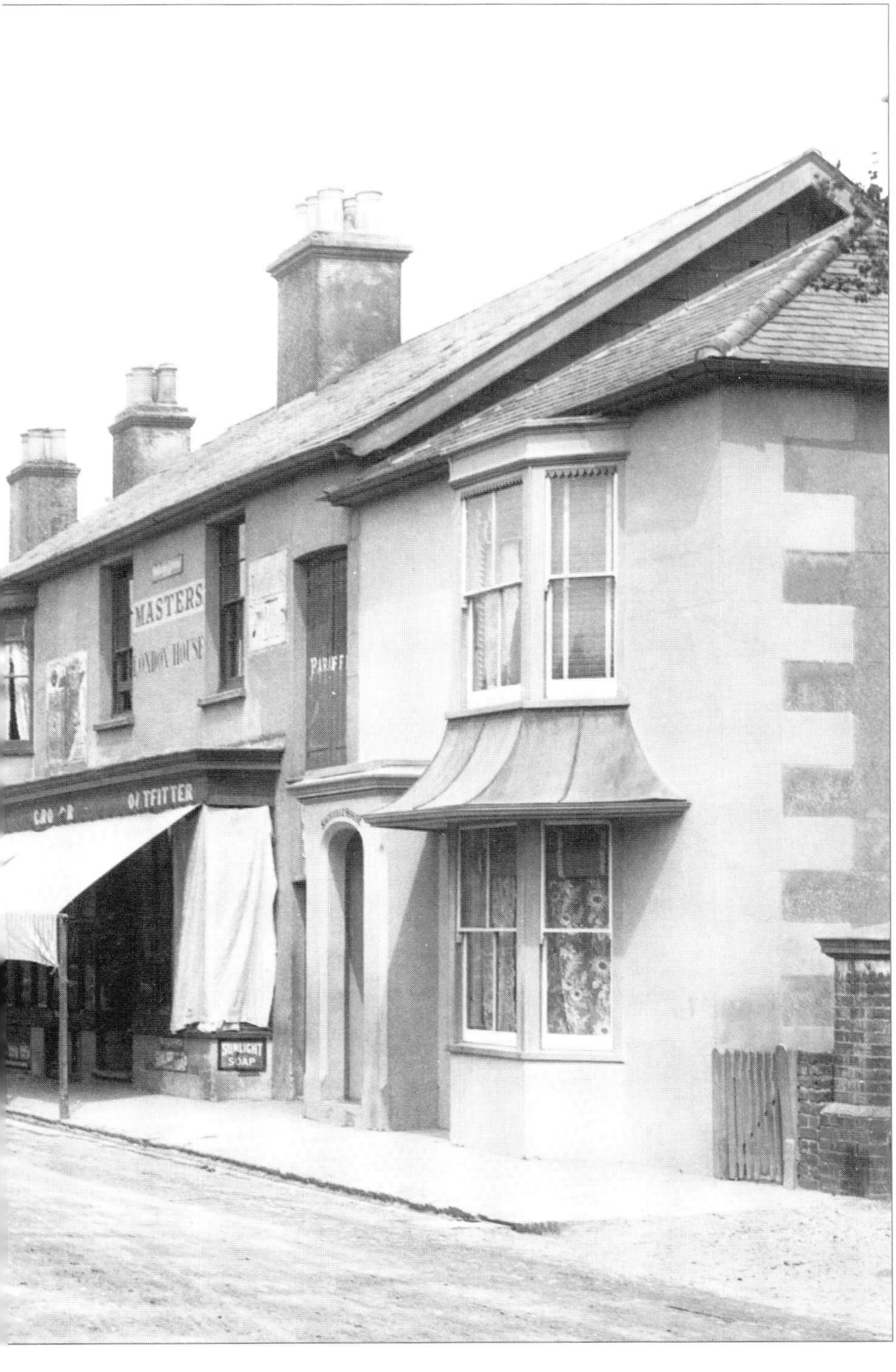


**HAILSHAM**
*High Street 1900* 44955

Hailsham, an old market town, lies about seven miles north of Eastbourne. For about 200 years its main industry was rope making, which was started by Thomas Burfield; his shop was in the High Street. In the late 19th century over a hundred people were working in the industry, and a central warehouse was also located in the High Street.

**UPPER DICKER**
*The Dicker c1955*
U50018

About two miles west of Hailsham is Upper Dicker, which has a Gothic-style church. Standing on a hill at a crossroads is the unusual house named The Dicker, built in 1908 for Horatio Bottomley MP. This is now St Giles School.

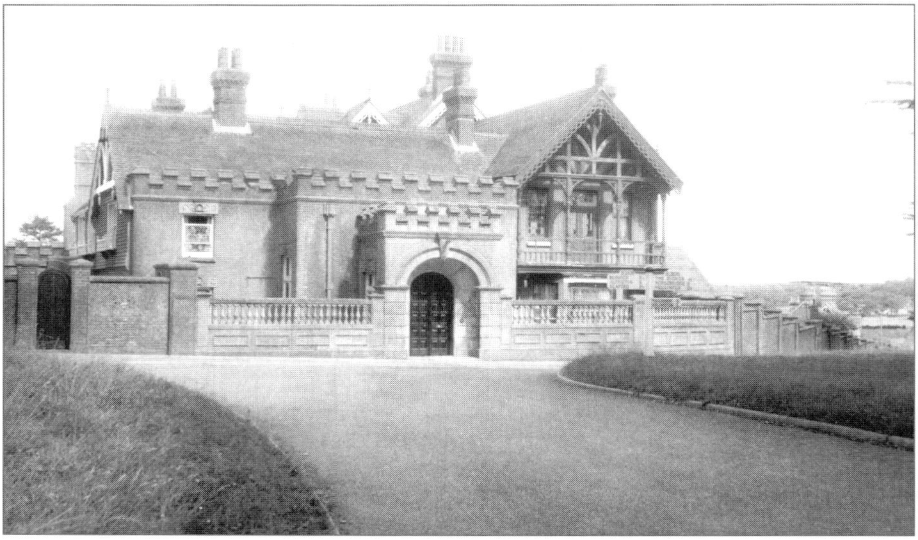

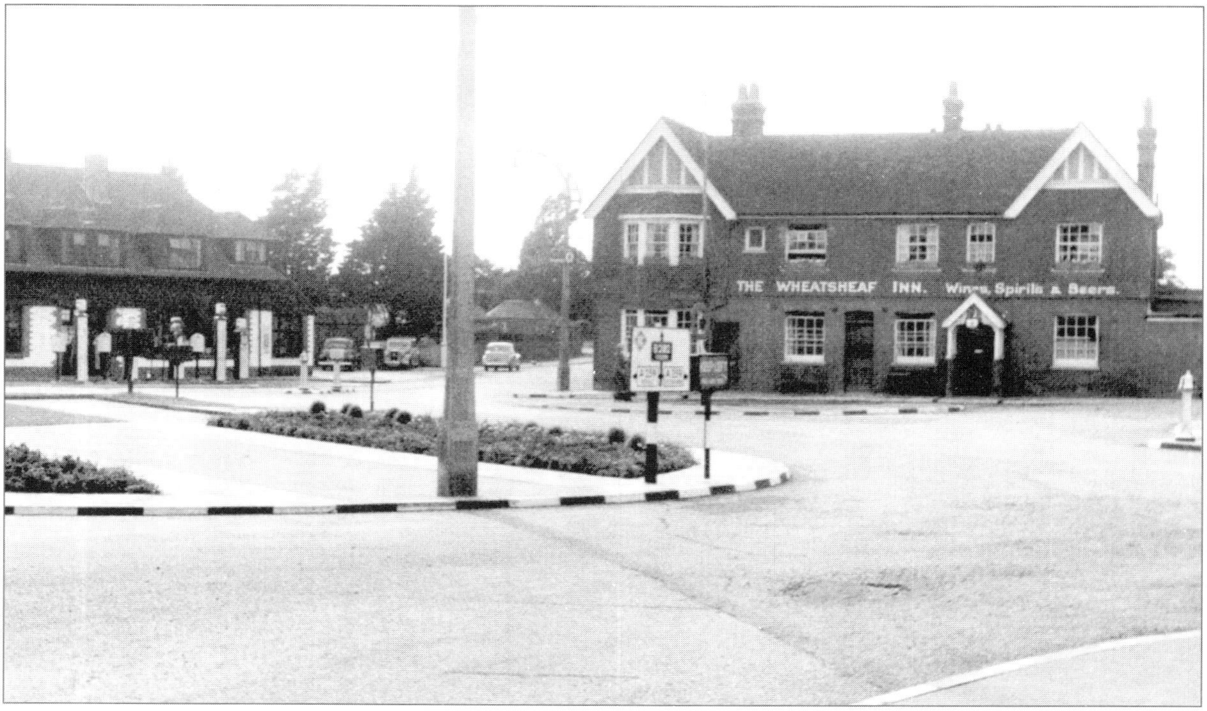


**LITTLE COMMON,** *The Wheatsheaf Inn c1960* L368003

Little Common, the name now used to describe this area, did not appear on maps before 1813. The name may well be synonymous with a piece of land known anciently as Slyders Common. The Wheatsheaf Inn, for many years an important staging post on the Brighton to Hastings route, was rebuilt in 1886.

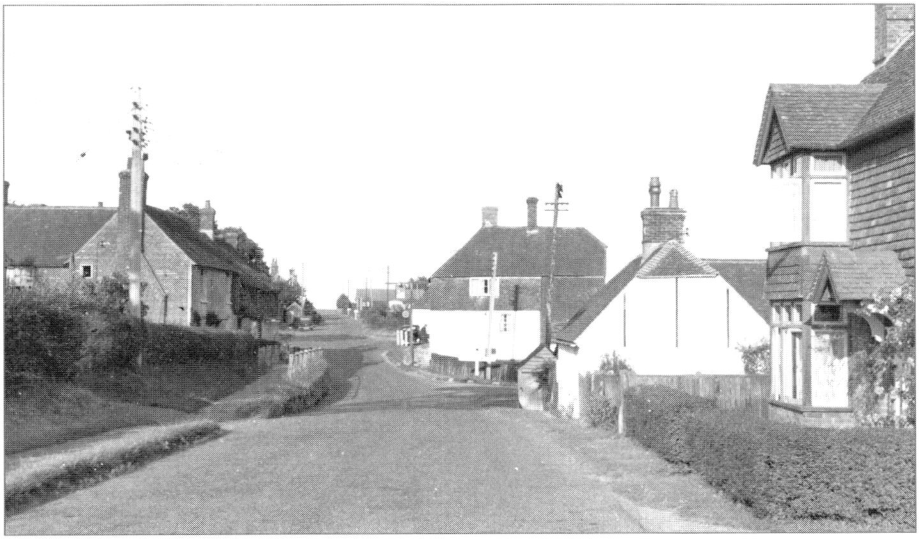

**DALLINGTON**
*Woods Corner c1955*
D156005

Woods Corner is a hamlet in the parish of Dallington, about four miles north-east of Herstmonceux. It is one of the late 18th-century settlements which developed on commons and wastes lying on the flat-topped ridgeways, after leases were granted to anyone who wanted to settle there. Other similar communities in the vicinity include Broad Oak and Punnett's Town.

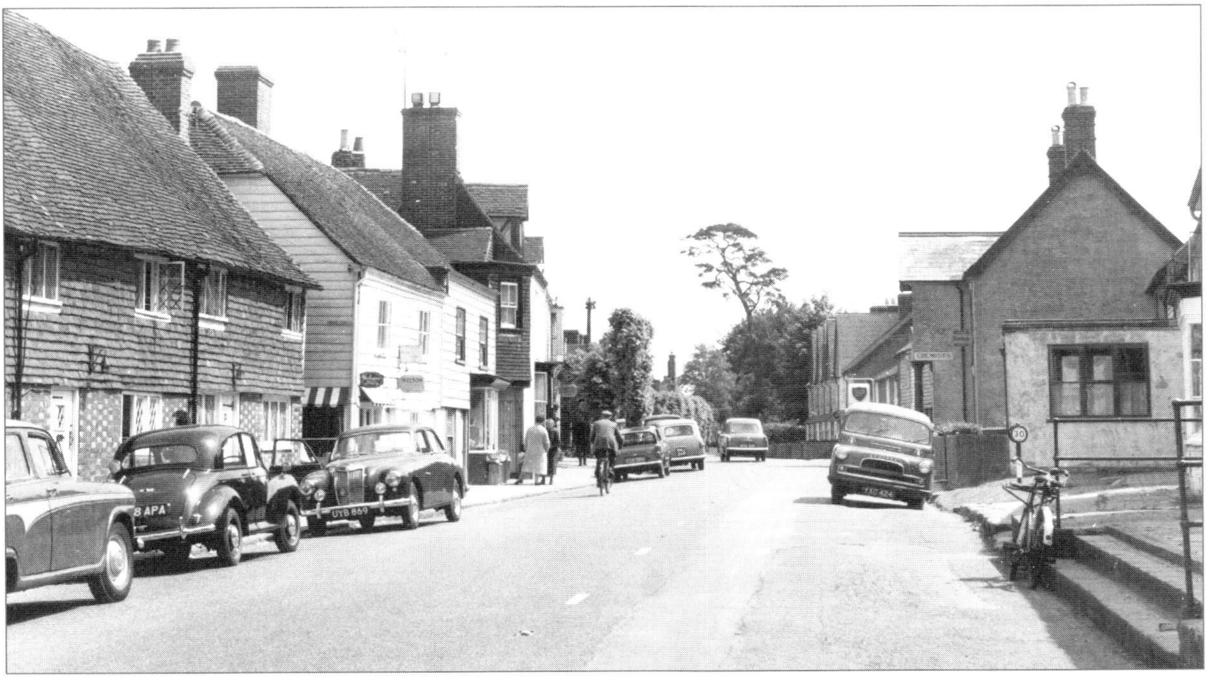

**BURWASH,** *High Street c1960* B291042

The picturesque village of Burwash was once a centre of the Wealden iron industry. Nearby stands Batemans, a 17th-century iron-master's house, the home of Rudyard Kipling for many years. Several fine period dwellings survive in the village. On the left is Shadwell Row: although greatly modified over the years, it incorporates two original houses dating from the late medieval period.

▼ **TICEHURST,** *The Square 1925* 76997

The village of Ticehurst is situated on a gentle slope surrounded by fertile valleys and hills, where hops were once extensively grown. The village was built around a crossroads to the south-east of the church. On the right is the 14th-century Bell Hotel, used as the headquarters of the British Legion from 1921. The war memorial was dedicated in 1923.

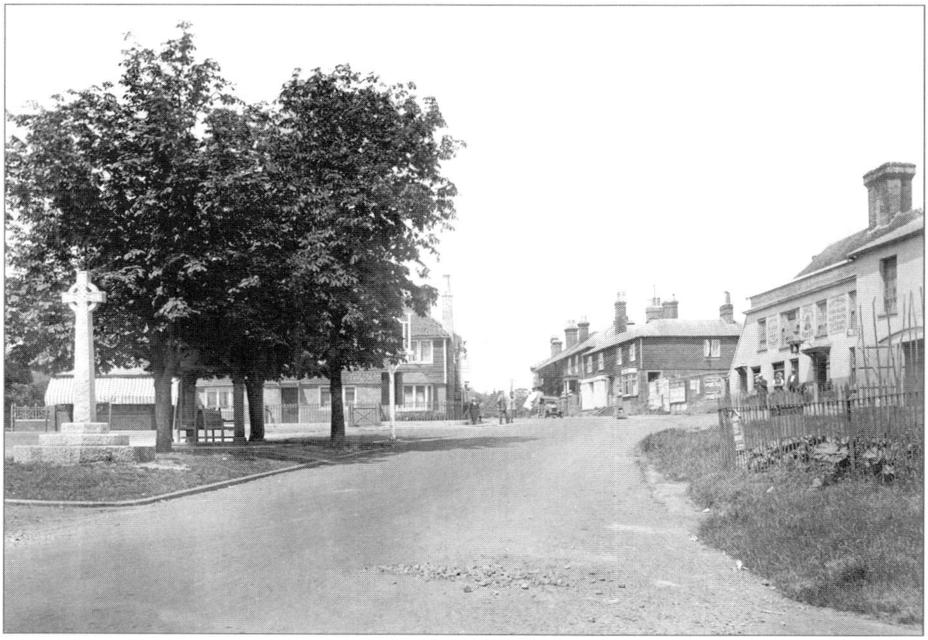

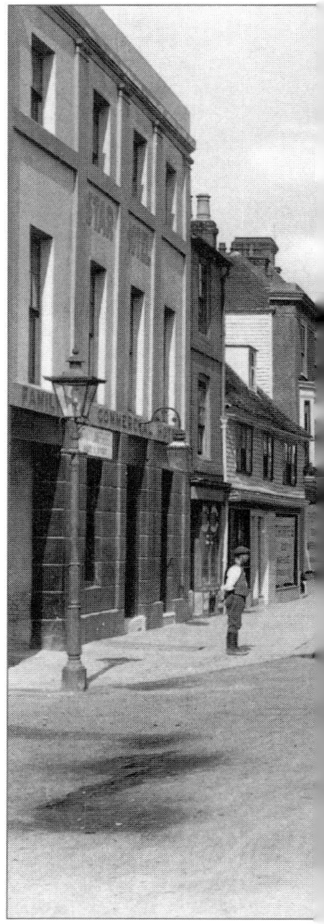

► **WADHURST**
*High Street 1903* 49368

Wadhurst, a village about six miles south-east of Tunbridge Wells, was a centre of the iron industry during the 16th and 17th centuries. At the time of this photograph, several of the older properties in the village were clad in the characteristic weatherboarding of the eastern Weald. In 1956 an RAF plane crash demolished the Queens Head Hotel in the High Street, along with several other buildings.

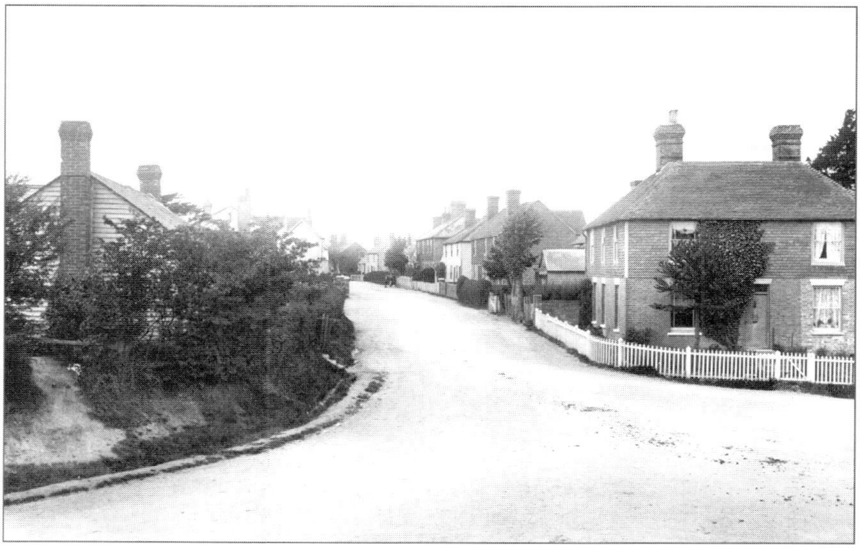

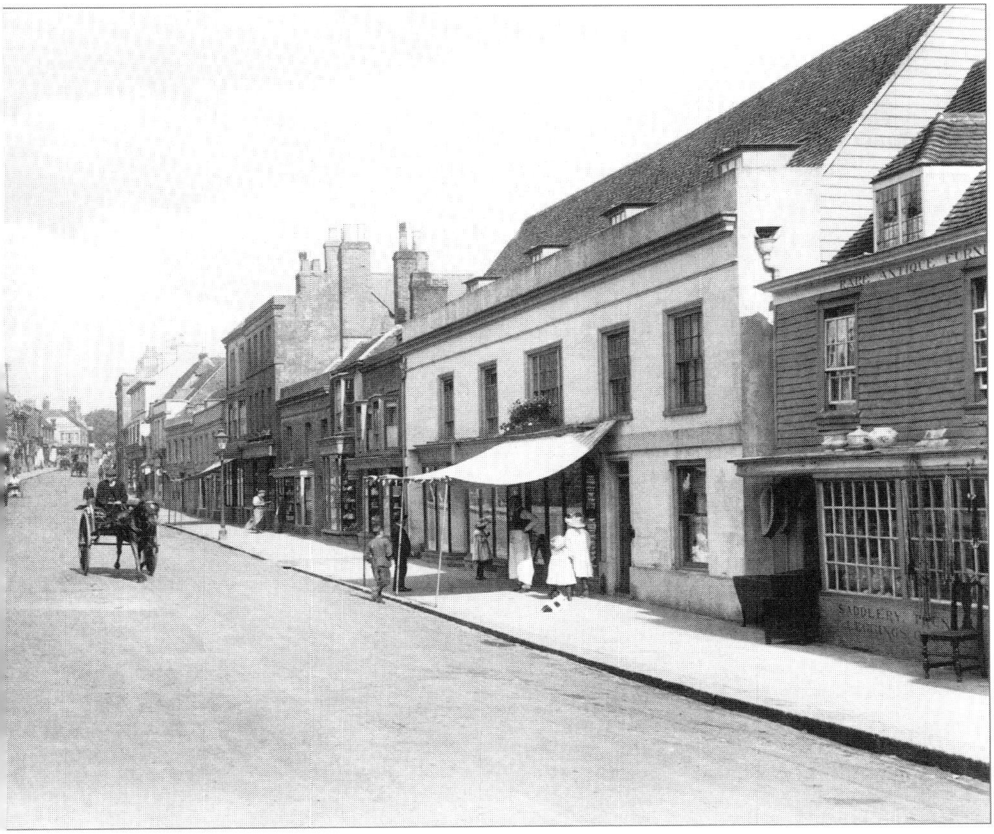

**BATTLE**

*High Street 1910*

62992

William I founded Battle Abbey on Senlac Moor, the site of the Battle of Hastings. The small town of Battle grew up when the people who built and maintained the abbey and its buildings settled there. The High Street is part of the main road, which passes through the town.

**BATTLE**

*High Street 1927*

80407

The old market place, on which the vehicles are parked, is a reminder of Battle's former identity as a market town. This triangular piece of ground contains the old Bull Ring, and lies immediately north of the abbey gatehouse (out of picture, bottom left). About half the buildings in the High Street area are 18th-century or earlier, although several have been disguised externally.

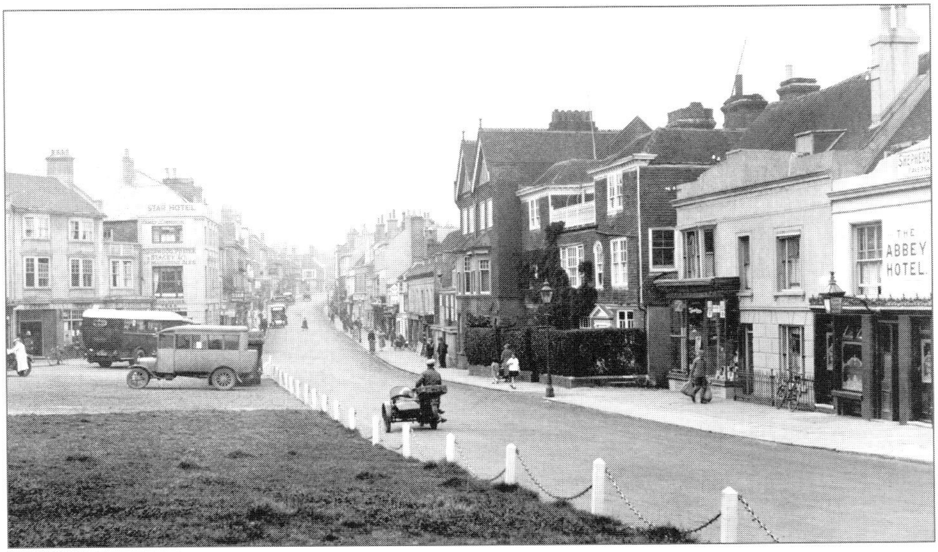

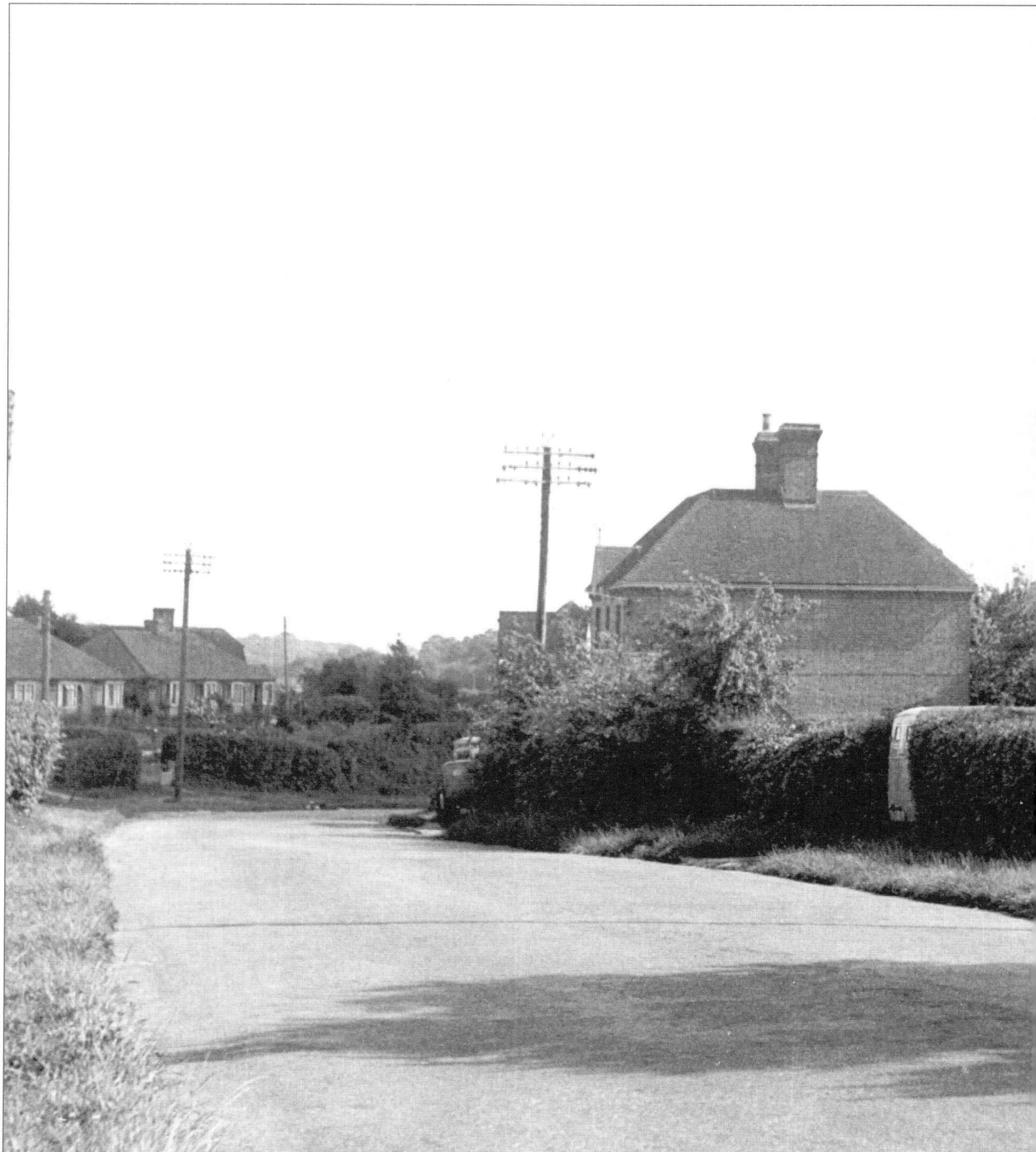

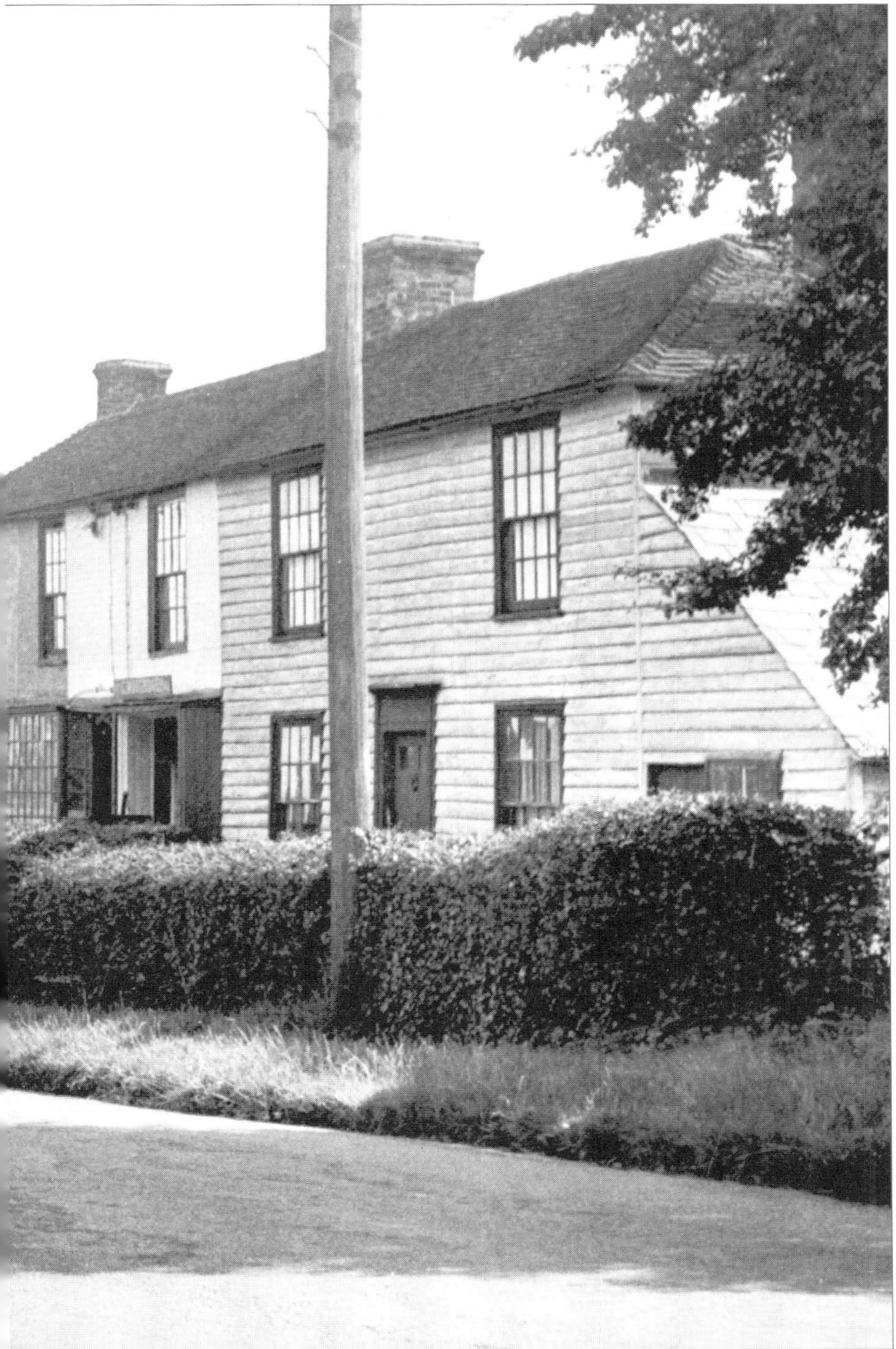

**PEASMARSH**
*High Street c1955*
P257004

The parish of Peasmarsh is situated between the River Rother on the north and the River Tillingham on the south. The village, about three miles north-west of Rye, lies on the Beckley to Rye road. During the 19th and early 20th centuries, hops were recorded as its main crop. The house on the right is clad in weatherboarding, a typical Wealden building material.

# RIVER VALLEYS, ANCIENT PORTS AND CASTLES

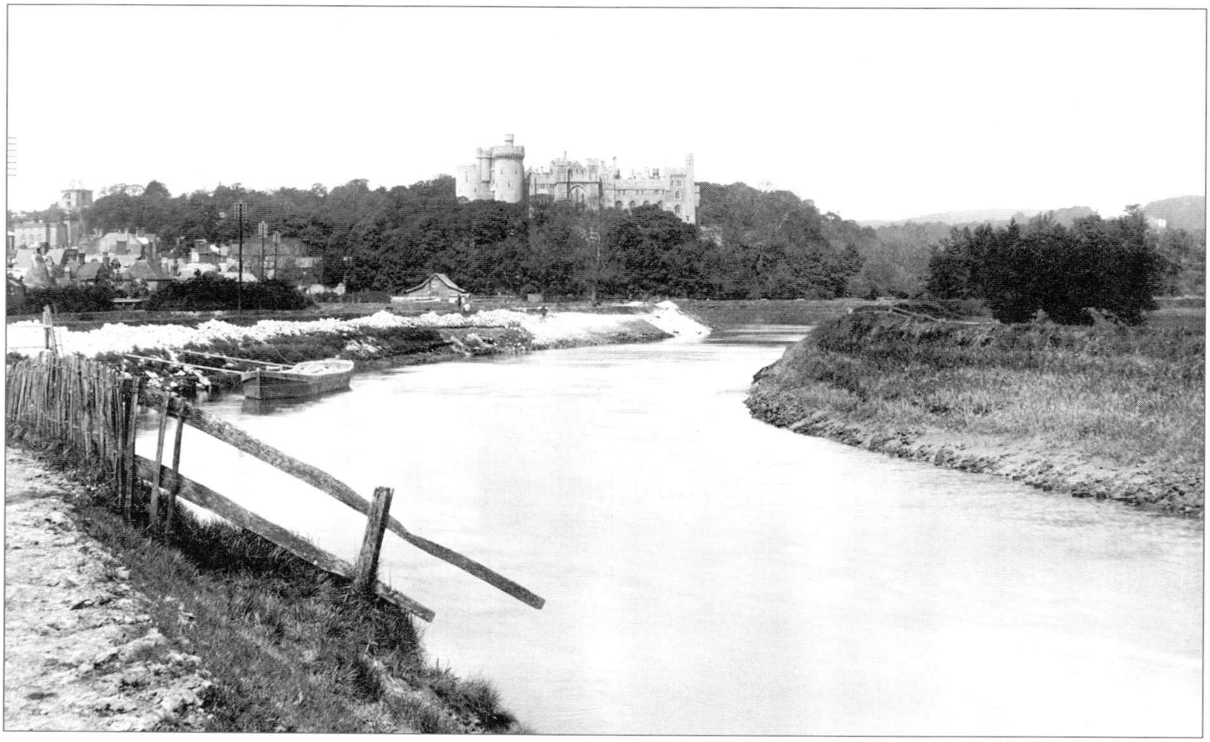

**ARUNDEL,** *The Castle and the River 1923* 73623

Markets and ports were an important part of the trading network during the Middle Ages. Indeed, by Domesday Arundel was already an important river port. Its impressive castle, re-built in the 19th century, overlooks the Arun valley. With its fine chalk cliffs at Amberley, this is possibly the most scenic of all the river valleys in Sussex.

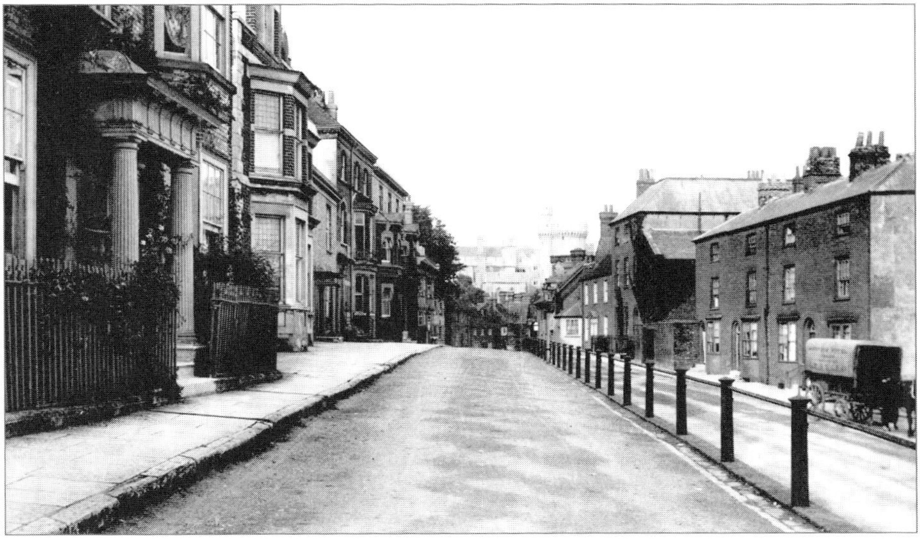

**ARUNDEL**
*Maltravers Street*
*1906* 56727

Maltravers Street is one of Arundel's three main streets. Its ancient name was Chepynge Street. During the 18th century it was known as Old Market Street and was the site of Arundel's market, which is one of the most ancient privileges of the Borough. Cattle markets were later recorded in the Square at Arundel, but have long since been discontinued.

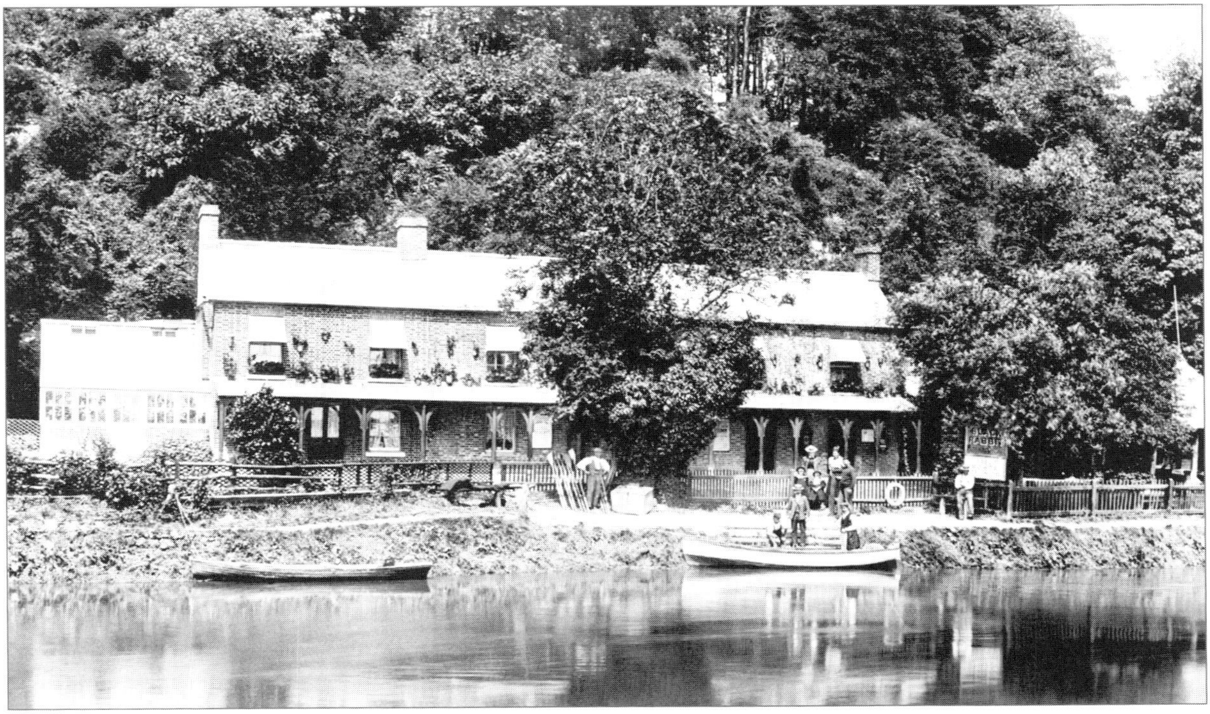

**ARUNDEL,** *The Black Rabbit 1898* 42551

The Black Rabbit Inn, still popular today, was first recorded as the Black Coney in the 1780s. It served riverside traffic - initially boatmen, and later excursionists from Arundel to Littlehampton; they came in large numbers to view Arundel Castle and to enjoy dancing, bowls, croquet and the tea garden at the Black Rabbit, which was laid out in the 1890s.

**AMBERLEY**
*The River Arun*
*c1960* A44031

At the time of the Norman Conquest it appears that the River Arun was only navigable from the sea to Ford, and was not tidal until the later Middle Ages. After improvements to the river channel, tides reached as far as Amberley by 1842. Houghton Bridge, with its tea gardens and boats for hire, remains a popular tourist attraction.

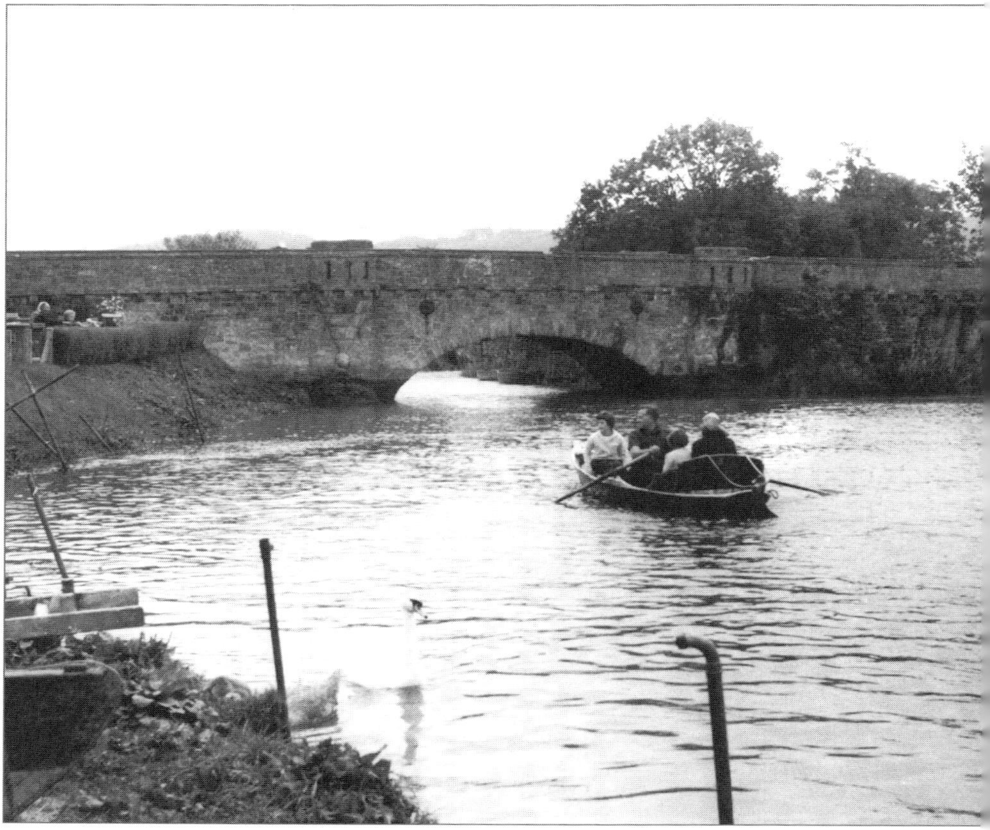

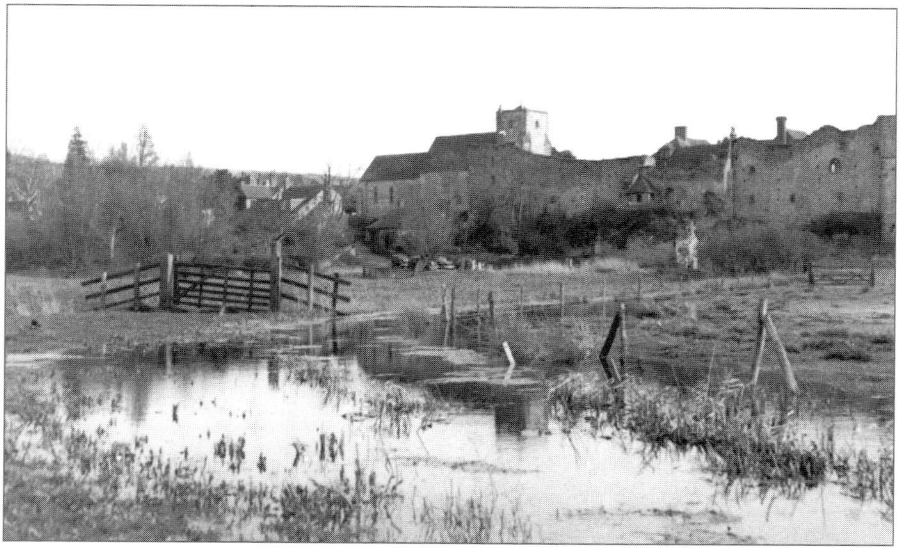

**AMBERLEY**
*Amberley Castle*
*c1955* A44004

Amberley Castle, which lies on higher ground above the River Arun's flood plain, is in fact a fortified manor house constructed between the 13th and 16th centuries by the Bishops of Chichester as part of their extensive but scattered estate. The castle was dismantled during the Civil War, but has since been refurbished and is currently a hotel and restaurant.

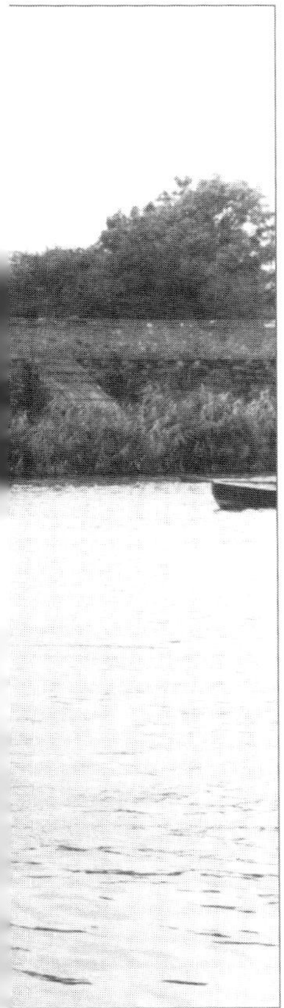

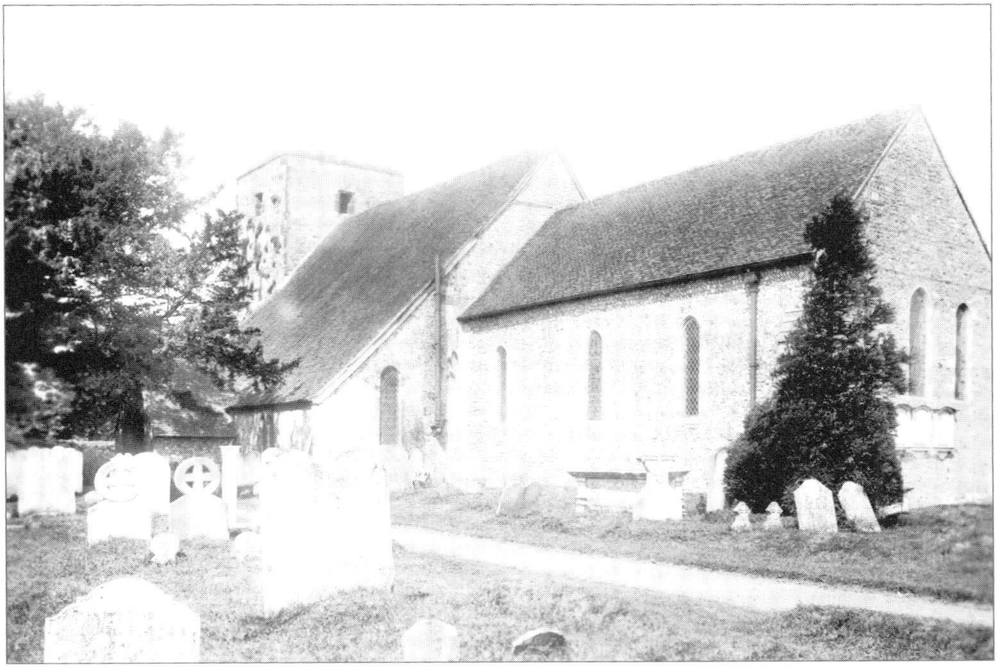

▲ **AMBERLEY,** *The Church 1899* 42555

Amberley church lies between the castle and the village at the western end of a ridge of high ground, which is about one mile north of Houghton Bridge. The church was built at about the same time as the castle by the Bishop of Chichester, Ralph I (1091-1123) - he also built Chichester Cathedral.

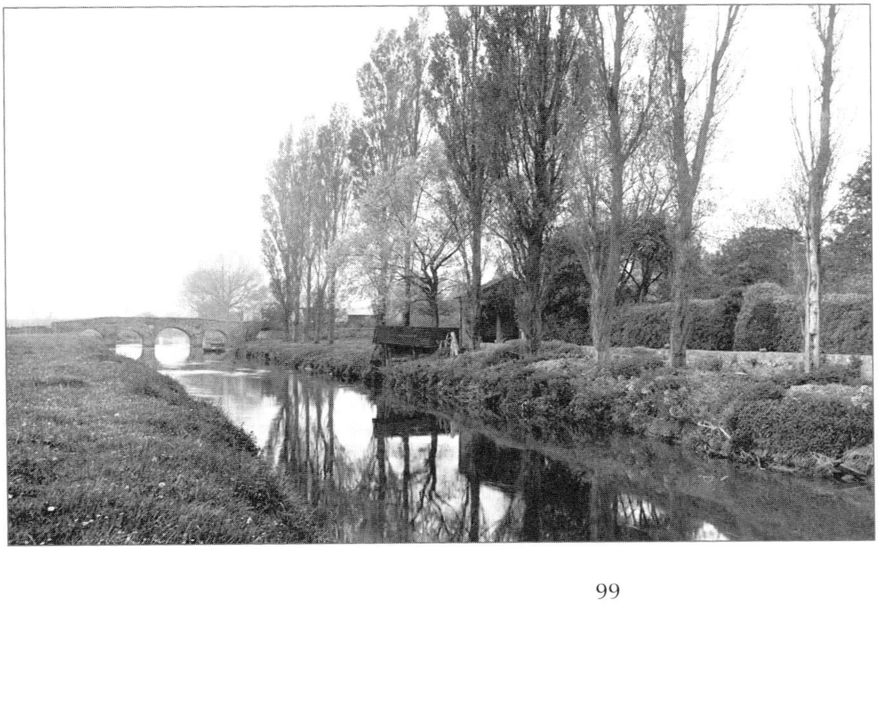

◄ **PULBOROUGH**
*Swan Bridge 1921* 70071

The Arun, described as the second fastest-flowing river in the country, had strong tides; by the 1930s, they reached Pulborough, where two old stone bridges crossed the river. The surviving old Swan bridge was built in 1738 to replace an earlier wooden one, and it has been preserved after a more modern bridge and carriageway were constructed alongside it.

**FITTLEWORTH**
*The Mill 1898*
42847

Just south-east of Stopham Bridge is the confluence of the Arun and its most important tributary, the Western Rother, previously known as the Turning Stream or Westwater, which extended to Fittleworth, Midhurst and beyond. A record of the 17th century reveals that Fittleworth Mill was used for the production of flour and malt.

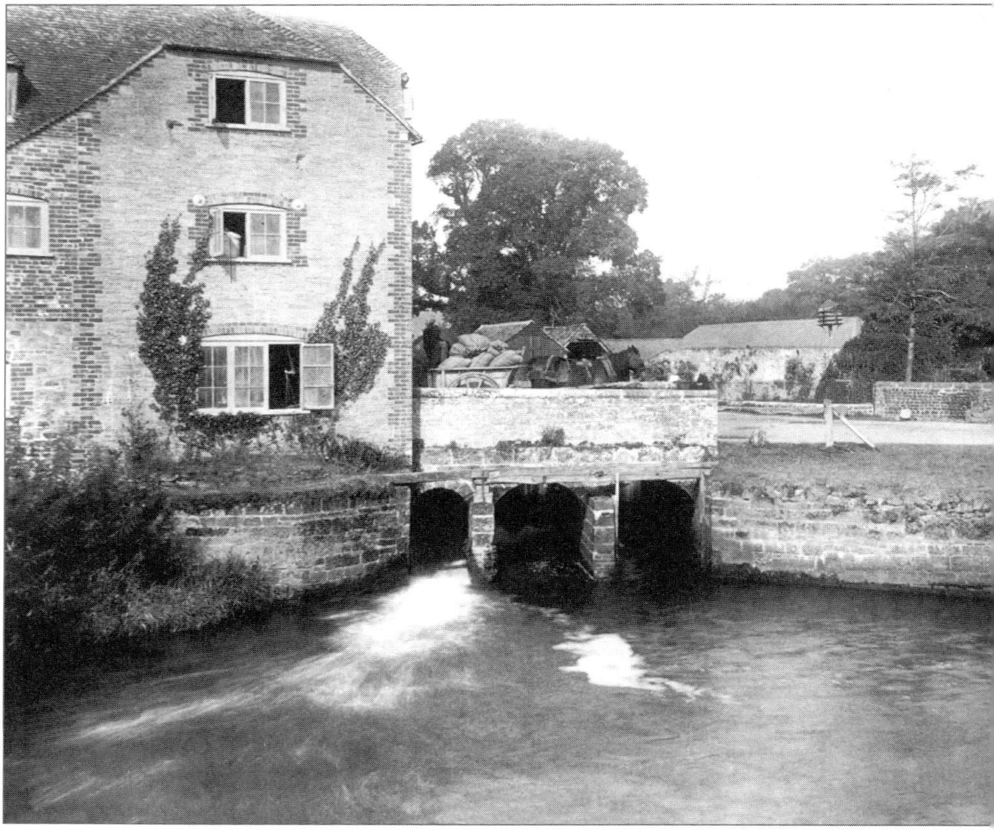

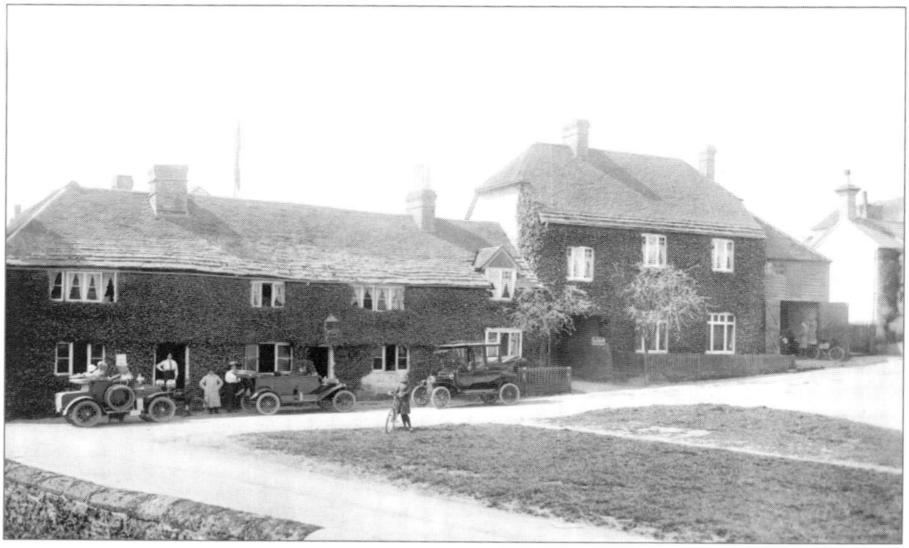

**FITTLEWORTH**
*The Swan Hotel 1914*
66921

The Swan, near the river in Lower Fittleworth and recorded in a document dated 1640, is possibly one of the two alehouses mentioned earlier in 1536. By the early 1900s it was described as 'a venerable and rambling building' popular with cyclists, motor car enthusiasts and particularly artists, many of whom decorated the Swan's little parlour with their paintings.

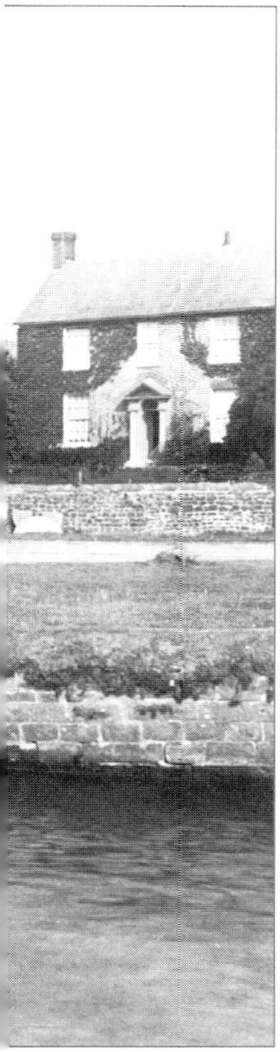

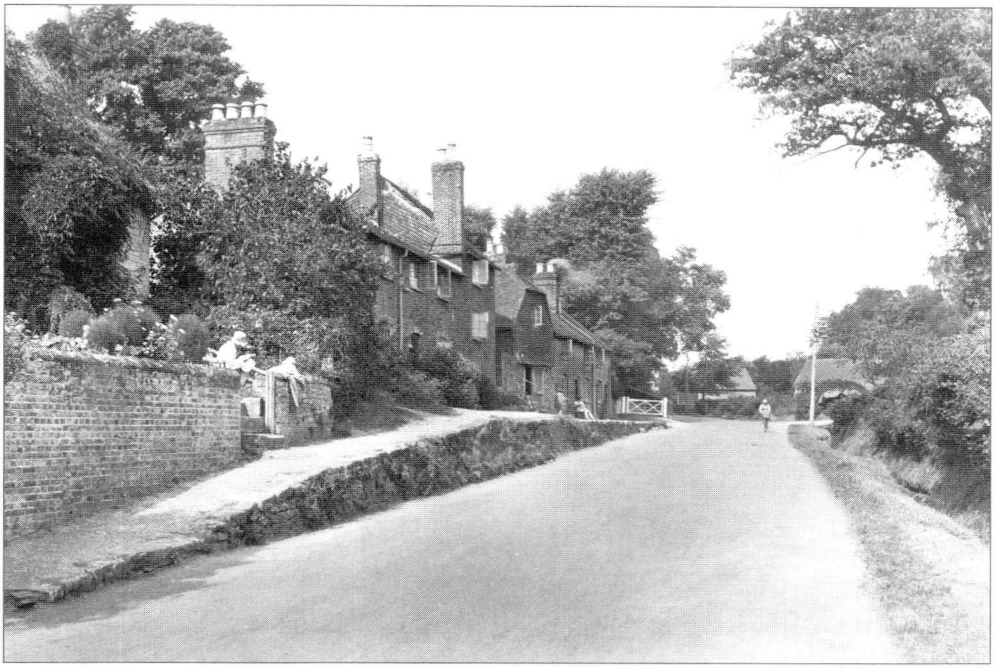

▲ **FITTLEWORTH,** *The Terrace 1928* 81409

By the 1920s, Fittleworth had become an artists' mecca owing to its pretty woods, its fine views from its commons, its quaint architecture and, it has been suggested, the warm welcome offered at the Swan Inn. Lower Fittleworth, by the river, was particularly popular with anglers, while the higher, sandier ground and commons in Upper Fittleworth attracted walkers.

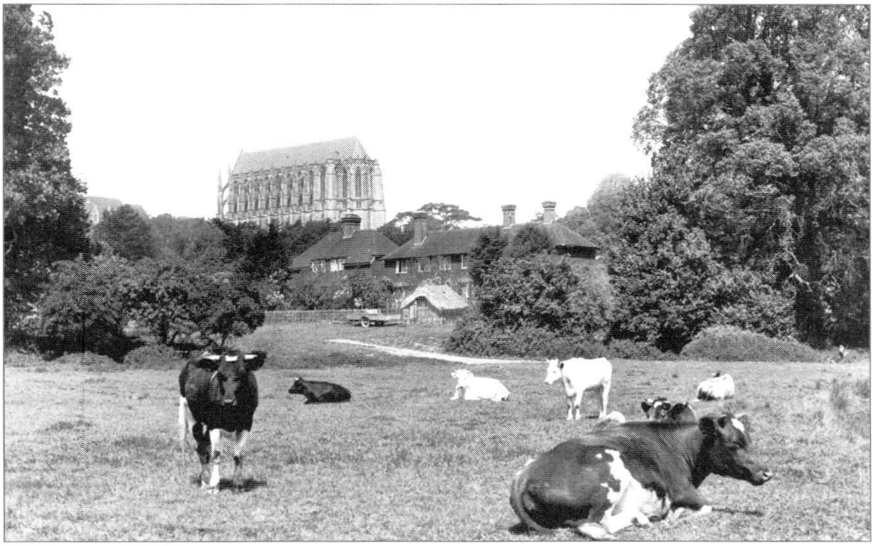

◄ **LANCING**
*The College c1955*
L517026

Lancing College and its chapel overlook the Adur estuary and Shoreham. In ancient times the estuary was much wider. Subsequent silting of the river mouth and its movement to the east thanks to a shifting shingle beach led to the decline of the port at Steyning, and the establishment of the town of New Shoreham by the De Broase family between 1086-1096.

▼ **UPPER BEEDING,** *The River Adur c1955* U40039

Today the River Adur's main channel passes under Beeding Bridge, from which this photograph was taken. Before the 17th century, the river was divided into two large channels south of Beeding; the eastern channel flowed under the old wooden bridge at Beeding, while the western channel flowed under Great Stone Bridge at Bramber.

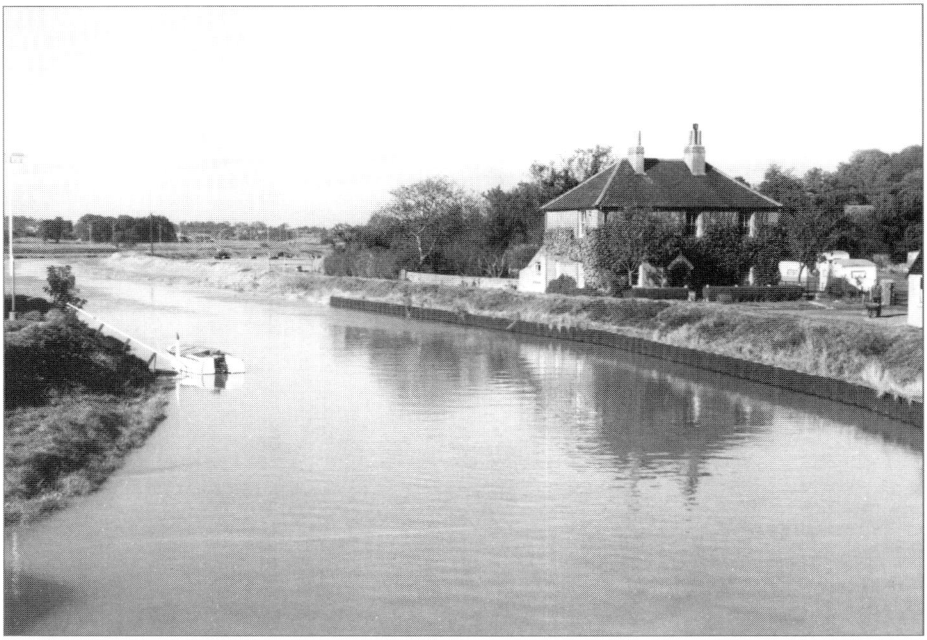

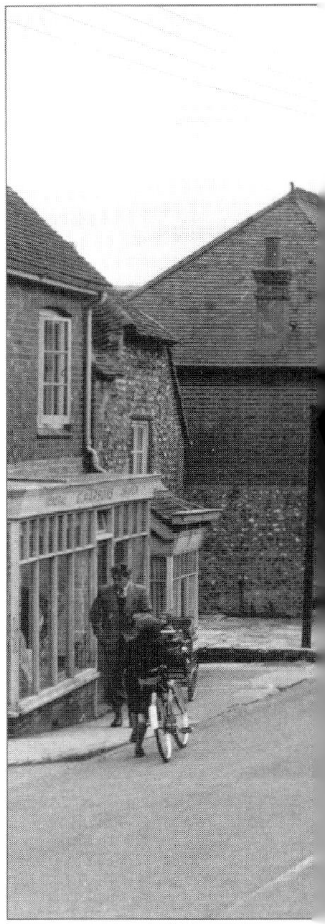

► **UPPER BEEDING**
*The Village c1955*
U40017

In the Middle Ages, the parish of Beeding also included a large detached portion in the Weald near Horsham, which was separated and named Lower Beeding by 1838. The remaining southern portion is today Upper Beeding, and its main street and houses lie along a causeway leading westwards towards Bramber.

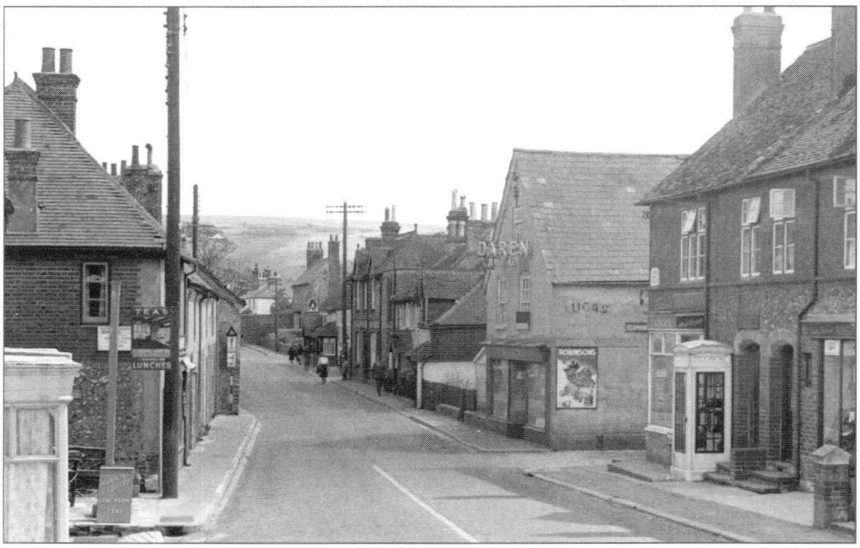

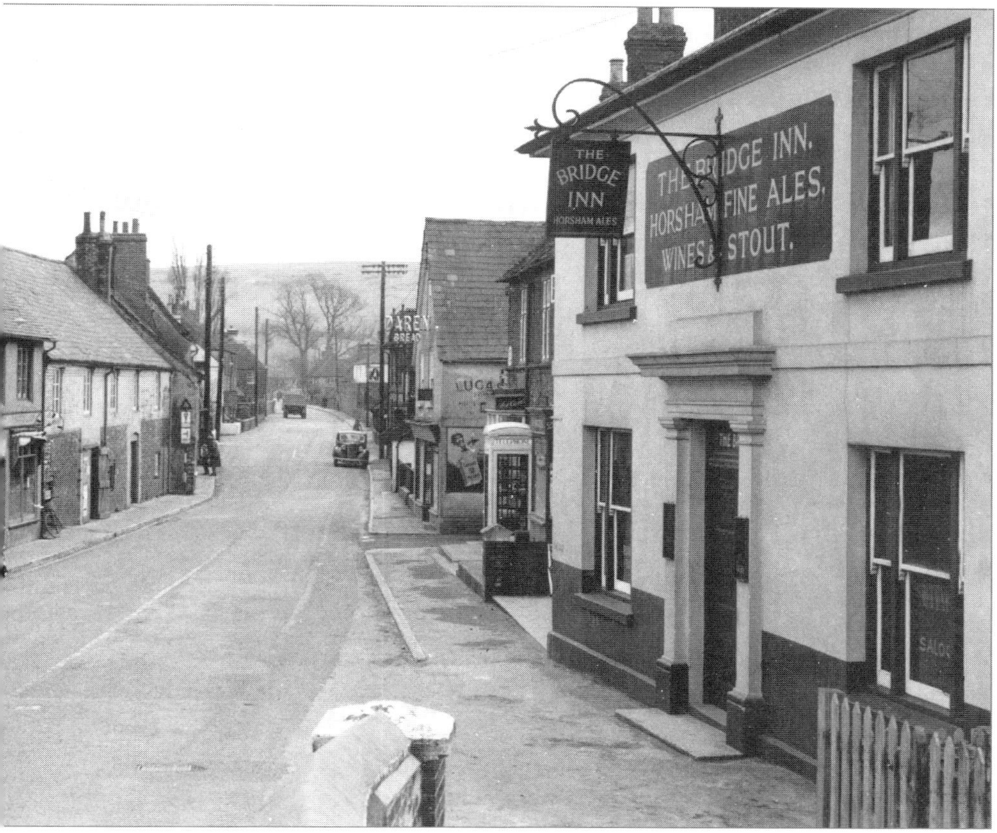


**UPPER BEEDING**
*From the Bridge*
*c1955* U40002

The High Street was named in the 13th century, when buildings were recorded east of Beeding Bridge. By the end of the 18th century, the western half of the High Street contained about fifteen houses, which by 1842 had increased to about twenty-five. Several of these still survive. The Bridge Inn on the eastern side of the bridge was recorded in 1913.

**UPPER BEEDING**
*The King's Head*
*c1955* U40006

Part of Beeding's Bridge is just visible on the small rise at the far western end of the High Street, next to the Bridge Inn on the left. The old King's Head was recorded by 1788, when the Burbeach Hundred Court first held their meetings there. The vestry meetings were also held there during the 1820s and later.

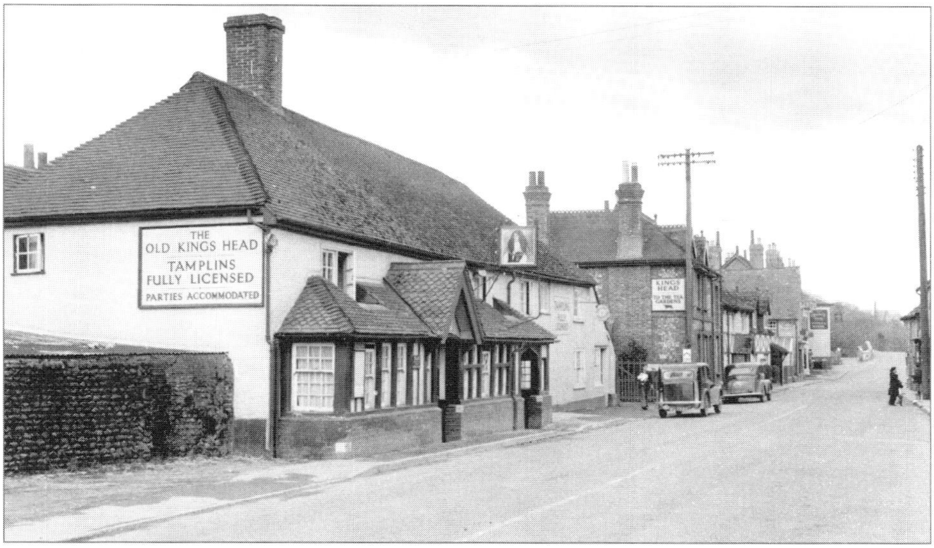

▼ **BRAMBER,** *St Mary's c1960* B179022

St Mary's dates from the 15th century, and stands on the site of an earlier Knights Templar house. The suggestion that the present house was built for the warden of the bridge was possibly confirmed when piers from the Great Stone Bridge were discovered in the garden during road repairs in 1839.

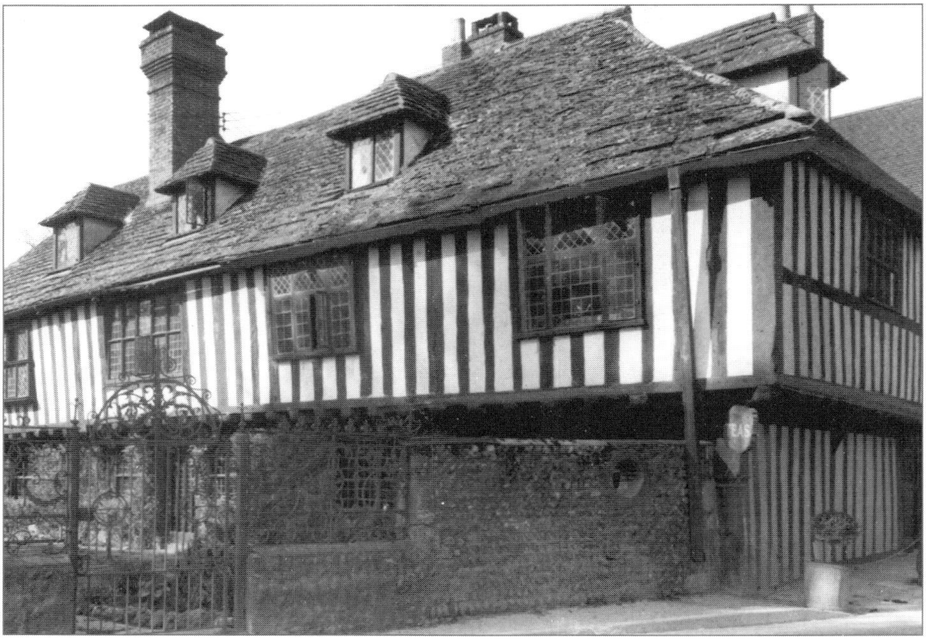

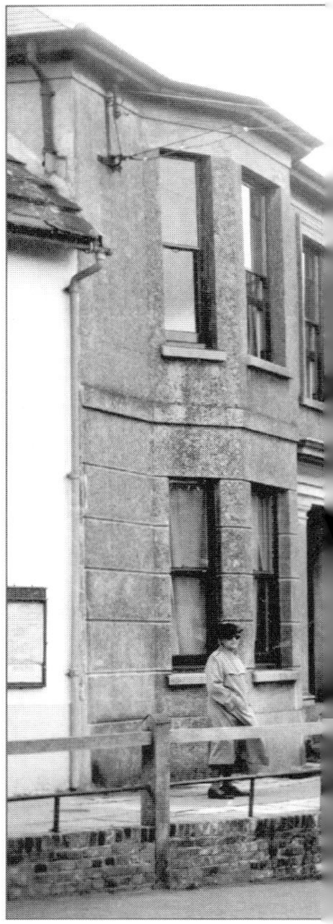

► **BRAMBER**
*The Village c1955*
B179003

The village of Bramber probably dates from the building of its Norman castle, since there is no evidence of a pre-Conquest settlement. Initially the village developed along a road constructed on a causeway across the marshes between the castle and a possible wharf near Bramber Bridge. Most of today's surviving buildings only date from the 18th century.

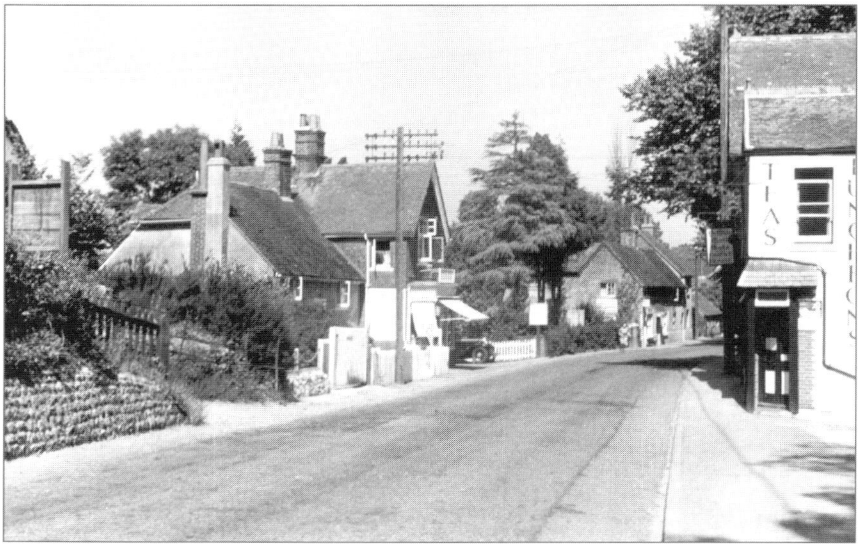

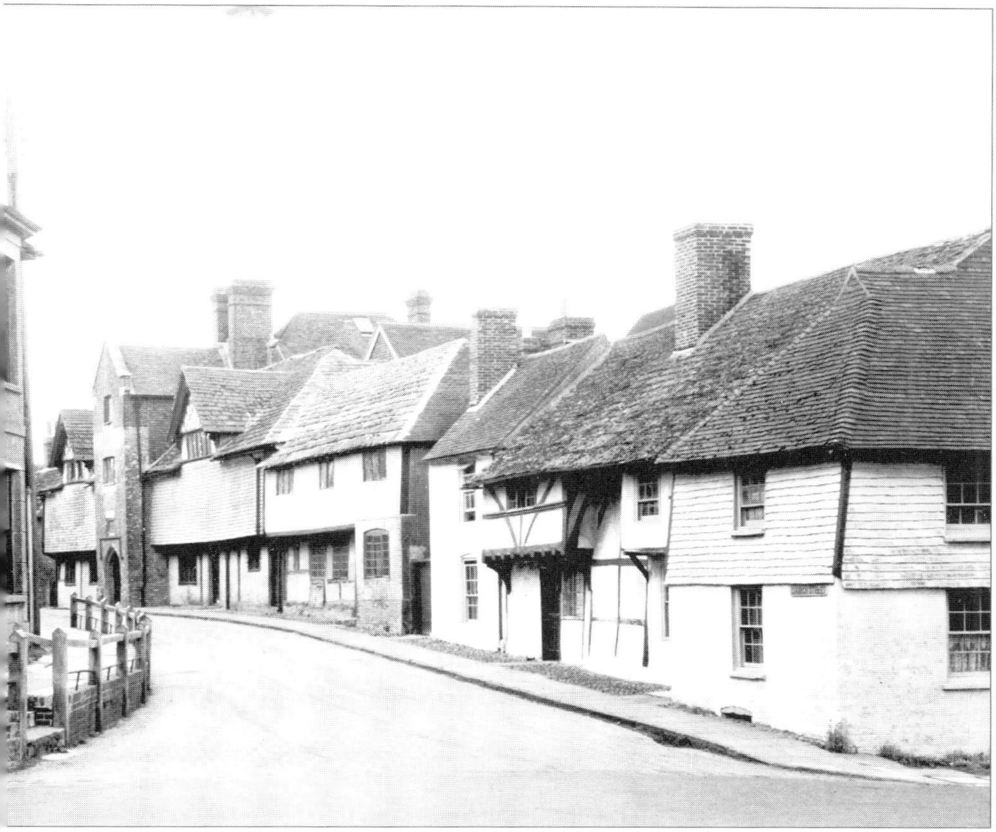

◄ **STEYNING**
*Church Street c1960* S192006

Following the decline of Steyning's port during the Middle Ages, the focus of the town shifted southwards from around the church and became centred on the junction of Church Street and the High Street. The building on the far right (now Numbers 1-5 Church Street) was originally a medieval Wealden timber-framed building, and is regarded as one of Steyning's treasures.

► **STEYNING**
*High Street c1955*
S192007

Many of Steyning's fine old buildings are now within a Conservation Area, which includes the High Street and Church Street. In the High Street, also known as Market Street in 1622, the chemist's (on the left) occupies part of a 16th-century building of the continuous jetty type. Opposite are three medieval properties, each with a Horsham stone roof.

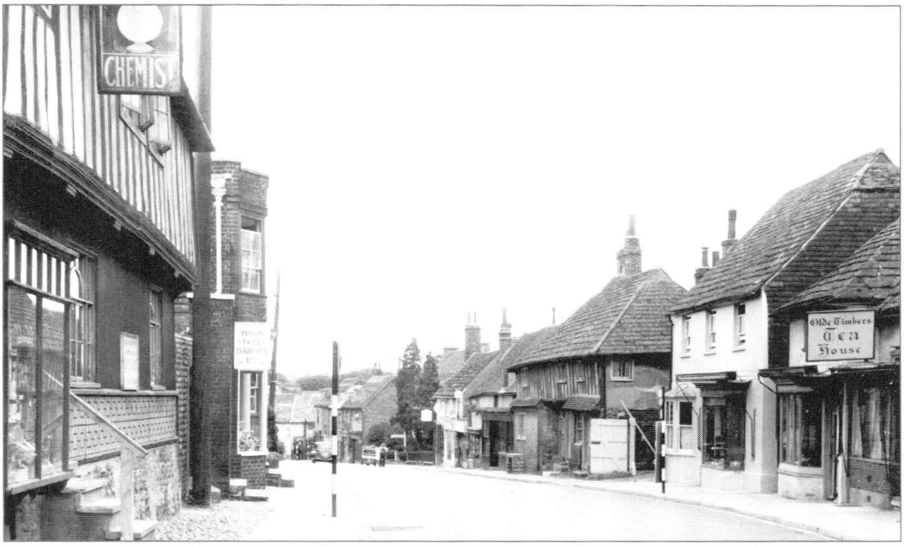

**HENFIELD**
*High Street c1955*
H313015

The High Street is part of the old London to Brighton route through Henfield, which lies to the east of the River Adur on a belt of Wealden clay behind the South Downs. On its eastern side is the George Inn, an old posting inn where post chaises and saddle horses could be hired in c1800.

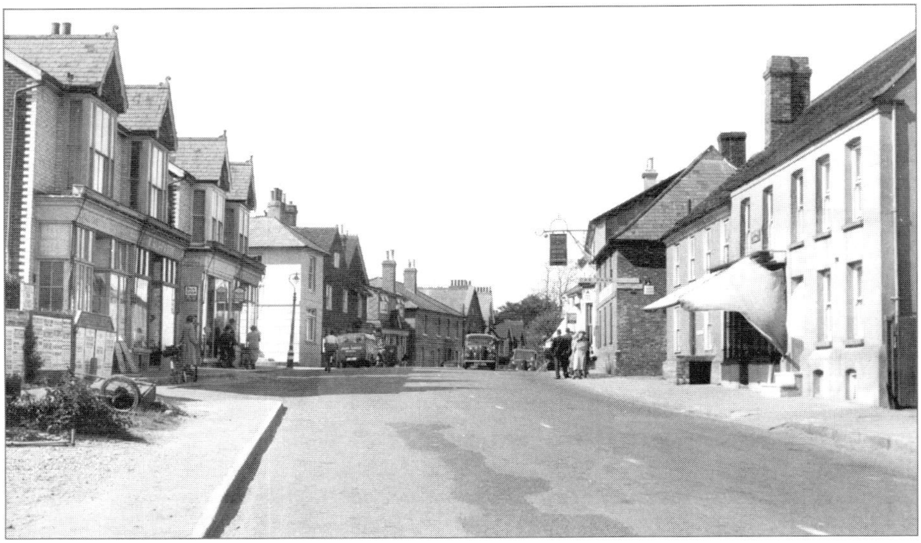

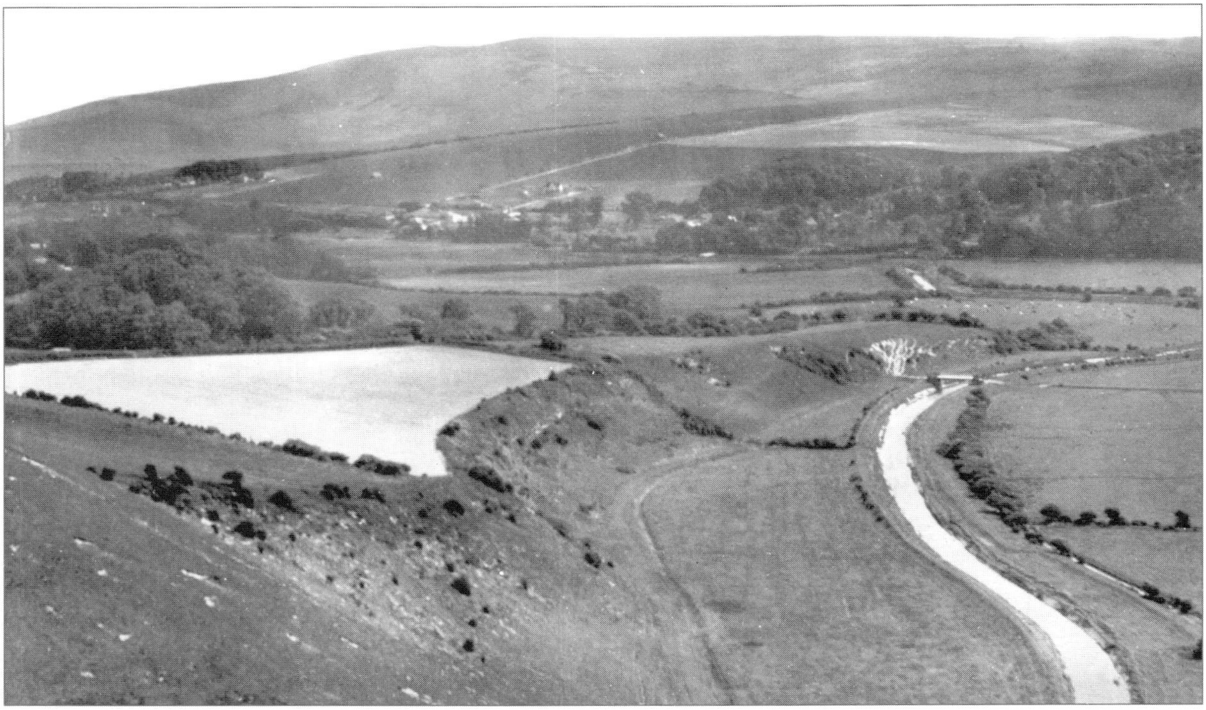

**ALFRISTON,** *The Cuckmere Valley c1955* A33001

The Cuckmere Valley is a charming and as yet unspoilt river valley. The River Cuckmere, whose Saxon name means 'flowing water', rises in the Weald and meanders southwards past Alfriston to enter the sea at Cuckmere Haven between Seaford Head and the Seven Sisters. It is the only river mouth in Sussex on which no port has been built.

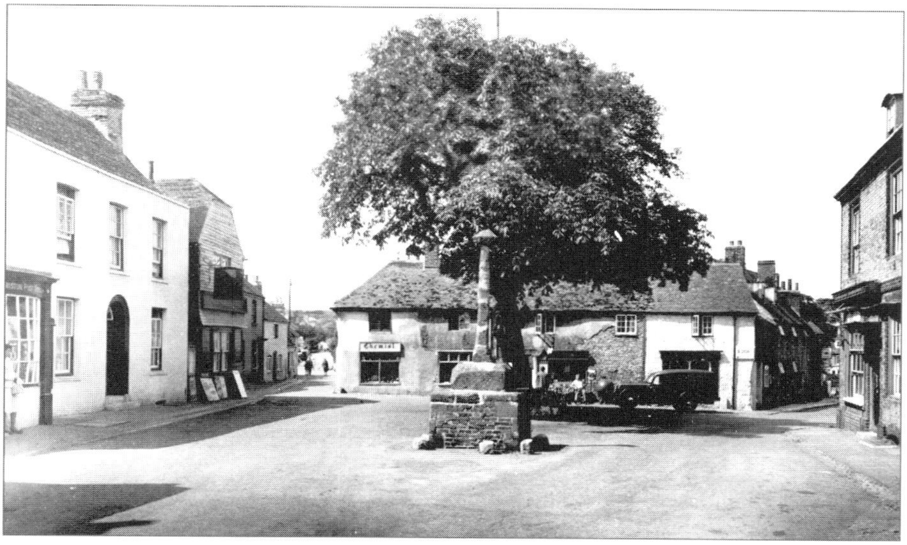

**ALFRISTON**
*The Village Square c1955* A33004

Behind the chestnut tree in the village square, once known as Waterloo Square, the shops were originally a small row of cottages, which were apparently used as a quartermaster's stores and to billet soldiers in 1800. On the left is the Georgian bow-windowed stores and post office. This has been a grocers' shop for over a hundred years.

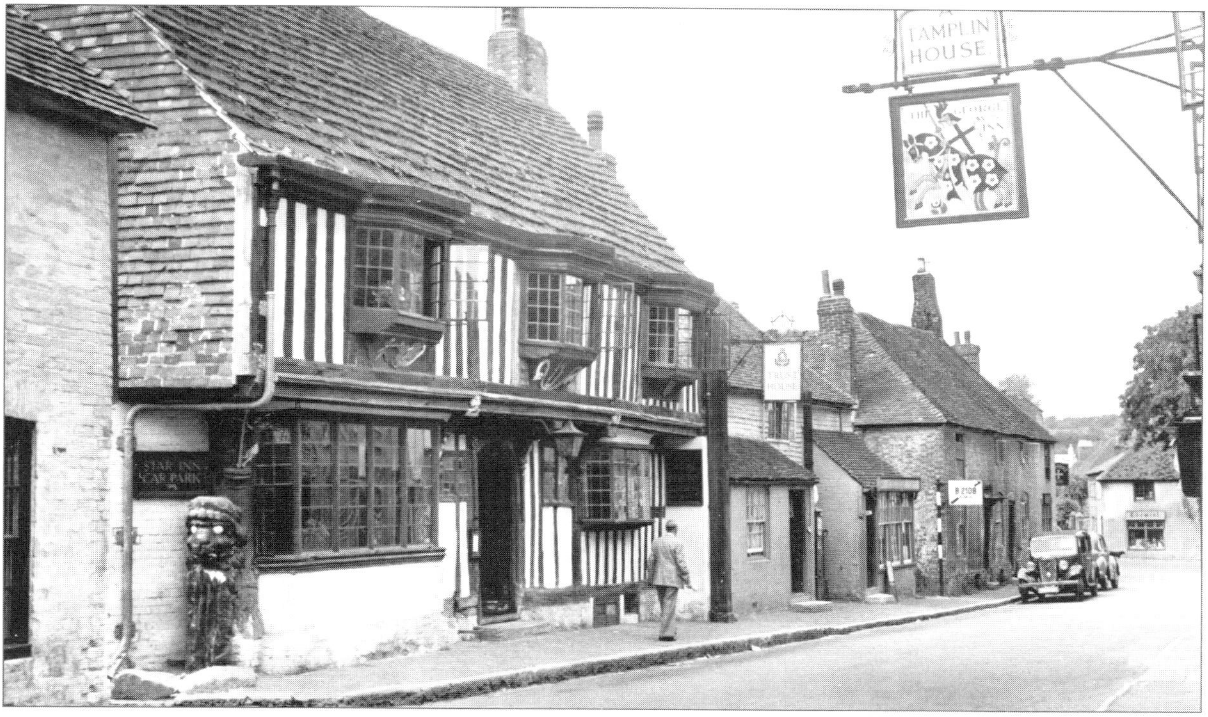


**ALFRISTON,** *The Star Inn c1955* A33014

The Star in the High Street, built in the early 16th century, was a hostelry and resting place for abbots and monks from surrounding priories and manors and also for pilgrims. The exterior of the inn exhibits many interesting carvings. The red lion standing at the corner (left) is a figure-head from a Dutch ship wrecked off Cuckmere Haven in the 19th century.

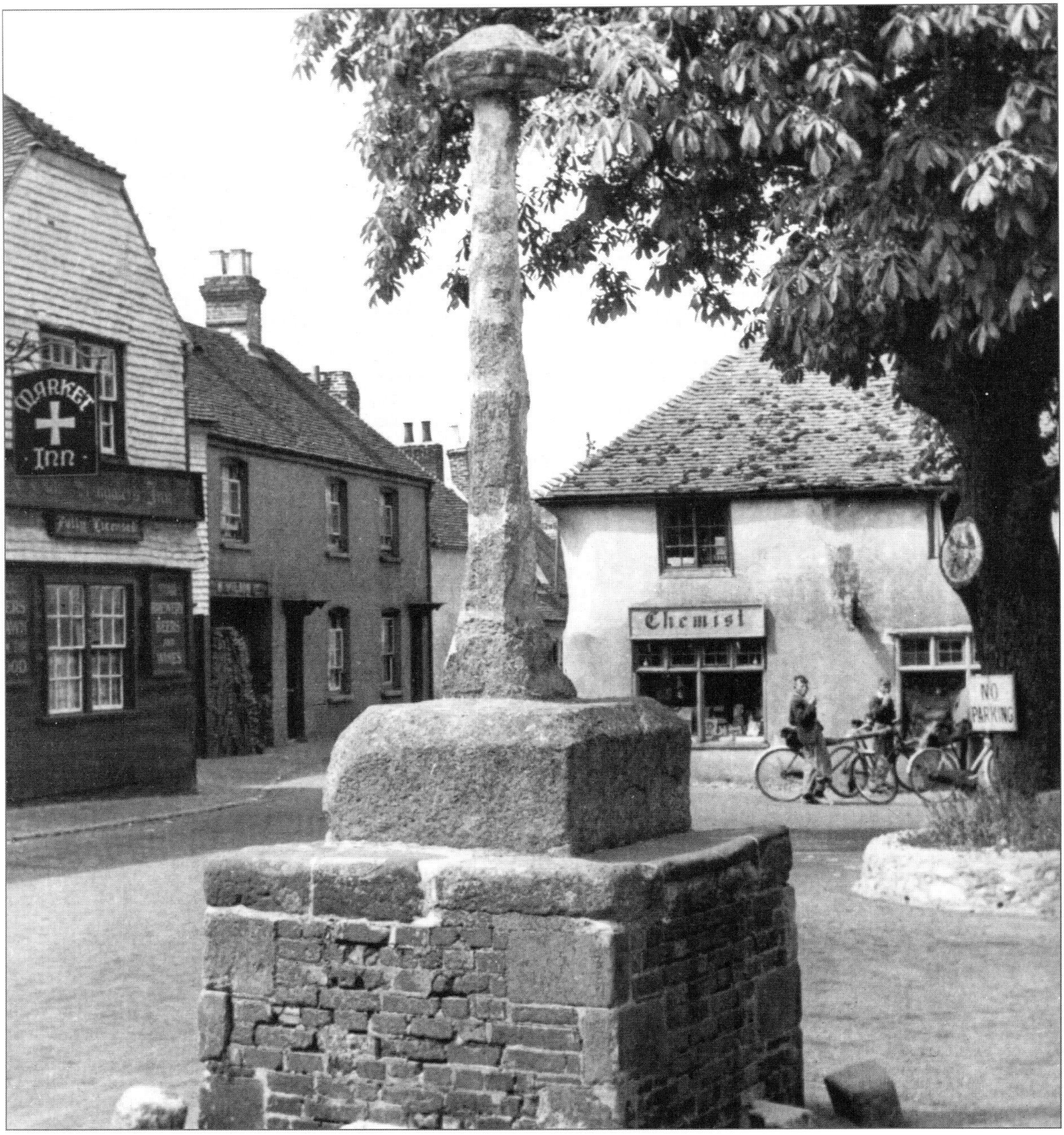


**ALFRISTON,** *The Ancient Market Cross c1960* A33021

The medieval market cross was erected when Alfriston was granted the right to hold a weekly market. It has been much mutilated over the years; the original cross has been missing since at least 1787, when the structure was higher. In 1833 a hat-like stone was placed on top, and the ancient steps around the base were removed because they impeded traffic.

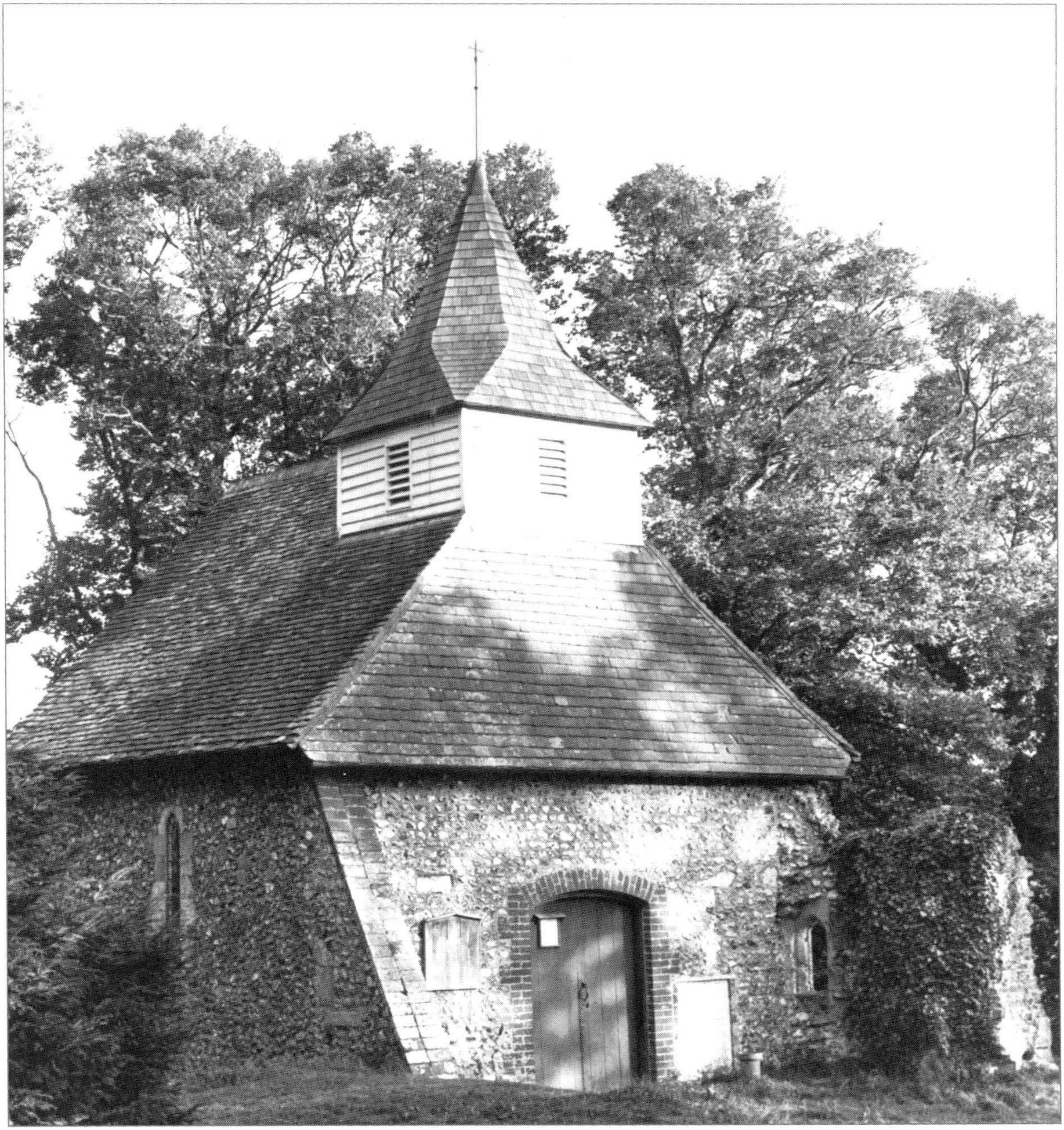

**LULLINGTON,** *The Church c1960* L524025

Lullington Church stands a short walk away from Alfriston village, across the White Bridge over the Cuckmere. It is one of the smallest churches in England - it seats about 20 people. All that remains today is part of the chancel of a once much larger 13th-century church.

▼ **PEVENSEY,** *The Village c1955* P50051

Situated on a small peninsula of higher ground above the surrounding ancient marshes between Eastbourne and Hastings, Pevensey was the principal town of the Rape of Pevensey in the medieval period. It had three roughly parallel medieval roads, and the route of the most northerly of these is still well-used today. The buildings exhibit the typical Wealden building materials of clay tiles and weatherboarding.

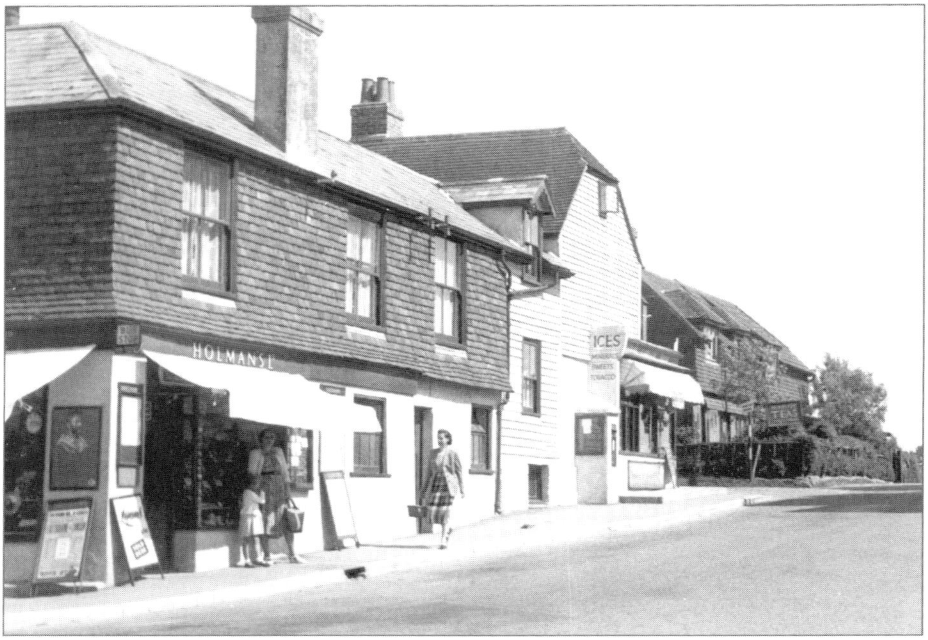


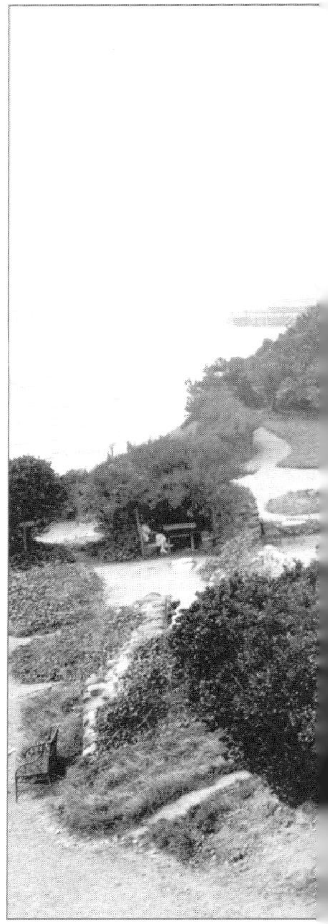

► **PEVENSEY**
*The Castle 1894* 34477

It is now believed that Pevensey was Anderida, a Roman fort, which in turn was probably Andredesceaster, the site of the battle between the Saxon invaders and the British in AD490. Within the Roman walled enclosure, William I built his Norman castle and moat in the south-eastern corner.

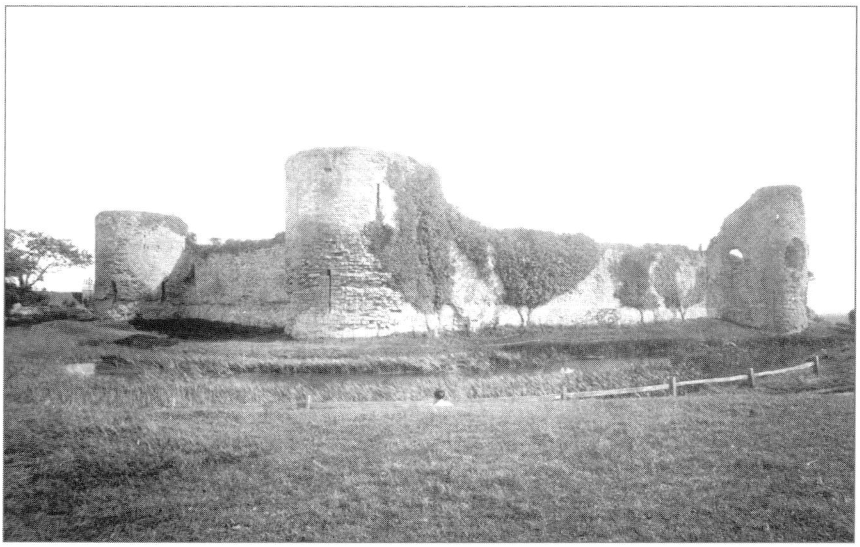

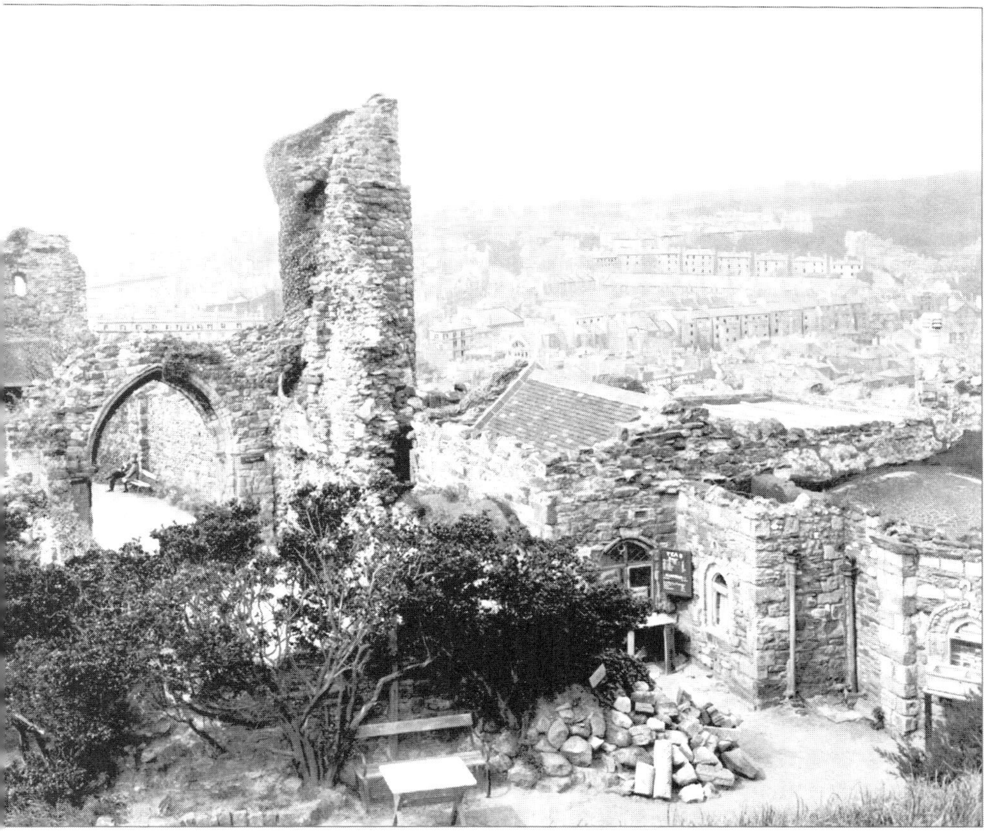

**HASTINGS**
*The Castle 1925*
77965

In the 12th century, Hastings was the headquarters of the Confederacy of the Cinque Ports. Its large Norman castle was built on a promontory that once stretched some distance out to sea, providing protection to the harbour that lay inland on the river estuary. The ruins of the castle still dominate the earlier fishing settlement that is now a modern seaside resort.

**WINCHELSEA**
*Castle Street 1912*
64944

Winchelsea is located on a sandstone rock, similar to the site of Rye, and was occupied in 1289 after Old Winchelsea was finally overwhelmed by the sea. New Winchelsea was laid out in a grid system, but only the north-eastern quarter is currently used. Several buildings of the 17th and 18th centuries were recorded in 1937, some of which had medieval vaults beneath them.

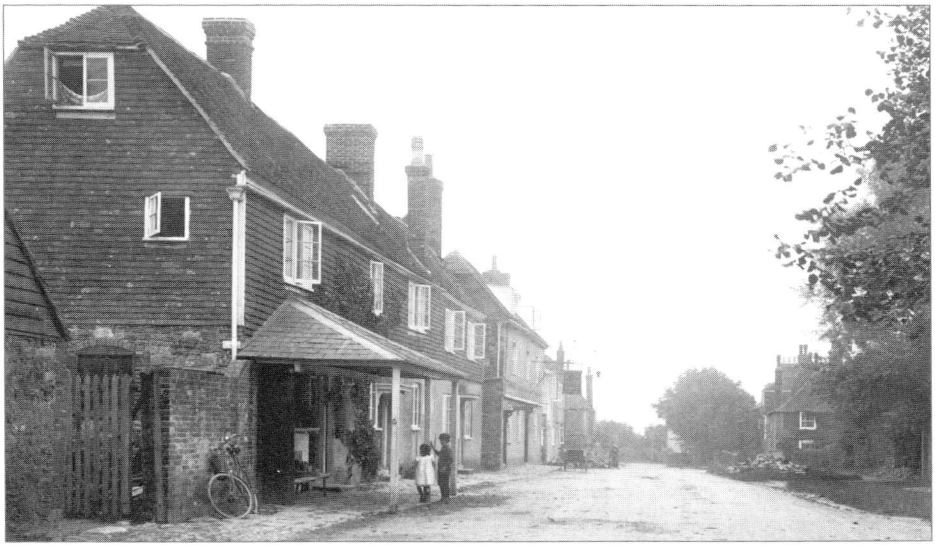

**RYE**
*The Canal 1912*
64933

The ancient town of Rye was built on a sandstone rock at the confluence of the Tillington and Rother rivers. The subsequent retreat of the sea and the reclamation of the surrounding marshes resulted in a lengthening coastline. In the interest of national security this was counteracted when the Royal Military Canal was built as a defence against Napoleon in 1807, linking the Rother with Hythe.

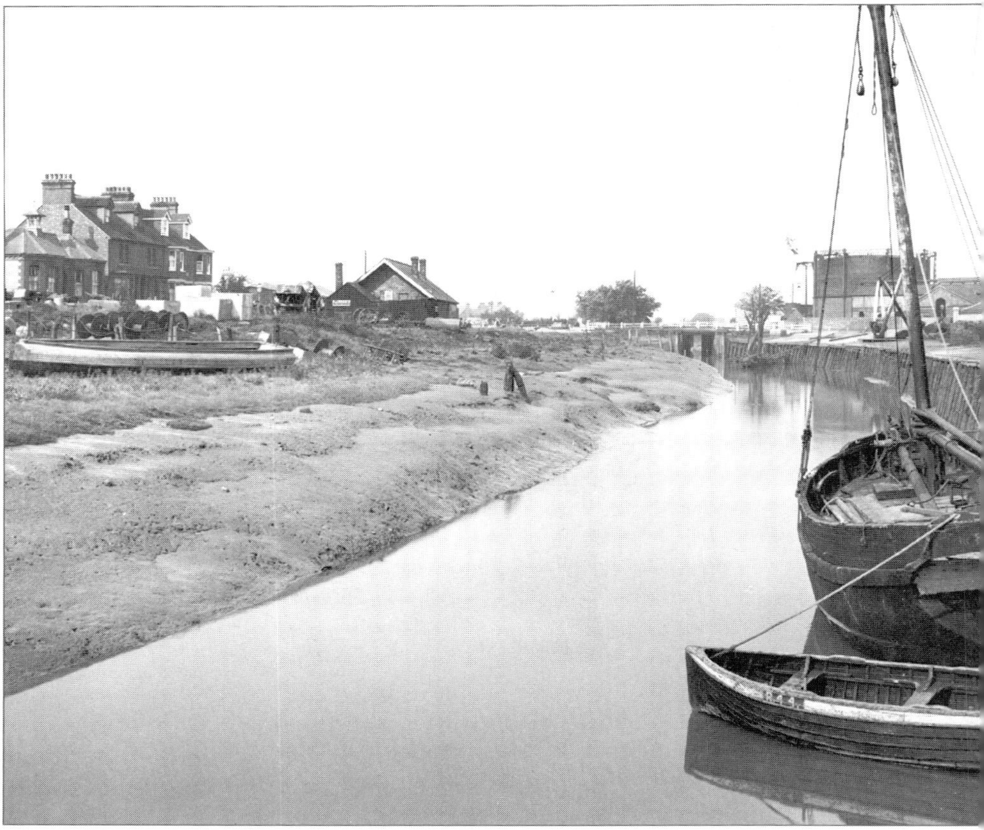

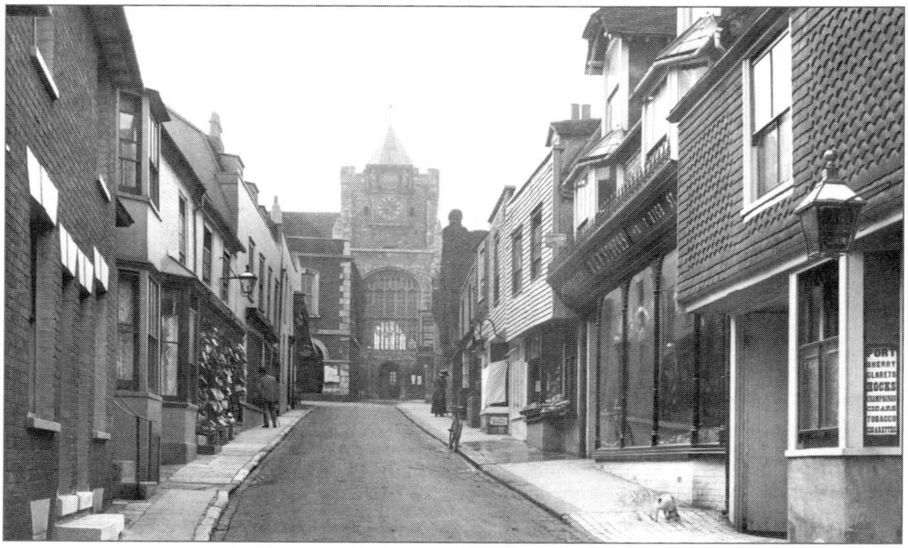

**RYE**
*Lion Street 1912*
64922

At the southern end of Lion Street, near its junction with Market Street, is Rye's large parish church of St Mary the Virgin, much of which is hidden by other buildings. This church was completely rebuilt after an earlier church on the site burnt down in 1377 along with most of Rye during an attack by the French.

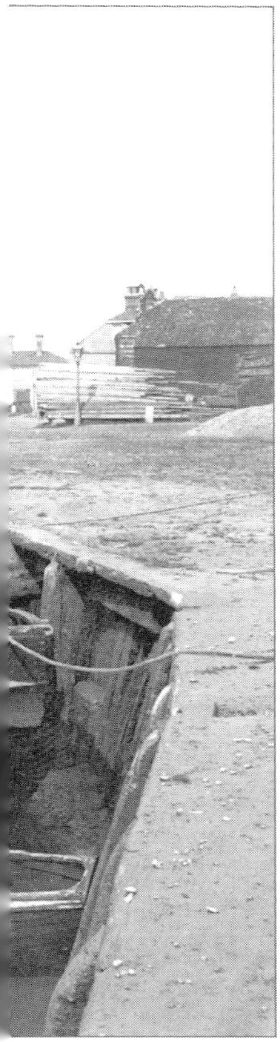

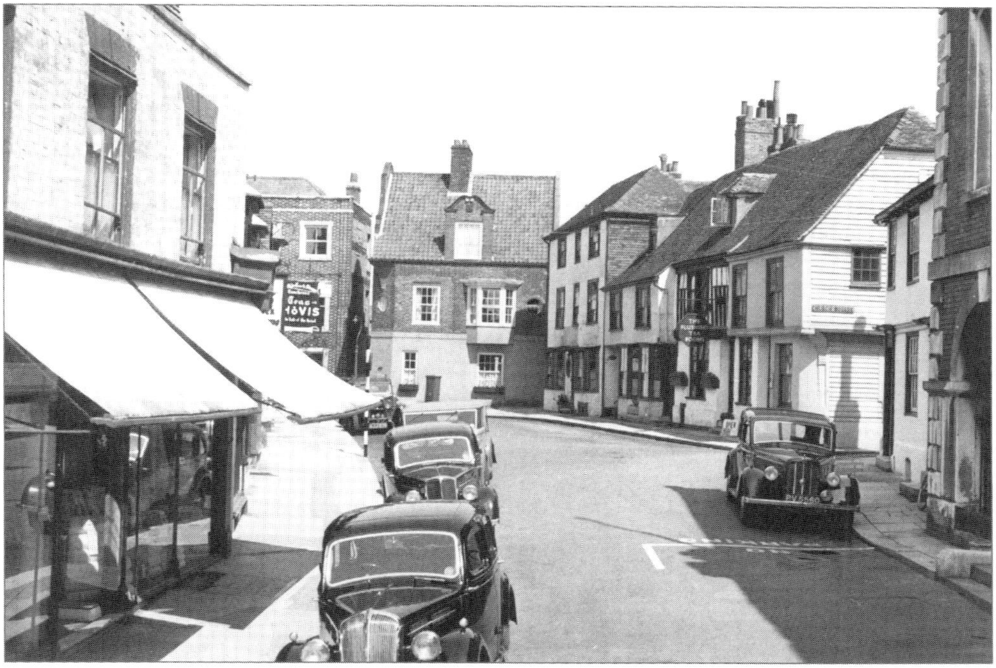

▲ **RYE,** *Market Street c1955* R77018

The present Market Street, formerly the Butchery, is a reminder of Rye's early market. The Town Hall, part of which can be seen on the right, was built in 1742 on the site of the Market Hall. The Old Flushing Inn (the Flushing Tea Rooms, right) faced the Market Square; the building dates from the 15th century.

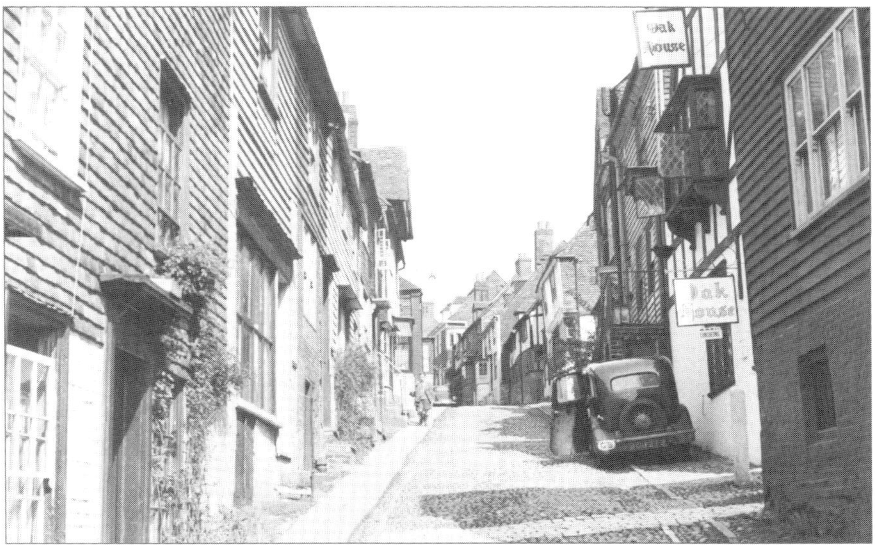


◄ **RYE**
*Mermaid Street c1955*
R77032

Mermaid Street, once known as Middle Street, has been described as Rye's principal Tudor street. Most of the buildings are timber-framed and date from the 15th to the 17th century, although several are now covered by weather-boarding. The cobbled street passes Oak House, one of the oldest houses in Rye; it dates from the 15th century, and replaced an earlier house that burnt down in 1377.

**HERSTMONCEUX**
*The Castle, the West Front 1890* 25345

It is suggested that the remains of Herstmonceux Castle form part of the oldest brick mansion in Britain; it was built in 1441, following a grant from the King to Roger de Fiennes to 'embattle' his manor-house at Herstmonceux. It was rebuilt in a military style, and in the towers are cross-crosslets from which cross-bow bolts could be discharged.

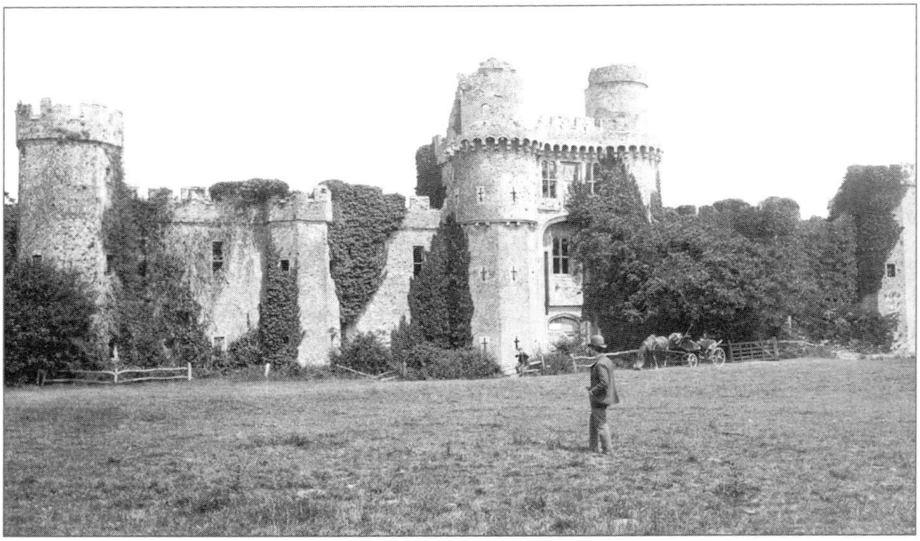

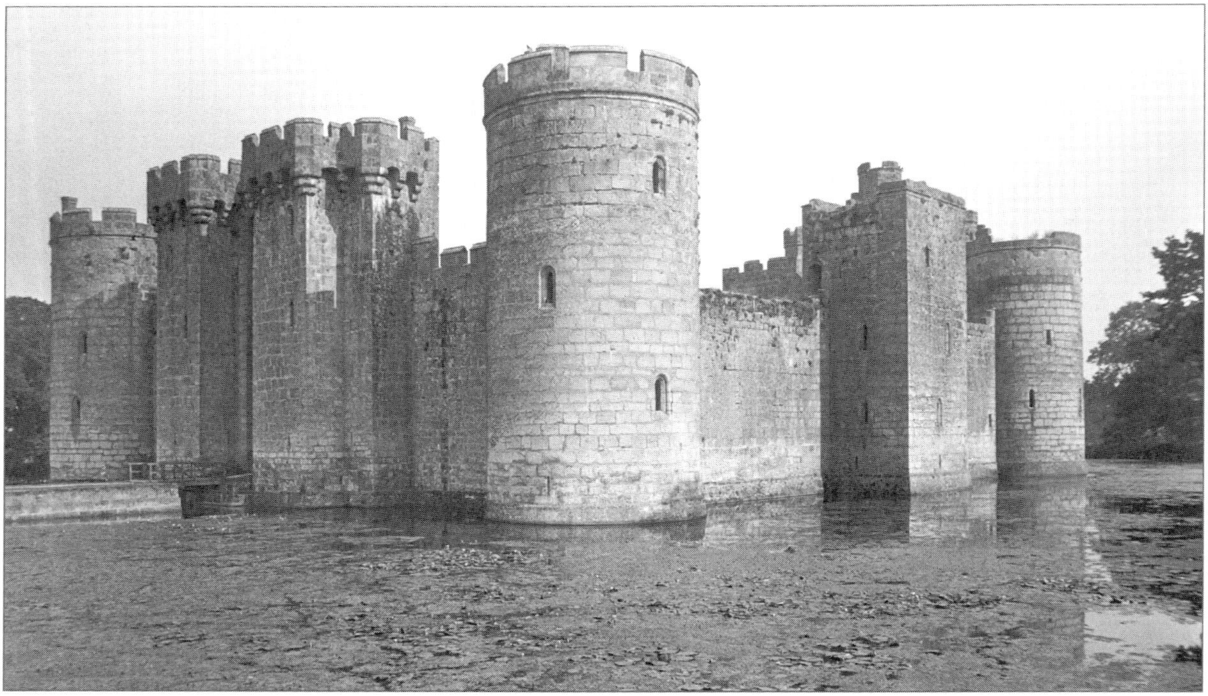

**BODIAM,** *The Castle 1925* 77005

Following the burning of Rye in 1377 and of Winchelsea in 1380, Bodiam Castle was built in 1385 because of the imminent threat of invasion by the French. As the Rother, navigable to Bodiam Bridge, was part of the port of Winchelsea, a licence was granted to Sir Edward Dalyngrigge 'to make a castle thereof in defence of the adjacent country against the King's enemies'.

# INDEX

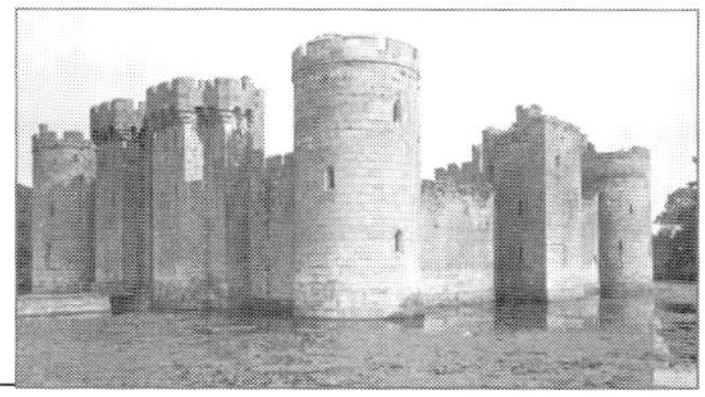

# Frith Book Co Titles

## www.francisfrith.co.uk

The Frith Book Company publishes over 100 new titles each year. A selection of those currently available is listed below. For latest catalogue please contact Frith Book Co.
***Town Books*** 96 pages, approximately 100 photos. ***County and Themed Books*** 128 pages, approximately 150 photos (unless specified). All titles hardback with laminated case and jacket, except those indicated pb (paperback)

| | | |
|---|---|---|
| Amersham, Chesham & Rickmansworth (pb) | 1-85937-340-2 | £9.99 |
| Andover (pb) | 1-85937-292-9 | £9.99 |
| Aylesbury (pb) | 1-85937-227-9 | £9.99 |
| Barnstaple (pb) | 1-85937-300-3 | £9.99 |
| Basildon Living Memories (pb) | 1-85937-515-4 | £9.99 |
| Bath (pb) | 1-85937-419-0 | £9.99 |
| Bedford (pb) | 1-85937-205-8 | £9.99 |
| Bedfordshire Living Memories | 1-85937-513-8 | £14.99 |
| Belfast (pb) | 1-85937-303-8 | £9.99 |
| Berkshire (pb) | 1-85937-191-4 | £9.99 |
| Berkshire Churches | 1-85937-170-1 | £17.99 |
| Berkshire Living Memories | 1-85937-332-1 | £14.99 |
| Black Country | 1-85937-497-2 | £12.99 |
| Blackpool (pb) | 1-85937-393-3 | £9.99 |
| Bognor Regis (pb) | 1-85937-431-x | £9.99 |
| Bournemouth (pb) | 1-85937-545-6 | £9.99 |
| Bradford (pb) | 1-85937-204-x | £9.99 |
| Bridgend (pb) | 1-85937-386-0 | £7.99 |
| Bridgwater (pb) | 1-85937-305-4 | £9.99 |
| Bridport (pb) | 1-85937-327-5 | £9.99 |
| Brighton (pb) | 1-85937-192-2 | £8.99 |
| Bristol (pb) | 1-85937-264-3 | £9.99 |
| British Life A Century Ago (pb) | 1-85937-213-9 | £9.99 |
| Buckinghamshire (pb) | 1-85937-200-7 | £9.99 |
| Camberley (pb) | 1-85937-222-8 | £9.99 |
| Cambridge (pb) | 1-85937-422-0 | £9.99 |
| Cambridgeshire (pb) | 1-85937-420-4 | £9.99 |
| Cambridgeshire Villages | 1-85937-523-5 | £14.99 |
| Canals And Waterways (pb) | 1-85937-291-0 | £9.99 |
| Canterbury Cathedral (pb) | 1-85937-179-5 | £9.99 |
| Cardiff (pb) | 1-85937-093-4 | £9.99 |
| Carmarthenshire (pb) | 1-85937-604-5 | £9.99 |
| Chelmsford (pb) | 1-85937-310-0 | £9.99 |
| Cheltenham (pb) | 1-85937-095-0 | £9.99 |
| Cheshire (pb) | 1-85937-271-6 | £9.99 |
| Chester (pb) | 1-85937-382 8 | £9.99 |
| Chesterfield (pb) | 1-85937-378-x | £9.99 |
| Chichester (pb) | 1-85937-228-7 | £9.99 |
| Churches of East Cornwall (pb) | 1-85937-249-x | £9.99 |
| Churches of Hampshire (pb) | 1-85937-207-4 | £9.99 |
| Cinque Ports & Two Ancient Towns | 1-85937-492-1 | £14.99 |
| Colchester (pb) | 1-85937-188-4 | £8.99 |
| Cornwall (pb) | 1-85937-229-5 | £9.99 |
| Cornwall Living Memories | 1-85937-248-1 | £14.99 |
| Cotswolds (pb) | 1-85937-230-9 | £9.99 |
| Cotswolds Living Memories | 1-85937-255-4 | £14.99 |
| County Durham (pb) | 1-85937-398-4 | £9.99 |
| Croydon Living Memories (pb) | 1-85937-162-0 | £9.99 |
| Cumbria (pb) | 1-85937-621-5 | £9.99 |
| Derby (pb) | 1-85937-367-4 | £9.99 |
| Derbyshire (pb) | 1-85937-196-5 | £9.99 |
| Derbyshire Living Memories | 1-85937-330-5 | £14.99 |
| Devon (pb) | 1-85937-297-x | £9.99 |
| Devon Churches (pb) | 1-85937-250-3 | £9.99 |
| Dorchester (pb) | 1-85937-307-0 | £9.99 |
| Dorset (pb) | 1-85937-269-4 | £9.99 |
| Dorset Coast (pb) | 1-85937-299-6 | £9.99 |
| Dorset Living Memories (pb) | 1-85937-584-7 | £9.99 |
| Down the Severn (pb) | 1-85937-560-x | £9.99 |
| Down The Thames (pb) | 1-85937-278-3 | £9.99 |
| Down the Trent | 1-85937-311-9 | £14.99 |
| East Anglia (pb) | 1-85937-265-1 | £9.99 |
| East Grinstead (pb) | 1-85937-138-8 | £9.99 |
| East London | 1-85937-080-2 | £14.99 |
| East Sussex (pb) | 1-85937-606-1 | £9.99 |
| Eastbourne (pb) | 1-85937-399-2 | £9.99 |
| Edinburgh (pb) | 1-85937-193-0 | £8.99 |
| England In The 1880s | 1-85937-331-3 | £17.99 |
| Essex - Second Selection | 1-85937-456-5 | £14.99 |
| Essex (pb) | 1-85937-270-8 | £9.99 |
| Essex Coast | 1-85937-342-9 | £14.99 |
| Essex Living Memories | 1-85937-490-5 | £14.99 |
| Exeter | 1-85937-539-1 | £9.99 |
| Exmoor (pb) | 1-85937-608-8 | £9.99 |
| Falmouth (pb) | 1-85937-594-4 | £9.99 |
| Folkestone (pb) | 1-85937-124-8 | £9.99 |
| Frome (pb) | 1-85937-317-8 | £9.99 |
| Glamorgan | 1-85937-488-3 | £14.99 |
| Glasgow (pb) | 1-85937-190-6 | £9.99 |
| Glastonbury (pb) | 1-85937-338-0 | £7.99 |
| Gloucester (pb) | 1-85937-232-5 | £9.99 |
| Gloucestershire (pb) | 1-85937-561-8 | £9.99 |
| Great Yarmouth (pb) | 1-85937-426-3 | £9.99 |
| Greater Manchester (pb) | 1-85937-266-x | £9.99 |
| Guildford (pb) | 1-85937-410-7 | £9.99 |
| Hampshire (pb) | 1-85937-279-1 | £9.99 |
| Harrogate (pb) | 1-85937-423-9 | £9.99 |
| Hastings and Bexhill (pb) | 1-85937-131-0 | £9.99 |
| Heart of Lancashire (pb) | 1-85937-197-3 | £9.99 |
| Helston (pb) | 1-85937-214-7 | £9.99 |
| Hereford (pb) | 1-85937-175-2 | £9.99 |
| Herefordshire (pb) | 1-85937-567-7 | £9.99 |
| Herefordshire Living Memories | 1-85937-514-6 | £14.99 |
| Hertfordshire (pb) | 1-85937-247-3 | £9.99 |
| Horsham (pb) | 1-85937-432-8 | £9.99 |
| Humberside (pb) | 1-85937-605-3 | £9.99 |
| Hythe, Romney Marsh, Ashford (pb) | 1-85937-256-2 | £9.99 |
| Ipswich (pb) | 1-85937-424-7 | £9.99 |
| Isle of Man (pb) | 1-85937-268-6 | £9.99 |
| Isle of Wight (pb) | 1-85937-429-8 | £9.99 |
| Isle of Wight Living Memories | 1-85937-304-6 | £14.99 |
| Kent (pb) | 1-85937-189-2 | £9.99 |
| Kent Living Memories(pb) | 1-85937-401-8 | £9.99 |
| Kings Lynn (pb) | 1-85937-334-8 | £9.99 |

**Available from your local bookshop or from the publisher**

# Frith Book Co Titles (continued)

| | | |
|---|---|---|
| Lake District (pb) | 1-85937-275-9 | £9.99 |
| Lancashire Living Memories | 1-85937-335-6 | £14.99 |
| Lancaster, Morecambe, Heysham (pb) | 1-85937-233-3 | £9.99 |
| Leeds (pb) | 1-85937-202-3 | £9.99 |
| Leicester (pb) | 1-85937-381-x | £9.99 |
| Leicestershire & Rutland Living Memories | 1-85937-500-6 | £12.99 |
| Leicestershire (pb) | 1-85937-185-x | £9.99 |
| Lighthouses | 1-85937-257-0 | £9.99 |
| Lincoln (pb) | 1-85937-380-1 | £9.99 |
| Lincolnshire (pb) | 1-85937-433-6 | £9.99 |
| Liverpool and Merseyside (pb) | 1-85937-234-1 | £9.99 |
| London (pb) | 1-85937-183-3 | £9.99 |
| London Living Memories | 1-85937-454-9 | £14.99 |
| Ludlow (pb) | 1-85937-176-0 | £9.99 |
| Luton (pb) | 1-85937-235-x | £9.99 |
| Maidenhead (pb) | 1-85937-339-9 | £9.99 |
| Maidstone (pb) | 1-85937-391-7 | £9.99 |
| Manchester (pb) | 1-85937-198-1 | £9.99 |
| Marlborough (pb) | 1-85937-336-4 | £9.99 |
| Middlesex | 1-85937-158-2 | £14.99 |
| Monmouthshire | 1-85937-532-4 | £14.99 |
| New Forest (pb) | 1-85937-390-9 | £9.99 |
| Newark (pb) | 1-85937-366-6 | £9.99 |
| Newport, Wales (pb) | 1-85937-258-9 | £9.99 |
| Newquay (pb) | 1-85937-421-2 | £9.99 |
| Norfolk (pb) | 1-85937-195-7 | £9.99 |
| Norfolk Broads | 1-85937-486-7 | £14.99 |
| Norfolk Living Memories (pb) | 1-85937-402-6 | £9.99 |
| North Buckinghamshire | 1-85937-626-6 | £14.99 |
| North Devon Living Memories | 1-85937-261-9 | £14.99 |
| North Hertfordshire | 1-85937-547-2 | £14.99 |
| North London (pb) | 1-85937-403-4 | £9.99 |
| North Somerset | 1-85937-302-x | £14.99 |
| North Wales (pb) | 1-85937-298-8 | £9.99 |
| North Yorkshire (pb) | 1-85937-236-8 | £9.99 |
| Northamptonshire Living Memories | 1-85937-529-4 | £14.99 |
| Northamptonshire | 1-85937-150-7 | £14.99 |
| Northumberland Tyne & Wear (pb) | 1-85937-281-3 | £9.99 |
| Northumberland | 1-85937-522-7 | £14.99 |
| Norwich (pb) | 1-85937-194-9 | £8.99 |
| Nottingham (pb) | 1-85937-324-0 | £9.99 |
| Nottinghamshire (pb) | 1-85937-187-6 | £9.99 |
| Oxford (pb) | 1-85937-411-5 | £9.99 |
| Oxfordshire (pb) | 1-85937-430-1 | £9.99 |
| Oxfordshire Living Memories | 1-85937-525-1 | £14.99 |
| Paignton (pb) | 1-85937-374-7 | £7.99 |
| Peak District (pb) | 1-85937-280-5 | £9.99 |
| Pembrokeshire | 1-85937-262-7 | £14.99 |
| Penzance (pb) | 1-85937-595-2 | £9.99 |
| Peterborough (pb) | 1-85937-219-8 | £9.99 |
| Picturesque Harbours | 1-85937-208-2 | £14.99 |
| Piers | 1-85937-237-6 | £17.99 |
| Plymouth (pb) | 1-85937-389-5 | £9.99 |
| Poole & Sandbanks (pb) | 1-85937-251-1 | £9.99 |
| Preston (pb) | 1-85937-212-0 | £9.99 |
| Reading (pb) | 1-85937-238-4 | £9.99 |
| Redhill to Reigate (pb) | 1-85937-596-0 | £9.99 |
| Ringwood (pb) | 1-85937-384-4 | £7.99 |
| Romford (pb) | 1-85937-319-4 | £9.99 |
| Royal Tunbridge Wells (pb) | 1-85937-504-9 | £9.99 |
| Salisbury (pb) | 1-85937-239-2 | £9.99 |
| Scarborough (pb) | 1-85937-379-8 | £9.99 |
| Sevenoaks and Tonbridge (pb) | 1-85937-392-5 | £9.99 |
| Sheffield & South Yorks (pb) | 1-85937-267-8 | £9.99 |
| Sherborne (pb) | 1-85937-301-1 | £9.99 |
| Shrewsbury (pb) | 1-85937-325-9 | £9.99 |
| Shropshire (pb) | 1-85937-326-7 | £9.99 |
| Shropshire Living Memories | 1-85937-643-6 | £14.99 |
| Somerset | 1-85937-153-1 | £14.99 |
| South Devon Coast | 1-85937-107-8 | £14.99 |
| South Devon Living Memories (pb) | 1-85937-609-6 | £9.99 |
| South East London (pb) | 1-85937-263-5 | £9.99 |
| South Somerset | 1-85937-318-6 | £14.99 |
| South Wales | 1-85937-519-7 | £14.99 |
| Southampton (pb) | 1-85937-427-1 | £9.99 |
| Southend (pb) | 1-85937-313-5 | £9.99 |
| Southport (pb) | 1-85937-425-5 | £9.99 |
| St Albans (pb) | 1-85937-341-0 | £9.99 |
| St Ives (pb) | 1-85937-415-8 | £9.99 |
| Stafford Living Memories (pb) | 1-85937-503-0 | £9.99 |
| Staffordshire (pb) | 1-85937-308-9 | £9.99 |
| Stourbridge (pb) | 1-85937-530-8 | £9.99 |
| Stratford upon Avon (pb) | 1-85937-388-7 | £9.99 |
| Suffolk (pb) | 1-85937-221-x | £9.99 |
| Suffolk Coast (pb) | 1-85937-610-x | £9.99 |
| Surrey (pb) | 1-85937-240-6 | £9.99 |
| Surrey Living Memories | 1-85937-328-3 | £14.99 |
| Sussex (pb) | 1-85937-184-1 | £9.99 |
| Sutton (pb) | 1-85937-337-2 | £9.99 |
| Swansea (pb) | 1-85937-167-1 | £9.99 |
| Taunton (pb) | 1-85937-314-3 | £9.99 |
| Tees Valley & Cleveland (pb) | 1-85937-623-1 | £9.99 |
| Teignmouth (pb) | 1-85937-370-4 | £7.99 |
| Thanet (pb) | 1-85937-116-7 | £9.99 |
| Tiverton (pb) | 1-85937-178-7 | £9.99 |
| Torbay (pb) | 1-85937-597-9 | £9.99 |
| Truro (pb) | 1-85937-598-7 | £9.99 |
| Victorian & Edwardian Dorset | 1-85937-254-6 | £14.99 |
| Victorian & Edwardian Kent (pb) | 1-85937-624-X | £9.99 |
| Victorian & Edwardian Maritime Album (pb) | 1-85937-622-3 | £9.99 |
| Victorian and Edwardian Sussex (pb) | 1-85937-625-8 | £9.99 |
| Villages of Devon (pb) | 1-85937-293-7 | £9.99 |
| Villages of Kent (pb) | 1-85937-294-5 | £9.99 |
| Villages of Sussex (pb) | 1-85937-295-3 | £9.99 |
| Warrington (pb) | 1-85937-507-3 | £9.99 |
| Warwick (pb) | 1-85937-518-9 | £9.99 |
| Warwickshire (pb) | 1-85937-203-1 | £9.99 |
| Welsh Castles (pb) | 1-85937-322-4 | £9.99 |
| West Midlands (pb) | 1-85937-289-9 | £9.99 |
| West Sussex (pb) | 1-85937-607-x | £9.99 |
| West Yorkshire (pb) | 1-85937-201-5 | £9.99 |
| Weston Super Mare (pb) | 1-85937-306-2 | £9.99 |
| Weymouth (pb) | 1-85937-209-0 | £9.99 |
| Wiltshire (pb) | 1-85937-277-5 | £9.99 |
| Wiltshire Churches (pb) | 1-85937-171-x | £9.99 |
| Wiltshire Living Memories (pb) | 1-85937-396-8 | £9.99 |
| Winchester (pb) | 1-85937-428-x | £9.99 |
| Windsor (pb) | 1-85937-333-x | £9.99 |
| Wokingham & Bracknell (pb) | 1-85937-329-1 | £9.99 |
| Woodbridge (pb) | 1-85937-498-0 | £9.99 |
| Worcester (pb) | 1-85937-165-5 | £9.99 |
| Worcestershire Living Memories | 1-85937-489-1 | £14.99 |
| Worcestershire | 1-85937-152-3 | £14.99 |
| York (pb) | 1-85937-199-x | £9.99 |
| Yorkshire (pb) | 1-85937-186-8 | £9.99 |
| Yorkshire Coastal Memories | 1-85937-506-5 | £14.99 |
| Yorkshire Dales | 1-85937-502-2 | £14.99 |
| Yorkshire Living Memories (pb) | 1-85937-397-6 | £9.99 |

# FRITH PRODUCTS & SERVICES

Francis Frith would doubtless be pleased to know that the pioneering publishing venture he started in 1860 still continues today. Over a hundred and forty years later, The Francis Frith Collection continues in the same innovative tradition and is now one of the foremost publishers of vintage photographs in the world. Some of the current activities include:

### *Interior Decoration*

Today Frith's photographs can be seen framed and as giant wall murals in thousands of pubs, restaurants, hotels, banks, retail stores and other public buildings throughout the country. In every case they enhance the unique local atmosphere of the places they depict and provide reminders of gentler days in an increasingly busy and frenetic world.

### *Product Promotions*

Frith products are used by many major companies to promote the sales of their own products or to reinforce their own history and heritage. Frith promotions have been used by Hovis bread, Courage beers, Scots Porage Oats, Colman's mustard, Cadbury's foods, Mellow Birds coffee, Dunhill pipe tobacco, Guinness, and Bulmer's Cider.

### *Genealogy and Family History*

As the interest in family history and roots grows world-wide, more and more people are turning to Frith's photographs of Great Britain for images of the towns, villages and streets where their ancestors lived; and, of course, photographs of the churches and chapels where their ancestors were christened, married and buried are an essential part of every genealogy tree and family album.

### *Frith Products*

All Frith photographs are available Framed or just as Mounted Prints and Posters (size 23 x 16 inches). These may be ordered from the address below. From time to time other products - Address Books, Calendars, Table Mats, etc - are available.

### *The Internet*

Already fifty thousand Frith photographs can be viewed and purchased on the internet through the Frith websites and a myriad of partner sites.

For more detailed information on Frith companies and products, look at these sites:

www.francisfrith.co.uk
www.francisfrith.com
*(for North American visitors)*

See the complete list of Frith Books at:
*www.francisfrith.co.uk*

This web site is regularly updated with the latest list of publications from the Frith Book Company. If you wish to buy books relating to another part of the country that your local bookshop does not stock, you may purchase on-line.

*For further information, trade, or author enquiries please contact us at the address below:*
**The Francis Frith Collection, Frith's Barn, Teffont, Salisbury, Wiltshire, England SP3 5QP.**
Tel: +44 (0)1722 716 376 Fax: +44 (0)1722 716 881 Email: sales@francisfrith.co.uk

**See Frith books on the internet at www.francisfrith.co.uk**

# FREE MOUNTED PRINT

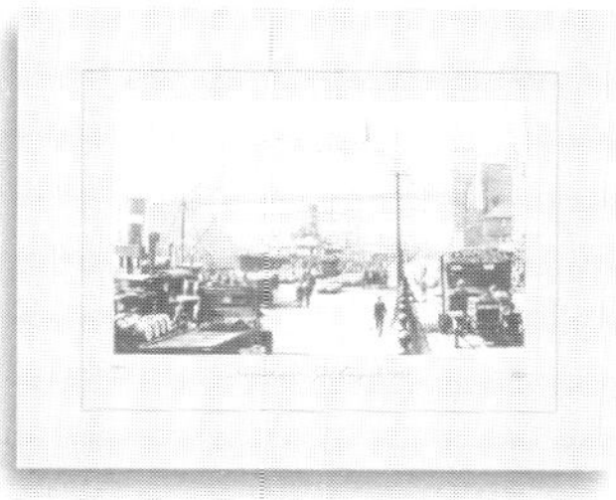

**Mounted Print**
*Overall size 14 x 11 inches*

**Fill in and cut out this voucher and return** *it with your remittance for £2.25 (to cover postage and handling). Offer valid for delivery to UK addresses only.*

***Choose any photograph included in this book.*** *Your SEPIA print will be A4 in size. It will be mounted in a cream mount with a burgundy rule line (overall size 14 x 11 inches).*

**Order additional Mounted Prints at HALF PRICE (only £7.49 each*)**
If you would like to order more Frith prints from this book, possibly as gifts for friends and family, you can buy them at half price (with no additional postage and handling costs).

**Have your Mounted Prints framed**
For an extra £14.95 per print* you can have your mounted print(s) framed in an elegant polished wood and gilt moulding, overall size 16 x 13 inches (no additional postage and handling required).

*** IMPORTANT!**

**These special prices are only available if you order at the same time as you order your free mounted print. You must use the ORIGINAL VOUCHER on this page (no copies permitted). We can only despatch to one address.**

*Send completed Voucher form to:*
**The Francis Frith Collection, Frith's Barn, Teffont, Salisbury, Wiltshire SP3 5QP**

# CHOOSE ANY IMAGE FROM THIS BOOK

## Voucher *for **FREE** and Reduced Price Frith Prints*

*Please do not photocopy this voucher. Only the original is valid, so please fill it in, cut it out and return it to us with your order.*

| Picture ref no | Page no | Qty | Mounted @ £7.49 | Framed + £14.95 | Total Cost |
|---|---|---|---|---|---|
| | | 1 | Free of charge* | £ | £ |
| | | | £7.49 | £ | £ |
| | | | £7.49 | £ | £ |
| | | | £7.49 | £ | £ |
| | | | £7.49 | £ | £ |
| | | | £7.49 | £ | £ |
| *Please allow 28 days for delivery* | | | * Post & handling (UK) | | £2.25 |
| | | | Total Order Cost | | £ |

Title of this book . . . . . . . . . . . . . . . . . . . . . . . . . . . . . .
I enclose a cheque/postal order for £ . . . . . . . . . . .
made payable to 'The Francis Frith Collection'

OR please debit my Mastercard / Visa / Switch / Amex card
*(credit cards please on all overseas orders)*, details below

Card Number

Issue No (Switch only) Valid from (Amex/Switch)

Expires Signature

Name Mr/Mrs/Ms ..........................................
Address ..........................................
..........................................
..........................................
.......................... Postcode ..................
Daytime Tel No ..........................................
Email ..........................................

Valid to 31/12/05

Free Print - see overleaf

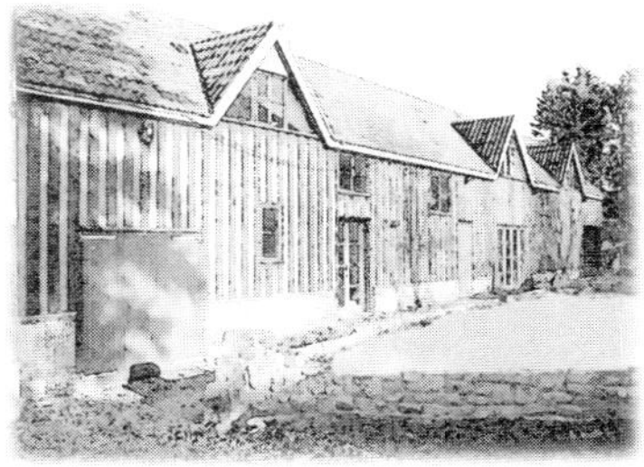

**Would you like to find out more about Francis Frith?**

We have recently recruited some entertaining speakers who are happy to visit local groups, clubs and societies to give an illustrated talk documenting Frith's travels and photographs. If you are a member of such a group and are interested in hosting a presentation, we would love to hear from you.

Our speakers bring with them a small selection of our local town and county books, together with sample prints. They are happy to take orders. A small proportion of the order value is donated to the group who have hosted the presentation. The talks are therefore an excellent way of fundraising for small groups and societies.

**Can you help us with information about any of the Frith photographs in this book?**

We are gradually compiling an historical record for each of the photographs in the Frith archive. It is always fascinating to find out the names of the people shown in the pictures, as well as insights into the shops, buildings and other features depicted.

If you recognize anyone in the photographs in this book, or if you have information not already included in the author's caption, do let us know. We would love to hear from you, and will try to publish it in future books or articles.

**Our production team**

Frith books are produced by a small dedicated team at offices in the converted Grade II listed 18th-century barn at Teffont near Salisbury, illustrated above. Most have worked with the Frith Collection for many years. All have in common one quality: they have a passion for the Frith Collection. The team is constantly expanding, but currently includes:

Jason Buck, John Buck, Douglas Mitchell-Burns, Ruth Butler, Heather Crisp, Isobel Hall, Julian Hight, Peter Horne, James Kinnear, Karen Kinnear, Tina Leary, David Marsh, Sue Molloy, Kate Rotondetto, Dean Scource, Eliza Sackett, Terence Sackett, Sandra Sampson, Adrian Sanders, Sandra Sanger, Julia Skinner, Lewis Taylor, Shelley Tolcher and Lorraine Tuck.